Financial Accounting and Management

Financial Accounting and Management

Edited by Rory Nolan

CLANRYE INTERNATIONAL
www.clanryeinternational.com

Clanrye International,
750 Third Avenue, 9th Floor,
New York, NY 10017, USA

ISBN: 978-1-63240-938-6

Cataloging-in-Publication Data

Financial accounting and management / edited by Rory Nolan.
p. cm.
Includes bibliographical references and index.
ISBN 978-1-63240-938-6
1. Accounting. 2. Financial statements. 3. Finance. 4. Finance--Management. I. Nolan, Rory.
HF5625 .F56 2020
657--dc23

For information on all Clanrye International publications
visit our website at www.clanryeinternational.com

CLANRYE
INTERNATIONAL

Printed in China.

Contents

Preface

This book was inspired by the evolution of our times; to answer the curiosity of inquisitive minds. Many developments have occurred across the globe in the recent past which has transformed the progress in the field.

Financial accounting is a sub-field of accounting that deals with the summary, analysis and reporting of financial transactions with respect to a business. It is governed by both local and international accounting standards. It involves the preparation of financial statement available for public use. Statements of cash flow, statement of profit and loss, and statement of financial position are the three components of financial accounting. The objectives of financial accounting are systematic recording of transactions, ascertainment of result of above recorded transactions, ascertainment of the financial position of business, providing information to the users for rational decision-making and to know the solvency position. This book is a compilation of chapters that discuss the most vital concepts of financial accounting. It also provides significant information of this discipline and helps to develop a good understanding of financial accounting and related fields. The extensive content of this book provides the readers with a thorough understanding of the subject.

This book was developed from a mere concept to drafts to chapters and finally compiled together as a complete text to benefit the readers across all nations. To ensure the quality of the content we instilled two significant steps in our procedure. The first was to appoint an editorial team that would verify the data and statistics provided in the book and also select the most appropriate and valuable contributions from the plentiful contributions we received from authors worldwide. The next step was to appoint an expert of the topic as the Editor-in-Chief, who would head the project and finally make the necessary amendments and modifications to make the text reader-friendly. I was then commissioned to examine all the material to present the topics in the most comprehensible and productive format.

I would like to take this opportunity to thank all the contributing authors who were supportive enough to contribute their time and knowledge to this project. I also wish to convey my regards to my family who have been extremely supportive during the entire project.

Editor

Financial ratios as performance measure: A comparison of IFRS and Nigerian GAAP

Zayyad Abdul-Baki [a,1], Ahmad Bukola Uthman [b] and Mubaraq Sanni[a]

[a] *University of Ilorin, Nigeria;* [b] *Al-Hikmah University, Ilorin, Nigeria*

Abstract: This study examines the effect of IFRS adoption on the performance evaluation of a case firm using some financial ratios selected from four major categories of financial ratios. The study was conducted through comparison of the ratios that were computed from IFRS based financial statements and Nigerian GAAP based financial statements. A One-Sample Kolmogorov-Smirnov Test was conducted to test for data normality. Mann-Whitney U test was employed in testing whether significant difference exists between the pair of ratios when the normality test showed a non-normal distribution of the data set. The result of the Mann-Whitney U test showed that there is no significant difference between the pair of ratios at 5% level of significance. It was concluded that the disclosure of IFRS compliant set of financial statements was not attributable to higher performance evaluation, through ratios, of the case firm. Rather, such disclosure could have been motivated by the capital needs theory or signaling theory.

Keywords: IFRS, financial ratios, Nigerian GAAP, capital needs theory, signaling theory

1. Introduction

Based on the premise that organizations exist to maximize profits (in the short-term) or wealth (in the long-term), any decision taken by organizations' drivers or agents are expected to enhance shareholders' wealth in the long-term. Wealth maximization does not imply maximizing shareholders' wealth alone; it extends to maximising the stakes of other financial claimants like the debt and warrant holders

[1] *Corresponding author:* Department of Accounting, University of Ilorin, PMB 1515, Ilorin, Nigeria Email address: abuzaytun2010@yahoo.com

(Jensen, 2001). According to Jensen (2001), an organization must not only have a score card, it must also make clear the way to measure 'better' as against 'worse'. The benchmark for measuring 'better' as against 'worse' is the increase in the stockholders' wealth (Jensen, 2001). It is in the light of the foregoing assertion that the adoption of IFRS in any jurisdiction is expected to create either in the long-term or short-term, an increase in stockholders' wealth. Hence the common benefits ascribed to international harmonization and adoption of a single set of accounting standards (IFRS).
The benefits ascribed to the adoption of IFRS are many and have been continually debated by several scholars of accounting. The adoption of IFRS arguably leads to "more accurate, comprehensive and timely financial statement information" (Ball, 2006: 11); reduction in adverse selection arising from information access differential among users of financial statements that may likely spur reduction in the cost of equity; better comparability of financial statements and much more, transparency in reporting; reduction in information processing cost leading to market efficiency; removal of barriers to cross-border acquisitions and divestitures, leading to increased takeover premiums; finally, better accounting quality and value relevant information resulting from less earnings management and more timely loss recognition (see Daske & Gebhardt, 2005; Ball, 2006; Barth *et al.*, 2008; Chua & Taylor, 2008; Gebhardt & Novotny-Farkas, 2010; Lee *et al.*, 2013). "The change from local standards to IFRS causes a change in the accounting representation of the firm's financial position and performance that may cause investors to revalue the equity of the firm" (Wang & Welker, 2010: 257).

In the light of these benefits, we seek to locate whether such benefits of IFRS adoption extend to a higher performance assessment of the case firm. Analysis of financial ratios from financial statements prepared based on IFRS and Nigeria GAAP is made and the results compared over seven years. The details of financial statement items used have been obtained from the firm's financial statement prepared from 2005 to 2012.

The objectives this study seeks to achieve are in three folds. First, given that the case company is not the only company to be listed on a foreign stock exchange (for example, Guaranty Trust Bank Plc., Diamond Bank and Afren Plc. are some of Nigerian companies listed on the London Stock Exchange), the voluntary publication of IFRS-based financial statements as far back as the year 2004 has aroused our interest to advance some theoretical explanations for the case firm's earlier disclosure of IFRS-based financial statements. Secondly, we also investigate whether significant difference exists among financial ratios prepared from IFRS financial statement and Nigeria GAAP financial statement of the case firm in order to ascertain whether financial ratios prepared from IFRS financial statement show higher performance than those prepared from Nigeria GAAP. These will help confirm whether significant change in the financial statement variables impacts on the performance assessment (using financial ratios) of the company. The study searches to answer the following research questions: (i) What theoretical explanations exist for the case firm's earlier disclosure of IFRS compliant financial statements?; (ii) Is there a significant difference among financial ratios prepared from IFRS financial statement and Nigerian GAAP of the case firm?; (iii) Do financial ratios prepared from IFRS financial statement show higher performance than those prepared from Nigerian GAAP?

2. Literature review

2.1 Theoretical framework

This paper adopts the value maximization theory for situating the study. The value maximization theory holds that the single objective of a firm's existence is to maximize profits in the short run and maximize shareholders wealth in the long run (Friedman, 1970; Jensen, 2001). The theory therefore explains that all the activities of organization, even when they seem eleemosynary, are profit-seeking. The theory explains further that the long run wealth maximization does not portend the maximization of shareholders' wealth alone but also the maximization of other financial claimants like debt and warrant holders. Therefore, we argue that the essence of the case firm's disclosure of IFRS compliant financial statements is to maximize firm's value. This assertion is further explained by the theories we explain herein in the next paragraphs and equally provides an answer to our research question one.

Capital needs theory holds that companies that have some growth opportunities in the capital market seek external financing opportunities from the capital market (Core, 2001). This, they achieve by issuing more share or borrowing from external parties. "Therefore, such finance requires some kind of competition among these companies in order to obtain corporate capital as cost-effectively as possible under the conditions of uncertainty by disclosing more information to outside investors in order to inform them about the corporate position and to increase the certainty of their future cash flow" (Alberti-Alhtaybat, Hutaibat & Al-Htaybat, 2012: 81). This theory perhaps, explains the reason for the case firm's disclosure of IFRS financial statement together with the Nigeria GAAP financial statement when the former was not even mandatory. This can further be justified from the growth of the company's debt and equity over the seven years examined in this study. The firm's equity grew from $2,162,000USD in 2004 to $2,896,000USD in 2006, to $3,541,000USD in 2008, to $3,542,000USD in 2009 and to $6,586,000USD in 2010. Equally, the firm's debt increased from $312,316,000USD in 2004 to $457,645,000USD in 2005, to $550,998,000USD in 2006, to $1,027,133,000USD in 2007, to $1,870,315,000USD in 2008, to $1,795,435,000USD in 2009, and to

$1,568,058,000USD in 2010. These increases in the company's capital are pointers to the fact that the disclosure of IFRS compliant financial statements by the case firm may be explained by this theory in that they are able to distinguish themselves form other companies that are listed on foreign exchanges by reporting IFRS-based financial statements which has reduced the information gap on the side of the investors. Thus, answering our research question one.

Furthermore, signaling theory holds that buyers of companies' shares are not in a position to distinguish between the quality of various products (companies' stock) if all firms choose to disclose standard and mandatory information alone. Hence sellers may provide additional voluntary information to show their betterment with respect to other firms in the market (see Akelof, 1970; Strong & Walker, 1987). This theory may also explain the reason for the case firm's disclosure of IFRS compliant financial statements. Thus, providing a second answer to our research question one.

2.2. Conceptual and empirical framework

Performance measure entails comparing actual results with an established standard. For example, the comparison of actual results with standards as in variance analysis or actual results with budgets as in budgetary control system or comparison of a company's financial ratios with the industry average as in ratio analysis or comparing a company's performance with best practices as in benchmarking. Ratios have been used as a measure of performance in various instances. Altman (1968) developed a model that uses ratios for bankruptcy prediction of firms. Prior to Altman, there was Beaver (1966) who also employed financial ratio in predicting the financial health of firms. Subsequently Beaver (1966) and Alltman's (1968) study were followed by other researches in predicting firms' bankruptcy (for example; Charitou *et al.*, 2004; Beaver *et al.*, 2005; Dewaelheyns & Van Hulle, 2006). All these studies have equally adopted financial ratios in predicting the financial health of the sampled firms. The use of financial ratios in measuring performance is not limited to bankruptcy prediction. Rather, they have been employed in various other contexts. Liu and O'Farrell (2009) employed financial ratios in comparing the strengths and weaknesses of US firms and China firms. Prior to Liu and O'Farrell (2009), other studies have equally adopted financial ratios in just a similar context, for example Fuglister (1997). Hagigi and Sponza (1990) equally adopted financial ratios in comparing the strengths and weaknesses of US firms and Italian firms and Lui and Wei (2008), compared the financial ratios of Chinese firms and Japanese companies.

In the context of adopting ratio for examining the effects of IFRS adoption on various variables, a number of studies have also been carried out. Blanchette *et al.* (2011) compared 26 ratios computed from IFRS financial statements and Canada

GAAP financial statements. Nine firms were used and the data were extracted from the financial statements prepared for under each accounting standard during the transition years. Their findings show that "IFRS's impact on financial ratios is driven by fundamental differences in application of fair value accounting and consolidation under IFRS and pre-changeover Canadian GAAP" (p. 7), "differences between IFRS and pre-changeover Canadian GAAP do not affect cash flows and most of the financial ratios under IFRS present a significantly higher volatility than those computed under pre-changeover Canadian GAAP" (p. 8). In the same vein, Lantto and Sahlstrom (2009) assessed the economic consequences of the adoption of IFRS in Finland. This was achieved by calculating ratios from sampled 91 firms' on Helsinki Stock Exchange. The result shows that after the adoption of IFRS, profitability ratios increased, liquidity ratios decreased and there was a decrease observed in a market based financial ratio- the PE ratio. Callao *et al.* (2007) examined the effect of IFRS on the comparability and relevance of financial reporting in Spain. Using IBEX-35 companies, they compared the accounting figures and the financial ratios under the IFRS and Spain GAAP to test whether a significant difference exist between the two groups of ratios. They found that comparability of accounts worsens when IFRS and local GAAP are used together in a country at the same time.

In the light of these researches, this study compares the financial ratios of a firm computed from its IFRS compliant financial statements and the Nigerian GAAP based financial statements' over seven years. The essence is to ascertain whether a significant difference exists and whether such difference, if any, is better for the company by increasing stakeholders' assessment of the company's performance thus increasing its value.

2.3. Accounting profession in Nigeria

The erstwhile issuer of the Statement of Accounting Standard (SAS) in Nigeria, the Nigerian Accounting Standard Board (NASB) gave the first unified and professional outlook to the regulation of accounting profession in Nigeria in 1982 when it was constituted as a board. The NASB, hitherto set up under the auspices of the Institute of Chartered Accountants of Nigeria (ICAN) was thence brought under government supervision by making it a component of the then Federal Ministry of Trade and Tourism in 1992 (ICAN, 2006). As a faction of a government parastatal, The NASB issued some standards which though, were not wholeheartedly followed by all players; serve effectively in providing a uniform basis for locally based companies and preparers of financial statements. The major setback of the NASB was the refusal of multinational companies to adopt the SASs as they considered it mere codifications of the extant International Accounting Standards (Nigeria's Financial Hub, 2011).

In May 2003, the NASB act was enacted into Nigerian law to make the NASB an independent body charged with the responsibility, among others, of regulating the accounting profession in Nigeria (Abdullahi, 2010). The act was to serve as a constitution that governs the operation of the NASB. This, it does by issuing accounting standards to be compulsorily adopted by preparers of financial statement in Nigeria (NASB Act, 2003). Although the standards were criticized as mere codification of existing international accounting standards (Nigerias Financial Hub, 2011), they cut across various industries and were applauded by users as elaborate and extensive set of standards. Until the NASB act was repealed in 2011, it had 31 SASs in operation (FRCN, 2014). Notwithstanding the oversight role of the NASB, plethora of sharp practices among accountants brought about disdain to the revered profession of accounting in Nigeria (Sanusi, 2010; Otusanya & Lauwo, 2012). Continual public outcry as well as the urgent need to adopt IFRS therefore necessitated the need for the enactment of the Financial Reporting Council of Nigeria (FRCN) in 2011.

In an effort to place Accounting and Financial Reporting Practices in Nigeria on the same footing as that of the world's best practices, the "FRCN Act" was enacted on 2011. In the presentation of a paper in 2012 at a retreat with Accounting Lecturers in Nigerian University, the Director of the council, Jim Obazee Osaynade noted that the "council will require management assessment of internal controls, including Information Systems Controls with independent attestation" (p. 25). He stated further that as part of the FRC oversight of professionals, "the FRC requires a good code of ethics for financial officers and certification of financial statements by chief executive officers and chief financial officers" (Osayande, 2012 p. 23) of reporting entities. More so, the council will reinvigorate efforts in restoring public confidence in financial reporting as it "issues code of corporate governance and guidelines, and develop a mechanism for periodic assessment of the codes and the guidelines" (Osayande, 2012 p. 23). Arguing further for the enactment of the FRCN act, Anao (2012) "considers that the development is timely as "it expands the scope of financial regulation beyond traditional spheres of accounting and financial reporting and also spans auditing and corporate governance" (p. 5). The increased involvement of government in financial reporting presents a picture that is ardently passionate about the public interest. Perhaps, because of the plethora of bank fraud exposures recorded in recent times in Nigeria and the urgent need to align with international best practices. The Financial Reporting Council of Nigeria therefore operates to enable the strict adoption of International Financial Reporting Standards, majority of which is embedded with fair value accounting (Ball, 2005). Further to that, the Nigeria's Federal Executive Council approved January 1 2012 as the effective date for the convergence of SAS with IFRS in Nigeria and charged the FRCN to swing into action by designing a conversion roadmap for all concerned entities (Robert, 2012).

2.4. IFRS and accounting quality

According to Chua and Taylor (2008), evidence regarding the accounting quality emanating from the adoption of IFRS is mixed. Accounting quality may be conceptualized in three major contexts: "on capital market effects (e.g., cost of equity capital or measures of liquidity); on attributes of analysts' forecasts (e.g., dispersion and accuracy); or on the extent of institutional ownership" (Chua and Taylor, 2008: 466). Barth *et al.* (2008) observe that 21 countries adopting IAS evident less earnings management, more timely loss recognition, and more value relevance of accounting amounts than matched firms adopting non-US domestic standards. Thus they conclude that firms adopting IAS evidence an improvement in accounting quality. However they caution that their findings may not be attributable to a change in reporting system but rather "to changes in firms' incentives and the economic environment" (p. 467).

Tendeloo and Vanstraelen (2005), using a sample of 636 firm-year observations of German listed companies adopting IFRS within the periods 1999-2001, observed that "IFRS-adopters do not present different earnings management behavior compared to companies reporting under German GAAP" (p. 155). In furtherance, Christensen *et al.* (2008) in their research found voluntary adoption of IFRS is associated with decreased earnings management and more timely loss recognition. However, they admit that such findings cannot be extended to firms that were forced to adopt IFRS. Jeanjean and Stolowy (2008) examined the effect of mandatory introduction of IFRS on earnings management in Australia, France and UK. They found that earnings management did not reduce in the sampled countries after the adoption of IFRS rather it increased in France.

Rainsbury *et al.* (2010) examined the effect of IFRS on adoption of New Zealand listed firms between 2005 and 2007. They found that the "adoption of IFRS resulted in statistically significant increases in earnings, assets and liabilities" (p. 1). They however submitted that "IFRS adoption did not improve the value relevance of the accounting numbers" (p. 1). Daske *et al.* (2013), examined the effect of voluntary and mandatory adoption of IFRS on liquidity and cost of capital. To test this, they split the sampled firms into 'label' and 'serious' adopters. By label adopters, they meant firms that may adopt IFRS only in name and just make few changes to their reports. On the other hand, serious adopters are those firms that adopt IFRS as a "strategy to increase their commitment to transparency" (p. 495). Their findings are summarized below:

> While on average liquidity and cost of capital often do not change around voluntary IAS/IFRS adoptions, we find considerable heterogeneity: "Serious" adoptions are associated with an increase in liquidity and a decline in cost of capital, whereas "label" adoptions are not. We obtain similar results when classifying firms around mandatory IFRS adoption (p. 496).

Devalle *et al.* (2010) investigated whether the value relevance of accounting data increased as a result of the adoption of IFRS. They sampled 3,721 firms on five European stock exchanges- Frankfurt, Madrid, Paris, London, and Milan. Their findings revealed a mixed evidence of an increase in value relevance of accounting data. While the influence on earnings on share price increased upon the adoption of IFRS in Germany, France and United Kingdom, the influence of book value of equity decreased except for the UK. Chen *et al.* (2010) also examined an increase in accounting quality around IFRS adoption of publicly listed companies in 15 member states of the EU. Using five proxies of accounting quality, they found that less of earnings management, lower magnitude of absolute discretionary accruals, and higher accruals quality are attributable to IFRS adoption. However, they equally found that "firms engage in more earnings smoothing and recognize large losses in a less timely manner in post-IFRS periods" (p. 221).

Ozkan *et al.* (2012) examined the impact of a mandatory adoption of IFRS in continental Europe on the contractual usefulness of accounting information in executive compensation based on pay-performance sensitivity (PPS) and relative performance evaluation. They found that "higher earnings quality and comparability brought by the adoption of IFRS facilitate executive compensation contracting" (p. 1078). Gebhardt and Novotny-Farkas (2011) assessed the implication of mandatory adoption of IFRS on accounting quality in 12 European banks. Their findings indicate that the recognition of incurred losses under IAS 39 reduces income smoothing. However they analyzed further that this result is less pronounced in banks with stricter supervision, widely spread ownership and in EU banks that are cross—listed in the US. Secondly they submit that the incurred loss approach under IAS 39 lead to less timely loan loss recognition.

Daske (2006) examined the impact of IFRS on the cost of equity of a set of German firms from 1993-2002. He found out that IFRS did not reduce the cost of equity of the sampled firms. The cost of equity, according to his findings rather increased.

Daske and Gebhardt (2006) examined the impact of IFRS adoption on accounting quality in three European countries- Austria, Germany and Switzerland. Using the annual reports of companies with annual report ratings by independent accounting scholars in these countries, they found that accounting quality significantly increased in the sampled companies that mandatorily and voluntarily adopted IFRS. Christensen, Lee and Walker (2008), examined the impact of incentives to adopt IFRS on accounting quality – earnings management and timely loss recognition- around IFRS adoption. They submit that improvement in accounting quality experienced around IFRS adoption can be isolated as being attributable to firms with incentives to adopt the IFRS.

3. Research methodology

This study adopts a case study research approach. This method is informed by the nature of data sourced and examined in this study. Obviously, compliance with IFRS by Nigerian firms has only been recently made compulsory in the year 2013. Thus only the case company has produced a pair of financial statements that comply with both IFRS and the domestic GAAP. The years observed are between 2004 and 2010 as there are no data produced for the later years by the company. The preliminary analysis of the data revealed that the values of the variable under study were not normally distributed as shown by the One-Sample Kolmogorov-Smirnov Test in Table 1. Consequently, the Mann-Whitney test statistics was employed to test whether a significant difference exists among the ratios calculated from the pair of financial statements. The result of the test was used to test the hypothesis generated from research question two and to provide an answer to research question three while a theoretical explanation was adopted to advance reasons for the earlier disclosure of IFRS compliant financial statements by the firm, thus answering research question one. This theoretical explanation is made in the next section under the theoretical framework. The hypothesis generated from the first research question and the second research question was answered in section three. In total, twelve ratios were examined under four categories with each category having three ratios each in order to have a holistic view of the case company's performance. The proposition tested in this study, derived from literature, is that there is no significant difference among financial ratios prepared from IFRS financial statement and Nigerian GAAP of the case firm.

Oando plc is one of Nigeria's leading Oil Company involving oil exploration and production (Upstream); energy services; gas and power (Midstream); marketing, supply and trading and Oando terminalling (Downstream). Founded in 1994 as Ocean and Oil limited to supply and trade petroleum products in Nigeria, it was incorporated as a Joint Venture between Oando Plc & and Ocean & Oil Services in 2004 after having acquired 60% stake in Unipetrol plc (oandoplc.com). The merger of Unipetrol and Agip in 2003 evolved Oando as the 2nd largest downstream oil and gas company in Nigeria with a market share of 15.64% in 2003(oandoplc.com).

With the company's involvement in a large-scale export and import of petroleum products and being a leading supplier of petroleum products to Nigeria, it "emerged to an integrated Energy group with varied interests and assets spanning the entire Oil and Gas Energy Value Chain" (Oandonews p.1). It is the first indigenous group to attain this height and has been growing until it won the battle for the acquisition of CononcoPhilips Nigerian Assets in a deal worth $1.79billion in 2012 (nigeriaoilandgasintelligence.com).

Oando's revenue grew from N336.8Million to N378.9Million between 2009 and 2010 amounting to 12.5% increase while its profits after tax in 2010 was

N14.4million, a 42% increase on 2009 as shown in Nigerian GAAP denominated financial statement. The company is the first (in Nigeria) to present the financial report of its operation covering the periods of 2005 accounting year to date denominated both in IFRS and Nigeria's GAAP. In 2005, the company was listed on the Johannesburg Stock Exchange (JSE) and by January 17, 2014, the company became listed on the Toronto Stock Exchange with a Market Capitalization of $184 Million. Meanwhile, the financial reports as presented on IFRS basis show a growth of 11.5% as opposed to 12.5% depicted under Nigerian GAAP. Thence, the need for a comparative evaluation of financial reports presented under the Nigeria's GAAP and those presented under IFRS.

4. Data presentation and analysis

Table 1 presents the One-Sample Kolmogorov-Smirnov Test of the distribution of the twenty four (24) financial ratios computed under both the Nigerian GAAP and IFRS.

Table 1. One-Sample Kolmogorov-Smirnov Test

N	Mean	Std Deviation	K-S Z value	Significant
24	3.9511	10.5315	1.992	0.001

Normality assumption is assumed if the significance level is greater than 0.05. The result as shown in this table indicates that the significant level is less than 0.05 implying that the data set does differ significantly from the normal distribution and therefore the violation of the normality assumption. In this instance, the non-parametric statistical mean should be considered as the best possible option (Abd Rahim, 2009). Consequently, the Mann-Whitney test, an equivalent non parametric test for the independent t test was used to determine whether the mean difference was significant at the 5% level.

Table 2. Summary of Mann-Whitney U test on overall financial ratios prepared from IFRS and Nigeria GAAP financial statements

Standards	N	Mean Rank	Sum of Ranks
Nigerian GAAP	12	13.08	157.00
IFRS	12	11.92	143.00
Total	24		
Test Statistics			
Z	-.404		
Asymp. Sig. (2-tailed)	.686		

Table two is the result of the Mann-Whitney U test. The result shows that there is no significant difference in the distribution of the ratio computed under the Nigerian GAAP and IFRS as the test statistic is 0.686 which is greater than 0.05 (i.e. at 5% level of significance). This result implies that the null hypothesis would not be rejected. Thus we accept that there is no significant difference among the financial ratios computed under Nigerian GAAP and under IFRS.

Table 3. Descriptive analysis of financial ratios prepared from IFRS and Nigeria GAAP financial statements

Variables		Nigerian GAAP				IFRS			
	Obs	Mean	Max	Min	Std. Dev.	Mean	Max	Min	Std. Dev.
Profitability									
Gross Profit Margin	7	0.1157	0.14	0.09	0.0172	0.1157	0.17	0.07	0.0341
Net Profit Margin	7	0.0214	0.04	0.01	0.0122	0.0229	0.03	0.01	0.0095
Return On Capital	7	0.0414	0.07	0.03	0.0135	0.0429	0.06	0.02	0.0125
Overall Mean		**0.0595**				**0.0605**			
Short- term solvency									
Current Ratio	7	0.8714	1.01	0.61	0.1264	0.8586	1.04	0.59	0.1399
Acid Test Ratio	7	0.7114	0.86	0.57	0.0886	0.6914	0.82	0.54	0.091
CRA	7	0.1657	0.26	0.09	0.0702	0.1643	0.26	0.09	0.0608
Overall mean		**0.5828**				**0.5714**			
Long Term solvency									
Debt Ratio	7	0.7514	0.88	0.66	0.0788	0.7514	0.85	0.66	0.0669
Gearing Ratio	7	0.5004	168.71	5.42	61.0653	0.3429	0.93	0.01	0.3784
Cash Flow Ratio	7	0.0729	0.2	-0.04	0.0793	0.0471	0.2	-0.12	0.1350
Overall mean		**0.4296**				**0.3805**			
Investment ratio									
Eearnings Per Share	7	13.3229	22.31	5.14	6.3152	12.9243	21.24	4.22	6.9250

Dividend Per Share	**7**	4.3371	6.67	2.34	1.6067	7.34	13.37	4	3.6688
Dividend Payout	**7**	0.4129	0.78	0.15	0.2487	0.6626	1.23	0.24	0.3179
Overall Mean		**6.0243**				**6.9756**			

Table 3 above summarizes the seven-year mean of the sampled ratio under each category of ratios. The individual as well as the overall profitability ratios depict fairly similar results for the financial statements of the duo. Although, the gross profit margins are the same under the IFRS and the GAAP, the net profit margin and the return on capital are higher under the IFRS.
The overall ratios of both the short and long term solvency indicate higher liquidity for GAAP denominated financial statement than the IFRS. All the individual ratios under the short-term and long-term solvency ratios are higher under GAAP than IFRS however; the debt ratio is the same under the two regimes. Inferring form this, financial ratios computed for solvency portray higher liquidity under GAAP than the IFRS.

The investment ratios present a mixed result as the GAAP has higher EPS than the IFRS while the DPS and the dividend payout ratios are higher under IFRS than the Nigerian GAAP.

Conclusively, the above comparison of ratios conveys to us that neither the Nigerian GAAP nor the IFRS has depicted a higher performance in terms of ratios as the results are mixed. Thus we can conveniently answer our research question three that the ratios under the IFRS do not depict a higher performance than the ratios under the Nigerian GAAP except for the profitability ratios and the investment ratios where the IFRS has two of the ratios under each category to be higher than the Nigerian GAAP.

Finally, to examine whether these differences are significant, we present the Mann-Whitney test for each category in the next table below.

Table 4: Summary of Mann-Whitney U test on each category of financial ratios prepared from IFRS and Nigeria GAAP financial statement

Ratios	Standards	N	Mean Rank	Sum of Ranks	Z statistics	Sig
Profitability	**GAAP**	3	4.67	14.00		
	IFRS	3	2.33	7.00	-1.528	0.127
Short term	**GAAP**	3	4.00	12.00		
	IFRS	3	3.00	9.00	-0.655	0.513

Long term	**GAAP**	3	4.33	13.00		
	IFRS	3	2.67	8.00	-1.091	0.275
Investment	**GAAP**	3	3.33	10.00		
	IFRS	3	3.67	11.00	-0.218	0.827

Preliminary analysis of the data revealed that in general, except some of the investment ratio and some of the profitability ratios, ratios computed under Nigerian GAAP have a higher mean scores than those computed under IFRS as indicated by the mean ranks of the groups of ratios in table 4 above. However the reason for the exception of the investment ratio may be attributable to the treatment of dividend under the different accounting standard regime. Typically, proposed dividends are treated as liability under Nigerian GAAP while they are not treated as liability under IAS. Overall, Nigerian GAAP shows higher mean rank (13.08- see table 2) than IFRS (11.92- see table 2). Thus, it can be inferred from this that IFRS does not show a higher performance in terms ratios comparison than Nigerian GAAP as none of the ratios has shown a significant difference, at all reasonable levels of significance, between the two ratios under each category.

5. Conclusions

While some studies have shown a significant difference in the financial ratios of the respective local GAAPs and IFRS (Blanchette *et al.*, 2011; Lantto & Sahlstrom, 2009), our result does not show a significant difference. The reason might perhaps be attributed to the fact that such local GAAPs were independently developed by the respective local Accounting Standards Setting bodies. Nigerian GAAP has always been an adaptation of IASs (now IFRS). This is evident in standards issued by the defunct Nigeria Accounting Standard Board (NASB) which had a section detailing the compliance of each Nigerian standard with IAS (NASB, 2009). Furthermore, the non-existence of a significant difference between Nigerian GAAP and IFRS based financial ratios implies that the company's disclosure of IFRS compliant set of financial statements may not be attributable to a short-term performance evaluation of the company's achievement using a number of financial ratios computed from IFRS rather, the theoretical inclinations of the firm may be to the capital needs theory and the signaling theory as discussed under the review of literature. Conclusively our result adds to the body of literatures that have examined the impact of IFRS on various financial ratios in different spheres.

We acknowledge the fact that, as it is common with most case study research, our findings' generalizability is hampered as we have only examined a company from which we could only source for data. Nonetheless, this study gives an insight into the likely outcome of future research covering a wider spectrum.

References

Abd Rahim M. N. (2009) *Statistical Methods for Research*, Prentice Hall, Selangor Malaysia

Abdullahi, N. A. (2010) "Celebrating 50 years of accounting profession in Nigeria", *The Cetified National Accountants* , pp. 23-36

Akerlof, G. (1970) "The market for "lemons": quality uncertainty and the market mechanism", *The Quarterly Journal of Economics,* vol. 84: 488–500

Alberti-Alhtaybat, L., Hutaibat, K. & Al-Htaybat, K. (2012) "Mapping corporate disclosure theories", *Journal of Financial Reporting & Accounting,* vol. 10 (1): 73-94

Altman, E. I. (1968) "Financial Ratios, discriminant analysis and the prediction of corporate bankruptcy", *The Journal of Finance*, vol. 23 (4), 589-609

Anao, R. A. (2012) FRC Act and Nigeria Roadmap to IFRS - implication for accounting education in Nigeria", Abuja: Financial Reporting Council of Nigeria

Ball, R. (2006) "International Financial Reporting Standards (IFRS): Pros and cons for investors", *Accounting & Business Research, International Accounting Policy Forum*, pp. 5-27

Ball, R. (2009) "Market and political/regulatory perspectives on the recent accounting scandal", Retrieved from DOI:10.111/j.1475-679x.2009.00325.x (Accessed on April 20, 2012)

Barth, M. E., Landsman, M. H. & Lang, W. R. (2008) "International Accounting Standards and accounting quality", *Journal of Accounting Research*, vol. 46 (3): 467-498

Beaver, W. H. (1966) "Financial ratios as predictors of failure", *Journal of Accounting Research,* vol. 4: 71-111

Beaver,W. H., Mcnichols, M. F. & Rhie, J. W. (2005) "Have financial statements become less informative? evidence from the ability of financial ratios to predict bankruptcy", *Review of Accounting Studies*, vol. 10: 93-122

Blanchette, M., Racicot, F. E. & Girard, J. Y. (2011) *The Effects of IFRS on Financial Ratios: Early Evidence in Canada*, Ottawa; Certified General Accountants Association of Canada

Callao, S. Jarne, J. I. & Laınez, J. A. (2007) "Adoption of IFRS in Spain: Effect on the comparability and relevance of financial reporting", *Journal of International Accounting, Auditing and Taxation*, vol. 16: 148–178

Charitou, A., Neophytou, E. & Charalambous, C. (2004) "Predicting corporate failure: Empirical evidence for the UK", *European Accounting Review*, vol. 13 (3): 465 – 497

Chen, H., Tang, Q., Jiang, Y. & Lin, Z. (2010) "The Role of International Financial Reporting Standards in accounting quality: Evidence from the European Union", *Journal of International Financial Management and Accounting*, vol. 21(3): 220-278

Chua, W. F. & Taylor, S. L. (2008) "The rise and rise of IFRS: An examination of IFRS diffusion", *Journal of Accounting and Public Policy*, vol. 27: 462–473

Core, J.E. (2001) "A review of the empirical disclosure literature: discussion", *Journal of Accounting and Economics*, vol. 31: 441-456

Daske, H. (2006) "Economic benefits of adopting IFRS or US-GAAP – Have the expected cost of equity capital really decreased?", *Journal of Business Finance & Accounting*, vol. 33(3) & (4): 329–373

Daske, H. & Gebhardt, G. (2005) "International Financial Reporting Standards and experts' perceptions of disclosure quality", *Abacus*, vol. 42: 461-498

Daske, H., Hail, L., Leuz, C. & Verdi, R. (2013) "Adopting a label: heterogeneity in the economic consequences around IAS/IFRS adoptions", *Journal of Accounting Research*, vol. 51(3): 495-547

Devalle, A., Onali, E. & Magarini, R. (2010) "Assessing the value relevance of accounting data after the introduction of IFRS in Europe", *Journal of International Financial Management and Accounting*, vol. 21 (2): 85-119

Dewaelheyns, N. & Van Hulle, C. (2006) "Corporate failure prediction modeling: distorted by business groups' internal capital markets?", *Journal of Business Finance & Accounting*, vol. 33(5) & (6): 909–931

FRCN Act (2011) Financial Reporting Council of Nigeria Act, *Federal Republic of Nigerial Official Gazette* . Lagos: Federal Government Printer.

FRCN (2014) *Financial Reporting Countil of Nigeria*, Retrieved February 13, 2014, from http://www.financialreportingcouncil.gov.ng/.

Friedman, M. (1970) "The social responsibility of business is to increase its profits", *The New York Times* Magazine, September 13

Fuglister, J. (1997) "A comparative ratio analysis between Chinese and US firms", *Advances in International Accounting*, vol. 10: 185-206

Gebhardt, G. & Novotny-Farkas, Z. (2010) "The effects of IFRS adoption on the financial reporting quality of European banks", *Marie Curie Research Training Network; the IFRS Revolution: Compliance, Consequences and Policy Lessons*

Gebhardt, G. & Novotny-Farkas, Z. (2011) "Mandatory IFRS adoption and accounting quality of European Banks", *Journal of Business Finance & Accounting*, vol. 38(3) & (4): 289–333

Hagigi, M. & Sponza, A. (1990) "Financial statement analysis of Italian companies: accounting practices, environmental factors, and international corporate performance comparisons", *The International Journal of Accounting*, vol. 25: 234-251

ICAN (2006) *Financial Reporting and Audit Practice.* Lagos: VI Publishing ltd.

Jensen, M .C. (2001) "Value maximisation, stakeholder theory and the corporate objective function", *European Financial management*, vol. 7(3): 297-317

Lantto, A. M. & Sahlstrom, P. (2009) "Impact of International Financial Reporting Standard adoption on key financial ratio", *Accounting and Finance*, vol. 48 (2): 341-361

Lee, E., Walker, M. & Zeng, C. (2013) *Does IFRS Convergence Affect Financial Reporting Quality in China?* London; Certified Accountants Educational Trust

Liu, C., & Wei, K. K. (2008) "A comparative ratio analysis of Chinese and Japanese corporations", *Proceedings of the 2008 International Accounting Conference, Shanghai, China, June 6-8*

Lui, C. & O'Farrell, G. (2009) "China and U.S. financial ratio comparison", *International Journal of Business, Accounting and Finance*, vol. 3 (2): 1-12

NASB (2009) *NASB Accounting Standards Handbook*. Lagos: Academy Press Plc.

NASB Act (2003) *Nigerian Accounting Standards Board Act*. Retrieved February 13, 2014, from http://www.placng.org/lawsofnigeria/node/315.

Nigeria's Financial Hub (2011) *History and Facts of the Nigerian Accounting Standard Board (NASB)*. Retrieved February 13, 2014, from http://www.nigerianaccounting.com/history-and-facts-of-the-nigerian-accounting-standards-board-nasb/.

NOGintelligence (2012) *Oando wins Battle for the Acquisition of ConocoPhillips Nigeria Assets*. Retrieved 29, 9, 2013, from http://www.nigeriaoilandgas intelligence.com/oando-wins-battle-for-acquisition-of-conocophillips-nigerian-assets.

Oandoplc (2006) Oando signs for OPL278 with NNPC, *Onadonews* , vol. 5 (1): 1-12

Oandoplc (2013) *History of Oando Plc*, Retrieved 29, 9, 2013, from http://www.oandoplc.com/oando-supply-and-trading/history.

Osayande, O. J. (2012) "Financial Reporting Council (FRC): A vehicle for improving Corporate Financial Reporting in Nigeria", Abuja, Nigeria: Financial Reporting Council of Nigeria

Otusanya, J. O., & Lauwo, S. (2012) "The Role of Auditors in the Nigerian Banking Crisis", *Accountancy Business and the Public Interest* , vol. 9: 159-204

Ozkan, N., Singer, Z. and You, H. (2012) "Mandatory IFRS adoption and the contractual usefulness of accounting information in executive compensation", *Journal of Accounting Research*, vol. 50 (4)" 1077-1107

Rainsbury, E. A., Diego, J. S. & Walker, L. (2010) "Evidence on the impact of International Financial Reporting Standards in New Zealand", A paper presented at the Second Quantitative Accounting Research Symposium 28 May 2010, Massey University, Albany Campus

Robert, D. (2012) Introduction and Preparation of Financial Statements, *ICAN IFRS Training*

Sanusi, S. L. (2010) "The Nigerian banking industry: what went wrong and the way forward", pp. 1-23, Kano

Strong, N. & Walker, M. (1987) *Information and Capital Market*, Basil Blackwell, New York, NY

Tendeloo, B. V. & Vanstraelen, A. (2008) "Earnings management and audit quality in Europe: Evidence from the private client segment market", *European Accounting Review*, vol. 17(3): 447-469

Wang, S. & Welker, M. (2010) "Timing equity issuance in response to information asymmetry arising from IFRS adoption in Australia and Europe", *Journal of Accounting Research*, vol. 49 (1): 257-307

2

The impact of accounting disclosure on emerging stock market prediction in an unstable socio-political context

Chaima Kooli[a], Raoudha Trabelsi[a,1] and Fethi Tlili [b]

[a] *Sfax Business School, Sfax University, Tunisia*
[b] *Tunis Higher School of Communication, Tunisia*

Abstract: The paper analyzes the impact of accounting disclosure on the prediction quality of stock market prices. The study also investigates whether a changing socio-political context affects the prediction quality. We focused on the Tunisian case, which has known a political turmoil in January 2011. Our sample includes 48,204 daily stock closing prices of 39 companies listed in Tunis Stock Exchange from 2009 to 2014. We used an Artificial Neural Network (ANN) with a Multi-layer Perceptron topology to predict the time series. The simulations showed that the average annual prediction error of the stock prices is the largest in the period relating to the January 2011 events. Thus, the country socio-political context impacts negatively the prediction quality of the stock market prices. Furthermore, the integration of an accounting variable improves the quality of the stock prices prediction for all the study periods, except the one that corresponds to the events of January 2011. In other words, it appears that accounting disclosure does not improve prices prediction quality in an unstable context.

Keywords: Accounting disclosure, Socio-political context, Stock prices prediction, Price discovery.

---

[1] *Corresponding author*: Department of Accounting, Sfax Business School.
Email address: raoudha.trabelsi@gmail.com

1. Introduction

It is a well-known fact that stock prices react to accounting-based earnings disclosures (Lev, 1989). Relatively few studies analyze the impact of these accounting disclosures on the prediction of stock prices, and specifically when it comes to an unstable country context.

For decades, Tunisia, an emerging country, has been considered one of the success stories in the African continent, characterized by a Gross Domestic Product growth of 4.2% in 2008, 3% in 2009 and 3.5% in 2010, according to the World Development Indicators database. Yet, on December 17, 2010 the self-immolation of a street vendor launched a revolution, and former President Zine El Abidine Ben Ali left power after a month of protests and violent confrontations.

In this changing socio-political context, it seems interesting to analyze the prediction quality of the stock market prices on the Tunis Stock Exchange, prior to and after the integration of an accounting variable. The idea here is to verify whether the integration of an accounting variable would have the same impact on the quality of the prediction in an unstable socio-political context as in a stable one.

To do this, the article aims to apply Artificial Neural Networks to predict the Tunis stock Exchange prices. Many authors question indeed conventional methods for quoted equities prediction relying on autoregressive prediction techniques and their derivatives. In fact, despite their efficiency for linear and invariant time series, these methods are not appropriate for the series of stock prices, which are known for their non-linearity and their non-stationarity. Therefore, more and more finance studies have started exploring other techniques and data analysis tools, such as artificial intelligence methods. According to Paquet (1997), contrary to the conventional approaches, these methods for intelligence simulation do not require any assumption on the variables. Accordingly, Artificial Neural Networks (ANN) which have been recognized as reliable in financial literature, are artificial intelligence techniques for processing and prediction, oriented especially for modeling complex functions.

The first objective of this work is to evaluate the prediction error of the stock market prices in different periods around the Tunisia events of January 2011, in order to verify if the socio-political events in a country impact its stock market prices prediction quality. In the second place, the research aims to compare the prediction error of the stock market prices prior to and after the integration in the prediction model of an accounting variable.

The remainder of this paper is organized as follows. Section 2 is dedicated to presenting a general overview of related literature on the impact of accounting disclosure on stock prices reaction and on the use of ANN in the prediction of financial time series. As for section 3, it depicts the data gathering and research sample preprocessing steps. In section 4, we expose the simulation scenario and the empirical results to be discussed in section 5. Finally, section 6 bears the paper's concluding remarks and proposed perspectives.

2. The literature review

The literature review will first focus on empirical studies related to the impact of accounting disclosure on stock prices. We then present the methodological aspect of the literature by exposing some of the studies that use ANN to predict financial time series.

2.1 The impact of accounting disclosure on stock prices reaction

There is a wide range of research showing the effect of accounting disclosure on stock prices reaction. In the following, we expose some of the existing literature first in developed markets then in emerging ones.

2.1.1 In developed markets

Ball and Brown (1968) worked on the Wall Street stock market and showed how the net income gets reflected in stock prices. Alford *et al.* (1993) conducted a cross-country study to measure the impact of accounting disclosure on US firm's stock prices, and in 16 other countries, within the period 1983-1990. First, the results showed that accounting-based earnings disclosures in Australia, France, the Netherlands and the United Kingdom have a greater impact on the determination of stock prices than in the United States. Second, the study showed that earnings variables in Denmark, Germany, Italy, Singapore and Sweden display lower levels of value relevance. Alford *et al.* (1993) explain these different results from a country to another by the diversity in accounting standards, in financial reporting practices and in corporate governance mechanisms.

The usefulness of accounting numbers for stock prices prediction was also emphasized in the works of Ohlson (1995), related to the US Market. The author identified book values and earnings as the two fundamental accounting variables used to explain stock prices.

Having worked on earnings and book values, Collins *et al.* (1997, 1999) showed that the explanatory power of these two accounting variables has increased over the time.

Boozer *et al.* (2017) considered corporate accounting disclosure in predicting the stock prices of American companies. They found a mixed relationship on the predictive power of accounting variables on stock prices before and after the 2007-

2009 financial crisis. The authors concluded that accounting disclosure has a predictive ability on stock prices, but only outside the crisis period.

2.1.2 In emerging markets

Graham and King (2000) examined the relationship between accounting disclosure and stock prices reaction among six Asian countries (Indonesia, Korea, Malaysia, the Philippines, Taiwan, and Thailand). They found significant differences across the six countries in the explanatory power of accounting variables for stock prices. The authors explained this result by diversity in accounting practices in these countries.

Using a sample of all listed firms in the Shanghai and Shenzhen Stock Exchanges from 1991 to 1998, Chen *et al.*(2001) provided evidence that accounting information based on Chinese GAAP impacts the stock market prices. The study also examined two competing explanations to the value-relevance of accounting information between A-share and AB-share companies. The authors found that accounting information in A-share companies impacts more the stock prices than in AB-Share companies. Different other researches (Lin & Chen, 2005; Liu & Liu, 2007) focused on the Chinese case and showed the relevance of accounting disclosure in stock prices determination.

Pirie and Smith (2008) showed that two accounting variables; earnings and book value, impact considerably the stock prices in Malaysia. Based on 30 accounting variables, Rounaghi *et al.* (2015) tried to predict Teheran stock prices using the MARS (Multivariate Adaptive Regression Splines) model and semi-parametric splines technique. As influencing variables on predicting stock prices, the authors selected 4 accounting variables (book value per share, predicted earnings per share, P/E ratio and risk) using the MARS model. Using the semi-parametric splines technique, they selected 4 other accounting variables; dividends, net EPS, EPS Forecast and P/E Ratio.

Finally, Zahedi and Rounaghi (2015) worked on the Teheran stock market, and showed the positive impact of the integration of accounting variables on the stock prices prediction quality. This study is among the few that used Artificial Neural Networks (ANN), rather than the usual econometric analysis tools. Since we also used ANN in our herein analysis of the Tunisian case, we expose in the following section some of the studies that used these tools in the prediction of financial time series.

2.2 Stock prices prediction : ANN versus traditional methods

Although some papers undermine the use of nonparametric machine learning models for market forecasts (Preethi & Santhi, 2012; Pyo *et al.*, 2017), the current body of empirical literature includes many studies showing the importance of ANN in predicting financial time series and particularly stock prices (Tkac & Verner, 2016).

In this context, Kimoto *et al.* (1990) and Slim (2004) worked on the prediction of the stock prices of respectively Tokyo and Tunis stock markets. For both studies, the prediction system achieved accurate predictions and the simulation on stocks trading has proved to be very interesting.

Donaldson and Kamstra (1996) focused on stock prices prediction with ANN in United States, Canada, Japan and British Kingdom stock markets and showed the efficiency of this tool to treat noisy data, compared to conventional tools. Similarly, Maciel and Ballini (2010) analyzed the use of ANN to predict the trend of North American, European and Brazilian stock indexes. They compared ANN and traditional methods such as GARCH (Generalized Autoregressive Conditional Heteroscedasticity) and concluded the superiority of ANN. Bagherifard *et al.* (2012) also used ANN to predict stock prices. In the same way, the study confirmed that ANN is a better performing tool than ARIMA models (AutoRegressive Integrated Moving Average).

Furthermore, other studies focused on the ANN tool itself testing different architectures in the prediction of financial time series. As an example, Naeini *et al.* (2010) worked on stock indexes prediction in Teheran stock market, using several variants of ANN schemes. In this research, two types of networks were compared; MLP (MultiLayer Perceptron) and the recurrent Elman model. The results showed that while MLP provides better prediction quality of stock prices, Elman model predicts better their change direction.

Finally, Zahedi and Rounaghi (2015) worked on Teheran stock market, and showed the impact of the integration of accounting variables, as additional inputs in the ANN tool, on the stock prices prediction quality. Yet, this research focused on a sample that has been selected based on, amongst others, the stability of all the research period.
In fact, this literature review, whether it concerns developed or emerging markets, shows the lack of studies interested in the analysis of the impact of accounting disclosure on share prices, while taking into account the stability or not of the context.

That's why, within this framework, our study aims to analyze the impact of the integration of an accounting variable on the Tunis Stock Exchange prices prediction quality, within an unstable context.

3. Data gathering and research sample preprocessing

The Tunis Stock Exchange was founded in 1969. Up to January 2018 it includes 81 listed companies. While realizing our study, the stock exchange reports available on the Tunis Stock Exchange website go back to 2008. Thus, the adopted duration for our sample was chosen to be 2008-2014. The stock prices reports provide four daily records for each company: "Lowest", "Highest", "Opening" and "Closing", the latter was chosen in our sample selection. In this research, the sample selection was led in two steps.

Elimination of the year 2008 from the study period

A close observation of the collected stock prices dataset revealed that only 48 firms are continuously present over the 7 years period (2008-2014). Moreover, given that the introduction of relevant number of firms in the market took place throughout 2008, and in order to avoid this lack of information, the 2008 data were removed from the sample, and the period was limited to 6 years (from 2009 to 2014).

Outliers elimination or rectification

In order to check data integrity, and given the large size of the sample, the evolution of the stock prices of the 48 companies over the 6 years (2009-2014) was represented graphically. These visual representations allow effective outliers detection. To do this, a linear scale representation was performed as depicted in Figure 1.

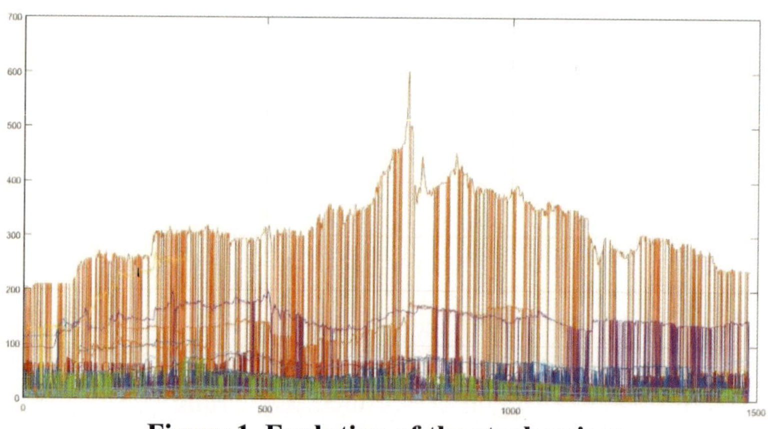

Figure 1. Evolution of the stock prices (48 companies - 2009 to 2014): Linear scale

As shown in the Figure 1, most of the 48 curves are overlapping and do not allow fine interpretation. This could be explained by the large dynamic of the stock prices over the different firms. To overcome this issue, a logarithmic scale representation is adopted as shown in Figure 2.

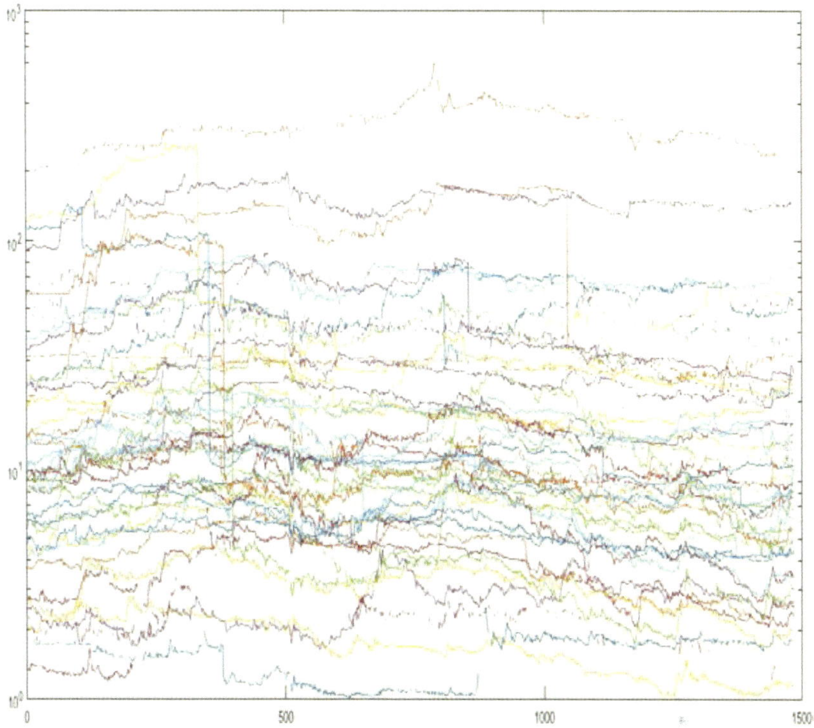

Figure 2. Evolution of the share prices (48 companies - 2009 to 2014): Logarithmic scale

A thorough analysis of the different curves reveals some aberrations in the collected data. Mainly, some curves look to be as dash line for given dates, which reflects quotation interruptions. For each of those particular cases, it was decided to duplicate the previous stock price value observed. Otherwise, ANN simulation tool would consider the missing values due to quotation interruptions as zero-valued, which would compromise the prediction quality.

In addition, it can be noticed a sharp drop of the stock prices for some firms, that stems from a distribution of bonus shares, whether through a stock split, or the creation of new free shares (following an incorporation of reserves in the capital). Based on historical values, the stock prices prediction would be obviously skewed by such outliers. That's why we decided to remove from our sample all the firms concerned by a split or an allocation of free additional shares.

It should also be noted that, all special cases were individually analyzed through a documentary research based on the firms' annual reports and their general meetings' minutes. Table 1 summarizes all the companies that had a distribution of free shares. It specifies for each case, whether it is a split or a creation of new free shares.

Table 1. Free shares distributions during the study period

Firms	Split			Allocation of free additional shares		
	Date		Split ratio	Date		Ratio
	General meeting	Application		General meeting	Application	
BT	May 7, 2010	May 28, 2010	1/10	May 26, 2009	Jun. 10, 2009	1/3
UBCI				Jun. 25, 2010	Jul 16., 2010	1/2
Monoprix	Apr. 6, 2010	May 3, 2010	1/5			
SOPAT				Feb. 9, 2010	Aug 2., 2010	1/8
SOTETEL	Jul. 21, 2011	Aug. 23, 2011	1/2			
SOTUVER	Jun. 14, 2010	Jul 8, 2010	1/10			
Amen Bank	Jun. 5, 2012	Jun. 14, 2012	1/2			
ICF				Jan. 5, 2012	Apr. 10, 2012	1/4
Magasin Général	26 Feb 2013	25 Mar 2013	1/5			

This analysis allowed us to remove from our sample the 9 firms concerned by the distributions of free shares. This would avoid indeed that such an isolated decision taken by the Extraordinary General Meeting alters the quality of the prediction of all the share prices. Hitherto, the sample used is made up of the daily stock closing prices of 39 companies, over the period from 2009 to 2014.

3.1 Data organization

Knowing that the publication of financial statements of a given year shall take place by the end of March of the next year, and similarly to Olson and Mossman (2003), the data collected were organized in such a way to redefine the period of the study from April 1st to March 31st of the following year, so we can integrate the accounting variable to the prediction model. Thus, the periods from January 1st to March 31st, 2009 and from April 1st to December 31st, 2014 were excluded from the sample, which redefines the study period to five subdivisions. Table 2 shows the period of the study, as well as the size of the final sample.

Table 2. Presentation of the final sample and the study period

	Apr.1, 2009 to Mar. 31, 2010	Apr. 1, 2010 to Mar. 31, 2011	Apr.1, 2011 to Mar. 31, 2012	Apr.1, 2012 to Mar. 31, 2013	Apr.1, 2013 to Mar. 31, 2014
Sample size by year and by firm	251	236	255	247	247
Total number of observations per firm	1,236 observations per firm				
Total number of observations over the entire period	1236 x 39 = **48,204 Observations**				

4. Empirical results

4.1 The simulation scenario

The prediction of the stock prices time series by means of the (ANN) toolbox in MATLAB® (R2013a edition) can receive input in various data formats; vectors in the form of rows, columns, or matrix. In this study, a matrix variable is created from the data table (stock market prices of the 39 companies, during the 5 periods of the study), and then injected in the ANN.
The ANN architecture that was adopted for our simulations has a Multi-layer Perceptron topology made up of an input layer, a hidden layer with 10 neurons and an output layer. The transfer function is a sigmoid in the hidden layer and a linear transfer function in the output layer. The training phase of the ANN was based on the Levenberg–Marquardt algorithm which is well known for its execution time efficiency. The chosen temporal prediction memory corresponds to 7 business days.

Following the injection of the time series to be analyzed in the ANN, data is then divided into three interlaced subsets, each intended for use in one of the three phases of processing: training, validation and test. The training phase (70% of our sample) aims to determine the settings of the ANN, in order to minimize through multiple iterations, the prediction error, i.e. the difference between predicted values and the actual injected data, which are known beforehand.

The validation phase (15% of our sample) is launched in order to confirm or, if needed, to adjust the chosen configuration of the ANN, whenever the generated prediction error exceeds a given threshold. Finally, the test phase (15% of our sample) operates on the third samples subset and performs data prediction by means of the ANN architecture as configured and set up by the two previous phases.

During the training phase, it should be noted that the ANN gives different prediction results, from one iteration to another, depending on the path followed when searching for the minimum prediction error. This is commonly well known in multiple local minima problem, for which the search operation may provide different results every time a new simulation is run.

One of the ways to deal with this inconvenience is to apply the Monte Carlo analysis (Metropolis & Ulam, 1949), which is abundant in the related literature (Andor & Bohák, 2017). In fact, we run a sufficient number of simulations (10 in our case), with the same time series as input, and to carry out the calculation of the result average. This allows to ensure a certain consistency of results.

For example, Figure 3 shows a simulation for the company "ADWYA", realized in the first research period. It shows the evolution of the real price's curve, mentioned "Target" in the figure, as well as that of the evolution of the price predicted by the ANN, mentioned "Output". The prediction error is thus presented through the vertical lines, linking each actual share price to the predicted one. The smallest the lines are, the most efficient the ANN is. An error free prediction would be presented by a dot instead of a line.

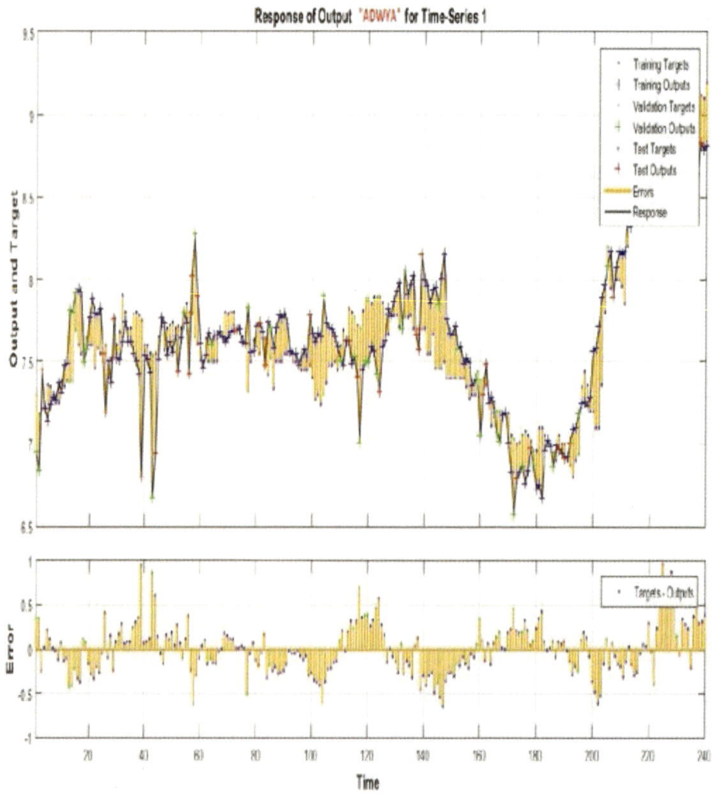

Figure 3. Curve of the market stock price of the company "ADWYA" on the first period: Real price, Predicted price and Prediction error

4.1 Simulation of the stock market prices prediction before and after the accounting variable integration

In order to carry out a twofold analysis of the prediction quality of stock prices, simulation was run with the research sample (48,204 observations from 39 companies over five study periods) without and with integration of an accounting variable “Operating income”.

4.1.1 Stock market prices prediction before the accounting variable integration

As previously explained, the ANN provides the value of the prediction error for each of the 48,204 observations from the 39 companies over the five study periods. It is worth mentioned that the only input to be injected for the simulation of the share prices prediction is their time series.
The following model has been applied in the present study to obtain stock prices prediction, namely:

$$y(t) = f(y(t-1), \dots y(t-d)),$$

where d stands for the temporal prediction memory, corresponding to 7 business days in our case.

Moreover, since the prediction error may have a positive or negative sign (over-estimation or under-estimation of the real stock price), the average error per company and per period was evaluated considering the absolute values of the prediction errors of all observations, and it is therefore estimated in Tunisian Dinar. Also, given the very varying range of the stock prices, the average error was reported at the average value in order to provide the relative average prediction error. Table 3 gives the overall average prediction error, for the 39 companies of the research sample, and for the five research periods, which corresponds to 0.84%.

Table 3. Average prediction error before integration of the accounting variable

Apr.1, 2009 to Mar. 31, 2010	Apr. 1, 2010 to Mar. 31, 2011	Apr.1, 2011 to Mar. 31, 2012	Apr.1, 2012 to Mar. 31, 2013	Apr.1, 2013 to Mar. 31, 2014	Average prediction error
0.56%	1.22%	0.95%	0.82%	0.63%	**0.84%**

After calculating the stock price prediction error based solely on historical stock prices, the following subsection presents a new estimate of this prediction error after integration of the accounting variable "operating income".

4.1.2 Stock market prices prediction with the accounting variable integration

For a prediction scheme based on two inputs (stock price history and the accounting variable "operating income"), we adopt the non-linear autoregressive model, with an external input, where the predicted stock prices are function of the past samples of time series (*y(t)*) and the variable " operating income" (*x(t)*):

$$y(t) = f(x(t-1), \dots x(t-d), y(t-1), \dots y(t-d)),$$

where *d* stands for the temporal prediction memory, corresponding to 7 business days in our case. Table 4 shows that the overall average prediction error, for the 39 companies and upon the five study periods, becomes 0.81% after the integration of the accounting variable “operating income”.

Table 4. Average prediction error with integration of the accounting variable

Apr.1, 2009 to Mar. 31, 2010	Apr. 1, 2010 to Mar. 31, 2011	Apr.1, 2011 to Mar. 31, 2012	Apr.1, 2012 to Mar. 31, 2013	Apr.1, 2013 to Mar. 31, 2014	Average prediction error
0.53%	1.86%	0.65%	0.43%	0.65%	**0.81%**

5. Discussion

In this study we evaluate the prediction quality of market stock prices, based on historical prices and accounting variables for listed companies, using the Artificial Neural Networks. To do so, we analyze the average prediction error of the stock prices, since its small or high value would respectively reflect a good or poor quality of prediction.

Exposing the averages of annual prediction errors for all companies of the sample, with or without accounting variables integration (the history of the variable "operating income"), Tables 3 and 4 show that, over the five periods of the study, the overall average of prediction error of all companies stock prices, does not exceed 1% (respectively 0.84% and 0.81% according to Tables 3 and 4).

In general, this result reflects a good quality of prediction of the stock prices of the Tunis Stock Exchange Market. In order to deepen the analysis, it is now necessary to analyze the impact on the prediction quality of two factors of different natures: the January 2011 events, and the integration in the prediction model of an accounting variable.

5.1 Impact of the socio-political context on the prediction quality of the stock market prices in Tunis Stock Exchange

With or without accounting variable integration in the prediction model, tables 3 and 4 show that the average annual prediction error of the stock prices for the 39 companies is the largest in the same period relating to the January 14th, 2011 events. In other words, as shown in Table 5, the degradation of the prediction quality for the second research period may be explained by the socio-political disturbances that the country and therefore the Tunisian stock market experienced. This result corresponds to the conclusions of Kaizoji and Miyano (2016), who, having studied the divergence rate measuring the spread between the observed prices and the intrinsic values corresponding to economic fundamentals, found that prices are overvalued during financial prosperity, and underestimated during periods of financial crisis. Furthermore, our results confirm those of Ormos and Timotity (2016), showing that in periods of great uncertainty, large deviations from fundamental prices are observed.

Table 5. Highlighting the impact of the socio-political context on the stock prices prediction quality in the Tunis Stock Exchange

Average prediction error	Apr.1, 2009 to Mar. 31, 2010	Apr. 1, 2010 to Mar. 31, 2011	Apr.1, 2011 to Mar. 31, 2012	Apr.1, 2012 to Mar. 31, 2013	Apr.1, 2013 to Mar. 31, 2014
Before integration of an accounting variable (%)	0.56%	**1.22%**	0.95%	0.82%	0.63%
After integration of an accounting variable (%)	0.53%	**1.86%**	0.65%	0.43%	0.65%

5.2 Impact of an accounting variable integration on the prices prediction quality

In order to evaluate the impact of the accounting variable "Operating income" on the quality of the stock prices prediction, it is necessary to compare the prediction errors obtained before and after integration of the given accounting variable, for the 39 companies and over the five study periods.

Thus, a positive difference reflects an improvement of the prediction quality, due to the consideration of the "operating income" in the stock prices prediction. Otherwise, a negative difference shows that the integration of the accounting variable in the simulation model does not improve the stock prices prediction quality. Table 6 summarizes the obtained results.

Table 6. Highlighting the impact of an accounting variable integration on the quality of prices prediction

Average prediction error	Apr.1, 2009 to Mar. 31, 2010	Apr. 1, 2010 to Mar. 31, 2011	Apr.1, 2011 to Mar. 31, 2012	Apr.1, 2012 to Mar. 31, 2013	Apr.1, 2013 to Mar. 31, 2014
Before integration of an accounting variable (%)	0.56%	**1.22%**	0.95%	0.82%	0.63%
After integration of an accounting variable (%)	0.53%	**1.86%**	0.65%	0.43%	0.65%
Variation of Annual prediction quality	0.03%	**- 0.86%**	0.65%	0.43%	0.56%
Improvement / Degradation	**Improvement**	**Degradation**	**Improvement**	**Improvement**	**Improvement**

Table 6 shows that the integration of the "Operating income" variable in the Artificial Neural Network simulation improves the quality of the prediction of market stock prices in four research periods among the five considered ones. Our results are consistent with those of Zahedi and Rounaghi (2015), based on Teheran stock market, and showing the positive impact of the integration of accounting variables, as additional inputs in the ANN tool, on the stock prices prediction quality. Indeed, taking into account the said accounting variable, the only period in which an increase in the prediction error and therefore a degradation of the quality of prediction is observed, is that during which the events of January 14th, 2011 took place in Tunisia. The same results were obtained by Boozer *et al.* (2017), who worked on American companies and found a mixed relationship on the predictive power of accounting variables on stock prices before and after the 2007-2009 financial crisis. The authors concluded that accounting disclosure has a predictive ability on stock prices, but only outside the crisis period.

These results can be interpreted by the fact that, whether in an emerging country (Tunisia) or developed one (US), in times of disruption, market efficiency, as defined by Fama (1965), is considerably altered. Indeed, according to this author, an "efficient" market is one "where there are large numbers of rational, profit-maximizers actively competing, with each trying to predict future market values of individual securities, and where important current information is almost freely available to all participants". Obviously, information risk increases in an unstable period in such a way that accounting disclosure becomes less reliable as a determinant of the market prices discovery. According to the same logic, it appears that accounting disclosure does not improve prices prediction quality in an unstable context.

6. Conclusions

This paper has been designed to predict, by Artificial Neural Network, the stock market prices on the Tunis Stock Exchange, given the socio-political country context, and by integrating an accounting variable in the prediction model. Considering a final sample of 48,204 daily stock closing prices of 39 companies, over the period from 2009 to 2014, some evidence consistent with the stock market prices prediction quality has been discovered to persist. Our empirical results demonstrate that the average annual prediction error of the stock prices for the 39 companies is the largest in the period relating to the January 14th, 2011 events. In other words, the Tunisian socio-political context impacts negatively the prediction quality of the stock market prices in Tunis Stock Exchange.

We also find that the integration of an accounting variable in the Artificial Neural Network simulation improves the quality of the prediction of market stock prices, with the exception of the period in which the events of January 14th, 2011 took place in Tunisia. In other words, it appears that accounting disclosure does not improve prices prediction quality in an unstable context.

As a matter of fact, the contribution provided by the present work is three-fold: theoretical, methodological and practical. Regarding the theoretical contribution, it involves validating the accounting variable disclosure positive impact and the unstable socio-political context negative impact on stock prices prediction quality. Methodologically, our research study has helped us assess the superiority of the non-linear autoregressive model with an external input (the accounting variable), compared to non-linear model based only on the past samples of time series, in predicting stock prices with ANN. This would constitute a test of the hypothesis of weak-form market efficiency, not through the conventional random walk test, but through an artificial neural network model. Moreover, our contributions can be clearly noticed at the practical level. Indeed, they serve to draw the investors' attention to the country contextual changes risks on the stock prices stability, even with accounting variable disclosure.

We highlight, still, that some limits are worth underlining as potential research perspectives. The first perspective concerns the possibility to integrate additional accounting variables in the prediction model. As for the second perspective, it has to do with the research period, which can be expanded. Finally, a further possible extension of this study would be to explore the institutional investors' impact on stock prices prediction.

References

Alford, A., Jones, J., Leftwich, R. & Zmijewski, M. (1993) "The relative informativeness of accounting disclosures in different countries", *Journal of Accounting Research*, Vol. 31: 183-223

Andor, G. & Bohák, A. (2017) "Identifying events in financial time series – A new approach with bipower variation", *Finance Research Letters*, Vol. 22: 1-280

Bagherifard, K., Nilashi, M., Ibrahim, O., Janahmadi, N. & Ebrahimi, L. (2012) "Comparative study of Artificial Neural Network and ARIMA models in predicting exchange rate", *Research Journal of Applied Sciences, Engineering and Technology*, Vol. 4, No. 21: 4397-4403

Ball, R. & Brown, P. (1968) "An empirical evaluation of accounting income numbers", *Journal of Accounting Research*, Vol. 6, No. 2: 159-178

Boozer, B.B., Rainwater, L.H. & Lowe, S.K. (2017) "Using financial statement variables to predict stock prices: Lessons from the 2007-2009 financial crisis", *Journal of Finance and Accountancy*, Vol. 21.

Chen, C. J., Chen, S. & Su, X. (2001) "Is accounting information value-relevant in the emerging Chinese stock market?", *Journal of International Accounting, Auditing and Taxation*, Vol. 10, No. 1: 1-22

Collins, D.W., Maydew, E.L. & Weiss, I. (1997) "Changes in the value-relevance of earnings and book values over the past forty years", *Journal of Accounting and Economics*, Vol. 24: 39-67

Collins, D.W., Pincus, M., & Xie, H. (1999) "Equity valuation and negative earnings: The role of book value of equity", *Accounting Review*, Vol. 79: 29-61.

Donaldson, R. G. & Kamstra, M. (1996) "Forecast combining with neural networks", *Journal of Forecasting*, Vol. 15, No. 1: 49-61.

Fama, E. F. (1965) "The behavior of stock market prices", *Journal of Business*, Vol. 38:31-105.

Graham, R. C. & King R. D. (2000) "Accounting practices and the market valuation of accounting numbers: evidence from Indonesia, Korea, Malaysia, the Philippines, Taiwan, and Thailand", *The International Journal of Accounting*, Vol. 35, No. 4: 445-470

Kaizoji, T. & Miyano, M. (2016) "Why does the power law for stock price hold?", *Chaos, Solitons & Fractals*, Vol. 88: 19-23

Kimoto, T., Asakawa, K., Yoda, M. & Takeoka, M. (1990) "Stock market prediction system with modular neural network", in *proceedings of the International Joint Conference on Neural Network, San Diego*, 1990, CA: 1-6.

Lev, B. (1989) "On the usefulness of earnings and earnings research: lessons and directions from two decades of empirical research", *Journal of Accounting Research*, Vol. 27: 153-192.

Lin, Z. J. & Chen, F. (2005) "Value relevance of international accounting standards harmonization: evidence from A- and B-share markets in China", *Journal of International Accounting, Auditing and Taxation*, Vol. 14: 79-103.

Liu, J. & Liu, C. (2007) "Value relevance of accounting information in different stock market segments: The case of Chinese A-, B, and H-shares, *Journal of International Accounting Research*, Vol. 6: 55-81

Maciel, L.S. & Ballini, R. (2010) "Neural networks applied to stock market forecasting: An empirical analysis", *Journal of the Brazilian Neural Network Society*, Vol. 8, Issue 1: 3-22

Metropolis, N. & Ulam, S. (1949) "The Monte Carlo method", *Journal of the American Statistical Association*, Vol. 44: 335-341.

Mossman, C. & Olson, D. (2003) "Neural network forecasts of Canadian stock returns using accounting ratios", *International Journal of Forecasting*, Vol. 19, No. 3: 453-465

Naeini, M.P., Taremian, H. & Hashemi, H.B. (2010) "Stock market value prediction using neural networks", in *Computer Information Systems and Industrial Management Applications (CISIM) 2010 proceedings of the international conference in Krakow, Poland, 2010*: 132-136

Ohlson, J. A. (1995) "Earnings, book values and dividends in security valuation", *Contemporary Accounting Research*, Vol. 11: 661–687

Ormos, M. & Timotity, D. (2016) "Market microstructure during financial crisis: dynamics of informed and heuristic-driven trading", *Finance Research Letters*, Vol. 19: 60-66

Paquet, P. (1997) "L'utilisation des Réseaux de Neurones Artificiels en finance", working paper No. 1997-1, Laboratoire Orléanais de Gestion, Orleans University, Orleans

Preethi, G. & Santhi, B. (2012) "Stock market forecasting techniques: a survey", *Journal of Theoretical and Applied Information Technology*, Vol. 46, No. 1

Pyo, S., Lee, J., Cha, M. & Jang, H. (2017) "Predictability of machine learning techniques to forecast the trends of market index prices: Hypothesis testing for the Korean stock markets", *PLOS ONE*, Vol. 12, No. 11

Rounaghi, M.M., Abbaszadeh, M.R. & Arashi, M. (2015) "Stock price forecasting for companies listed on Tehran Stock Exchange using multivariate Adaptive Regression Splines model and semi-parametric splines technique", *Physica A: Statistical Mechanics and its Applications*, Vol. 438: 625-633

Slim, C. (2004) "Forecasting the volatility of stock index returns: a stochastic neural network approach", in *Computational Science and Its Applications (ICCSA) 2004 proceedings of the international conference in Assisi, Italy, 2004*, Springer: 14-17

Tkac, M. & Verner, R. (2016) "Artificial neural networks in business: Two decades of research", *Applied Soft Computing*, Vol. 38: 788–804

Zahedi, J. & Rounaghi, M. M. (2015) "Application of artificial neural network models and principal component analysis method in predicting stock prices on Tehran Stock Exchange", *Physica A: Statistical Mechanics and Its Applications*, Vol. 438: 178-187

3

Analysis of the impact of first-time mandatory IFRS adoption on financial statements: The case study of the listed hotels in Turkey

İlhan Dalcı[a] and Hasan Özyapıcı[a,1]

[a] *Eastern Mediterranean University, North Cyprus, Turkey*

Abstract: This study aims to explore the impact of first-time IFRS adoption on the selected financial ratios of the hotels listed in ISE in Turkey. The selected liquidity, solvency, and profitability ratios were used. Both non-parametric Wilcoxon signed-rank test and paired-samples t-test have been applied to test the impact of IFRS adoption. The results show that the transition to IFRS does not influence the financial ratios of listed hotels in Turkey. Accordingly, it sheds light into whether or not transition to IFRS influences the financial performance of the hotel industry in an emerging country. In addition, this study provides better understanding of financial reporting theory and IFRS practices in hospitality sector. This study also provides useful information to the decision-makers such as hotel managers, accountants, investors from other emerging economies, and practitioners who are currently evaluating the merits of applying IFRS. To the best of our knowledge, there is no study investigating the quantitative impact IFRS transition in the hospitality industry in general and hotels in particular. Thus, the present study is expected to fill this gap.

Keywords: first-time mandatory IFRS, IFRS adoption, financial statements, financial ratios

---

[1] *Corresponding author*: Hasan Özyapıcı, Assistant Professor in the Department of Business Administration, Eastern Mediterranean University, Famagusta, North Cyprus, Via Mersin 10, Turkey. Address: Department of Business Administration, Eastern Mediterranean University, Famagusta, North Cyprus, Via Mersin 10, Turkey. E-mail: hasan.ozyapici@emu.edu.tr

1. Introduction

In 2002, the European Union (EU) Parliament approved a regulation (Regulation (EC) 1606/2002) that mandates all companies registered in the EU stock markets to adopt International Financial Reporting Standards (IFRS) in preparing consolidated and stand-alone financial statements commencing after 1 January 2005 (Delvaille *et al.*, 2005; Soderstrom & Sun, 2007; Aharony *et al.*, 2010; Moscariello *et al.*, 2014). The adoption of IFRS has been an important development not only in the EU member countries but also in other non-EU countries such as Turkey, Australia, New Zealand, and China. To illustrate, Turkey, which is one of the largest emerging economies among the non-EU countries, has ongoing negotiations to access the EU since October 2005 (Çelik & Ecer, 2009). In this regard, Turkey needs to apply IFRS in order to be consistent with the EU legislation. Parallel to this development, the adoption of IAS/IFRS which had been optional starting from 2003 has become mandatory since 2005 for all listed companies in İstanbul Stock Exchange (ISE) in Turkey (Balsari & Varan, 2014; Şenyiğit, 2014).

The mandatory adoption of IFRS has received considerable research interest and there have been a growing number of studies conducted to explore the impact of mandatory/voluntary IFRS adoption on financial statements; account numbers, net income, and financial ratios, in the EU and other countries (e.g. ; Clarkson *et al.*, 2011; Kabir *et al.*, 2010; Sahut *et al.*, 2011; Kim, 2013; Istrate, 2014; Grabinski *et al.*, 2014; Lueg *et al.*, 2014). On one hand, there are streams of research that investigate the impact of mandatory/voluntary adoption of IFRS on the financial statements (e.g. Aharony *et al.*, 2010; Sahut *et al.*, 2011; Cordazzo, 2013). On the other hand, some of the studies explored the value relevance of IFRS adoption as compared to local GAAP (e.g. Kabir *et al.*, 2010; Wan Ismail *et al.*, 2013). Some of the studies exploring the impact of IFRS adoption focus on a single country (e.g. Callao *et al.*, 2007; Haller *et al.*, 2009; Lin *et al.*, 2012; Lueg *et al.*, 2014), while some of them have international focus (e.g. Delvaille *et al.*, 2005; Gaston *et al.*, 2010; Moscarielloa *et al.*, 2014; Haller & Wehrfritz, 2014). There are two streams of research having international focus. One research stream focuses on regional country groupings (e.g. Delvaille *et al.*, 2005; Callao *et al.*, 2009; Aharony *et al.*, 2010), while the other one focuses on comparative groupings (Gaston *et al.*, 2010; Moscarielloa *et al.*, 2014).

The current study aims to explore the impact of IFRS adoption on the selected financial ratios of the first-time IFRS adopting hotels listed in ISE in Turkey. There are several motivations for carrying out this research. These motivations are outlined as follows: (1) A considerable global attention has been taken in the literature regarding the impacts of IFRS adoption. This study is encouraged from this development and it is expected to contribute to the literature on the outcomes of IFRS adoption. (2) Researches related to the impact of adoption of IFRS have focused largely on the member countries of the EU and other industrialized countries such as Australia and New Zealand (e.g. Trewavas *et al.*, 2012; Gastón *et al.*, 2010). However, there is a very limited number of studies (e.g. Mısırlıoğlu *et al.*, 2013; Terzi *et al.*, 2013) exploring the impact of IFRS adoption in developing countries such as Turkey which have also started to adopt IFRS. Hence, the current study will contribute to this issue. (3) Research related to the impact of adoption of IFRS has focused largely on the total sample of firms listed in the stock markets of the EU and other parts of the world (e.g. Aisbitt, 2006; Aubert & Grudnitski, 2011; Hellman, 2011; Trewavas *et al.*, 2012; Gastón *et al.*, 2010; Fitó *et al.*, 2013). Similarly, the studies investigating the impact of IFRS in Turkey have focused either on the whole sample of firms (except financial institutions) listed in ISE (e.g. Mısırlıoğlu *et al.*, 2013) or only on particular sectors such as manufacturing (e.g. Terzi *et al.*, 2013). However, the impacts of IFRS adoption on the financial statements of service firms in general and hotels in particular are likely to be different from the ones on the financial statements of manufacturing firms. For example, the non-current assets of manufacturing firms include machinery and equipment which depreciate fast and which may experience significant decreases in value. On the other hand, the non-current assets of service firms such as hotels do not encompass these types of assets and they are mainly composed of building and land which do not depreciate as fast as machinery and equipment and which do not experience such significant decreases in value. Just because of this reason, transition to IFRS that has brought new applications such as fair value adjustment and asset impairments may have different effect on the property, plant and equipment, total non-current assets, and equity of hotels when compared to manufacturing companies. To the best of our knowledge, there is no study investigating the quantitative impact IFRS transition in the hospitality industry in general and hotels in particular. Thus, the present study is expected to fill this gap and provide additional and comparable evidence to the results drawn in the other studies. Additionally, the results of the present study are expected to be useful for the users of the financial statements of the hotels such as creditors, managers, and the regulatory authorities. The present study mainly shows that transition to IFRS does not influence the financial ratios of listed hotels in Turkey.

The remainder of this article is organized as follows: Section 2 presents the literature review related to the impact of IFRS adoption. Section 3 gives detailed information regarding the differences between previous accounting standards and IFRS. Research methodology is given in Section 4. The results and conclusions are given in Section 5 and Section 6, respectively.

2. Literature review on the quantitative impact of IFRS adoption

In recent years, IFRS adoption has been an important issue in financial reporting, having global consequences (Kabir *et al.*, 2010). Parallel to this, the adoption of IFRS has triggered the empirical research to explore the impact of the change in the accounting regime on the financial statements both in Europe and other parts of the world. Previous literature on the impact of IFRS adoption is twofold. On one hand, there is a stream of research that investigate the impact of mandatory/voluntary adoption of IFRS on the financial statements, account numbers, and the financial ratios (e.g. Aharony *et al.*, 2010; Sahut *et al.*, 2011; Mısırlıoğlu *et al.* 2013; Cordazzo, 2013). On the other hand, some of the studies explored the value relevance of IFRS adoption as compared to local GAAP (e.g. Kabir *et al.*, 2010; Wan Ismail *et al.*, 2013). Some of the studies studying the impact of IFRS adoption focus on a single country (e.g. Callao *et al.*, 2007; Haller *et al.*, 2009; Lin *et al.*, 2012; Lueg *et al.*, 2014), while some of them have international focus (e.g. Delvaille *et al.*, 2005; Gaston *et al.*, 2010; Moscarielloa *et al.*, 2014, 2014; Haller & Wehrfritz, 2014). There are two streams of research having international focus. One research stream focuses on regional country groupings (e.g. Delvaille *et al.*, 2005; Callao *et al.*, 2009; Aharony *et al.*, 2010), while another one focuses on comparative groupings (e.g. Gaston *et al.*, 2010; Moscarielloa *et al.*, 2014). In the current study's context, we focus the literature review on the studies that have investigated the impacts of IFRS adoption on the account numbers and financial ratios. To the best of our knowledge, there is no study investigating the impact of IFRS adoption particularly in hotels. Therefore, the following literature review is based the studies focusing either on the total sample of firms including hotels or specific sectors such as manufacturing. In this regard, the literature review progresses as follows:

Haller *et al.* (2009) studied the effects of first-time mandatory IFRS adoption on equity and net income of 103 publicly traded companies in Germany. The results reveal statistically significant increases in the equity and net income after IFRS are adopted. Fitó *et al.* (2013) studied the impact of IFRS adoption on the main accounting numbers and ratios in Spain. The results demonstrate that the non-current assets, equity, reserves, and long-term liabilities changed significantly after the implementation of new IFRS-based standards. Callao *et al.* (2007) explored, by studying IBEX-35 companies in Spain, whether there are significant differences in the accounting numbers presented in the consolidated financial statements and financial ratios under Spanish accounting standards and IFRS. According to the results, IFRS adoption has significant effects in debtors, cash and cash equivalents, equity, long-term and total liabilities in the balance sheet. In the income statements, on the other hand, significant differences were found in the operating and extraordinary income.

In another study, Jermakowicz (2004) investigated the impact of mandatory application of IFRS on the consolidated financial statements of listed BEL-20 companies in Belgium. The findings of the study revealed that the application of IFRS caused significant changes in the equity and net income reported in companies' consolidated financial statements. Aisbitt (2006), on the other hand, examined the impact of transition from the UK GAAP to IFRS on the equity of companies that formed the UK's FTSE 100 index. The findings of that study did not yield overall effect on equity. Lueg *et al.* (2014) explored the impact of mandatory IFRS adoption on the financial ratios of the listed companies in the UK. According to the findings of that study; operating income margin, return on invested capital, and current ratio are some of the financial ratios affected by the adoption of IFRS.

Callao *et al.* (2009), conducted an international study and investigated the quantitative impact of IFRS on financial reporting of 11 European countries and evaluate if this impact is relevant in relation to the traditional accounting system in which each country is classified, either the Anglo-Saxon or the Continental-European accounting system. The results of that study revealed that the impact of IFRS on financial statements of European firms is not related to traditional accounting systems. The results also demonstrated that there are significant differences among the countries in all variables except inventories and returns. Similarly, Ferrer *et al.* (2008) explored the impact of IFRS adoption on the financial information reported by firms listed in 11 UE countries. The results demonstrated that the adoption of IFRS has a significant impact in Spain, France, Ireland, Sweden and UK on such accounting figures as fixed and current assets, short-term and total liabilities and net income. In another study having international focus, Gaston *et al.* (2010) examined the impact of first-time mandatory IFRS adoption on the account numbers and selected financial ratios of listed firms in the UK and Spain. The results reveal increases in fixed and total assets, long-term liabilities, short-term liabilities and indebtedness and decreases in current assets, current ratio and solvency for Spanish firms. For the UK firms, on the other hand, the results demonstrated statistically significant increases in fixed and total assets, long-term liabilities, short-term liabilities, operating income, net income, indebtedness and return on equity and decreases in current assets, equity, and solvency.

Outside the EU, Kabir *et al.* (2010) examined the impact of mandatory IFRS adoption on the account numbers and earnings quality using the firms in New Zealand Stock Exchange for 2002-2009. The results demonstrated that total assets, total liabilities, and net profit were significantly higher under IFRS when compared to local GAAP. In another study conducted in New Zealand, Stent *et al.* (2010) analyzed the impact of mandatory IFRS adoption on the consolidated financial statements and ratios using 56 listed firms during 2005 through 2008. The elements of financial statements most affected by IFRS are liabilities and equity. The IFRS adoption also influenced such ratios as return on assets, return on equity, and asset turnover. In another developing country, Turkey, Mısrlıoğlu *et al.* (2013) explored how mandatory transition to IFRS has changed measurement of accounts and disclosures in the consolidated financial statements of firms listed in İstanbul Stock Exchange (ISE). The authors also studied the factors that affected the overall measurement change. While the results found significant changes on some disclosure items, they revealed that there is little significant impact of transition to IFRS on the balance sheet. The findings of the study further demonstrated that the firm-specific factors do not have any impact on the change in financial ratios. According to the results, among the firm-specific factors only "gearing" had impact on the change in long-term debt to equity ratio.

3. Differences between PAS (Previous Accounting Standards) and IFRS

Before implementing IFRS on a mandatory basis, all listed firms in ISE had to prepare their financial statements in compliance with the first set of financial accounting standards that were developed in January 1989 by the CMB to be in effect on or after January 1, 1989 (CMB, 1989). For the purpose of the current study, the first set of accounting standards developed by the CMB is named Previous Accounting Standards (PAS). There are key differences between PAS and IFRS/IAS in relation to measurement of some financial statement items such as financial instruments, inventories, property, plant & equipment, intangible assets, provisions, and employee benefits. Some differences also exist in relation to treatment/classification of such items as extraordinary income and expenses, changes in foreign exchange rates, leases, and related party transactions (CMB, 1989, XI/1, XI/5; CMB, 2003, XI/25). However, some of the differences such as the ones concerning construction contracts are not applicable to the hotels. Therefore, they are omitted in this study. In addition to this, as pinpointed below, adjusted figures of the income statement items are not available for the listed firms in Turkey. Because of this reason, the differences between PAS and IFRS which are expected to impact income statement items are also omitted. The discussions concerning the differences between PAS and IFRS presented below are based on the serial publications of the CMB (CMB, 1989, XI/1 and XI/5; CMB, 2003, XI/25) as well as the previous research (e.g. Simga-Mugan & Hosal-Akman, 2005; Terzi *et al.*, 2013; Mısırlıoğlu *et al.*, 2013).

3.1. Differences between PAS and IFRS which are considered to affect property, plant & equipment, intangible assets, and investment property.

In compliance with taxation laws, the impairments of tangible and intangible assets are not allowed under PAS. According to IAS 36, on the other hand, impairment tests are required in case net recoverable values of the assets are less than book values. Once the impairment test is applied, property, plant & equipment and intangible assets are expected to decrease.

Another new application which is likely to diminish intangible assets is related to the treatment of research expenditures. While research expenditures can be recognized as intangible assets under PAS, they are separated from the assets and reported as expenses under IAS 38. Thus, transition to IAS 38 is expected to decrease intangible assets. According to PAS, tangible and intangible assets are measured with historical costs. However, according to IAS 16 for property, plant and equipment and IAS 38 for intangible assets, assets can be measured with fair values if value of the assets increases at material level.

Under PAS, investment property is not separated from property, plant & equipment and it is measured with its acquisition cost. In compliance with IAS 40, on the other hand, investment property is classified as a separate account from property, plant & equipment. Thus, this new application is expected to result in a decrease in property, plant & equipment and an increase in investment properties. Property, plant & equipment are also expected to increase as a result of a move to a new application regarding the treatment of financial leases. This is because while financial leases are not reported as assets under PAS, a property subject to a financial lease should be recognized as an asset in compliance with IAS 17.

Based on the above discussions, it can be concluded that: (1) IAS 40 is expected to increase investment property and decrease property, plant and equipment. (2) IAS 36 is expected to decrease property, plant and equipment and intangible assets. (3) IAS 38 is expected to increase or decrease intangible assets. (4) IAS 16 and 17 is expected to increase property, plant and equipment.

3.2. Differences between PAS and IFRS which are considered to affect current and non-current trade and/or other receivables, trade and/or payables, receivables/payables from/to related parties.

According to IAS 24, receivables/payables from/to related parties have to be classified in separate accounts. This reclassification requirement, therefore, is expected to decrease trade and/or other receivables/payables and increase receivables/payables from/to related parties. Another accounting standard which is likely to decrease trade payables is the adoption of IAS 21. Restatement of foreign trade payables at sell rates under new application will lead to a decrease in trade payables.

Consequently, the IAS 24 and 21 are expected to reduce trade and/or other payables. The IAS 24 is also expected to lead to a fall in trade receivables and an increase in receivables/payables from/to related parties.

3.3. Differences between PAS and IFRS which are considered to impact financial instruments

Revaluation of financial instruments on the basis of the fair value in line with IAS 39 is expected to increase or decrease current and non-current financial assets and liabilities. In addition to this, the impairment test that should be applied within the scope of IAS 39 will decrease the financial assets. On the other hand, in compliance with IAS 21, the foreign financial liabilities must be valued at buy rates rather than sell rates. Hence, financial liabilities are expected to decrease as a result of this application.

3.4. Differences between PAS and IFRS which are considered to affect inventories

Under PAS, inventories are valued at cost. According to IAS 2, however, inventories should be valued at lower of historical cost or replacement cost (LCM). Valuation of inventories at lower replacement cost will lead to a decrease in inventories. On the other hand, LIFO method can be used under PAS if specific conditions are met. However, LIFO is prohibited under IFRS. In this case, switching from LIFO to FIFO or average-cost in the transition period will result in an increase in inventories.

3.5. Differences between PAS and IFRS which are considered to affect deferred tax assets and deferred tax liabilities

Before IFRS were adopted, only current income tax liability is reported in the financial statements. In compliance with IAS 12, however, deferred tax liabilities as well as deferred tax assets should also be reported in addition to current tax liabilities. Therefore, the application of IAS 12 is expected to increase deferred tax assets and/or deferred tax liabilities.

3.6. Differences between PAS and IFRS which are considered to impact total current assets, total non-current assets, and total assets

As outlined above, transition to IFRS is likely to impact some of the current assets. The current asset items which are expected to change are: (1) Financial assets (IAS 21 and 39). (2) Inventories (IAS 2), and (3) Deferred tax assets (IAS 12). While some of these new application are expected to increase or decrease the current asset items (IAS 2 and 21), some of them have mixed effects (IAS 39).

Some of the current asset items, on the other hand, are influenced because of reclassification (IAS 24). However, this application is not expected to have any impact on the total amount of current assets because while it decreases one current asset item, it increases the other one by the same amount. As explained in section 4.1, while the IAS 38 and 17 are expected to increase total non-current assets, the IAS 36 is expected to decrease them. The IAS 40, on the other hand, is not expected to have any impact on total non-current assets.

Therefore, transition to IFRS is expected to have mixed effects on both total current and non-current assets. Parallel to the changes in total current and non-current assets, total assets may also increase or decrease depending on the magnitude of the change.

3.7. Differences between PAS and IFRS which are considered to impact total current and non-current provisions

Recognition of provisions and contingent liabilities is limited under PAS. According to IAS 37, on the other hand, provisions are recognized if certain conditions are met. Transition to IFRS, therefore, results in an increase in total provisions.

3.8. Differences between PAS and IFRS which are considered to affect total short-term liabilities, total long-term liabilities, and total liabilities

As it is the case for the total assets, transition to IFRS tends to have mixed effects on total liabilities. This is due to the fact that whereas some of the new applications are expected to increase several liability accounts, some of them tend to decrease others. One of the differences between PAS and IFRS that is expected to increase liabilities is related to IAS 12 which requires reporting of deferred tax liabilities. The other difference which tends to increase liabilities is in relation to the treatment of financial leases in compliance with IAS 17. Another difference which is expected to lead to an increase in liabilities is the treatment of provisions under IAS 37.

On the contrary, regarding the IAS 19 and 21, total liabilities are expected to decrease. Firstly, discounting of employment benefits in line with IAS 19 is likely to result in lower liabilities to be reported in the statement of financial position (balance sheet). Secondly, restatement of foreign liabilities at buy rates in compliance with IAS 21 tends to decrease foreign liabilities.

On the other hand, valuation of financial liabilities at fair value in conjunction with IAS 39 is likely to lead to an increase or a decrease in financial liabilities.

3.9. Differences between PAS and IFRS which are considered to affect equity

As stated above, impairment tests are required according to IAS 36 and 39. In this case, the impairment losses would decrease equity. Reporting of higher provisions through loss under IAS 37 is also expected to lead to a decrease in equity. Possible impairment of inventories at lower replacement cost through loss under IAS 2 is another new application which is likely to decrease equity.

The new application which is expected to lead to an increase in equity is in relation to the treatment of financial instruments. De-recognition of financial instruments through profit under IAS 39 is expected to lead to an increase in equity. The valuation of foreign liabilities at buy rates under IAS 21 is another application which is expected to result in a gain which will in turn increase equity. Discounting of employee benefits under IAS 19 which will result in lower provision loss is also expected to lead to an increase in equity.

On the other hand, the recording of deferred tax assets or liabilities through deferred tax expenses and/or revenues under IAS 12 is expected to have mixed effects on equity.

In summary, while some of the new applications are expected to increase/decrease equity, some of them are expected to have mixed effects.

3.10. Differences between PAS and IFRS considered to impact financial ratios
As explained above, the expected impact of IFRS on the total current assets, total non-current assets, total current liabilities, total long-term liabilities, total liabilities, and total equity is inconclusive. Therefore, it is expected that the ratios may not change because of the offsetting impacts of the mutual effects.

4. Research methodology

4.1. The selection of case studies

In order to explore the first-time impact of mandatory IFRS transition, comparable data is required. According to IFRS 1 "First-Time Adoption of IFRS", first set of IFRS-based financial statements should comprise comparative figures. In this regard, the statements of financial position to be disclosed in 2005 in Turkey should be compared with the statements of financial position of 2004 which have been adjusted according to IFRS (CMB, 2003, XI/25). However, comparative figures for income statements, cash flow statements, and statements of changes in retained earnings are not reported in the financial statements of 2005 (CMB, 2003, XI/25). Therefore, comparable data for the statements of financial position is only available under both the local accounting standards and the IFRS for the year, 2004.

The statements of financial position prepared under PAS are obtained from the 2004 financial statements. The statements of financial position adjusted according to IFRS, on the other hand, are extracted from the comparative figures reported in 2005. It is important to emphasize that the comparative figures for income statements are not reported in the financial statements of 2005. Because of this reason, the current study focuses only the statements of financial position of 2004 prepared according to both PAS and IFRS. These data have been downloaded from the website ISE. In fact, there are 8 hotels listed in ISE. Of those, 1 hotel's adjusted financial statements are not available. Therefore, the financial statements of 7

hotels are explored in this study. In other words, a total of 7 hotels listed in ISE in Turkey are selected as case studies. The brief information regarding the hotels can be given as follows (www.borsaistanbul.com):
Altın Yunus Resort & Thermal Hotel, located in Çeşme, is a subsidiary of Yaşar Holding. It was founded in 1974. The amount of total assets recorded on the balanced sheet prepared at the end of 2005 is 74.236.163 TL (Turkish Lira). *Marmaris Altınyunus Turistik Tesisler A.Ş.* is a subsidiary of the Koç Group. It was established in 1986. In 2005, it reported total assets of 54.351.834 TL. *Marmaris Marti Otel İşletmeleri A.Ş* is listed in Borsa İstanbul since 1990. The amount of total assets reported in 2005 is 124.886.130 TL. *Metemtur Otelcilik ve Turizm İşletmeleri A.Ş.* was established in 1985. The amount of total assets reported in 2005 is 24.059.193 TL. In addition, *Petrokent Turizm A.Ş., Net Turizm Ticaret Ve Sanayi A.Ş., and Tek-Art İnşaat Ticaret Turizm Sanayi Ve Yatirimlar A.Ş.* are also case hotels having total assets of 30.179.201 TL, 246.017.016 TL, and 46.584.031 TL, respectively. In this regard, it is concluded that the size of the case hotels differs from each other.

Although the number of case studies is likely to be small in this study, it is possible to obtain powerful results with a single case study or very small sample size. There is not any theoretical minimum sample size to be needed for the population that is normally distributed. Similarly, Wilcoxon signed rank test can also be applied for the population that is not normally distributed. This is because the validity is closely related to the selection of the appropriate method by considering the distribution of sample data (Lowry, 2010).

4. 2. Study variables

In this study, the analysis of the impact of first-time IFRS adoption refers to the account numbers in the statement of financial position and selected liquidity and solvency ratios that can be calculated using the statements of financial position. The overview of the statements of financial position reveals that the hotels did not report financial lease liability, current tax assets, non-current receivables/payables from/to related parties before and after IFRS. Therefore, although these variables are also expected to be influenced by IFRS, they are not analyzed in this study. As stated above, the adjusted income statements are not reported by the case hotels. Therefore, the current study does not explore the impact of IFRS transition on the income statement. It is also important to emphasize that current ratio, acid-test ratio, cash flow liquidity ratio, debt ratio, shareholder equity ratio, debt-to-equity ratio, tangible fixed assets to total assets, return on total assets, and return on equity have mainly been used to determine the effect of IFRS transition on liquidity, solvency, and profitability of case hotels.

4.3. Data analysis

As Appendix 1 portrays, the data are not normally distributed for majority of the variables. These variables can be seen in the Panel A of Appendix 2. This is due to the fact that, the skewness and kurtosis values for the distributions of these variables are higher than the threshold values of 1 and 3 respectively (Bulmer, 1979; Balanda & MacGillivray, 1988). Additionally, Kolgomarov-Smirnov and Shapiro-Wilk tests results reveal that these variables are significant at the level of $p<0.1$. This means that, the sample data for these variables are not normally distributed, are leptokurtic, and are positively skewed (Lueg *et al.*, 2014). On the other hand, for the rest of the variables as Panel B of Appendix 2 shows, the data are normally distributed.

In order to analyze the data that does not show normal distribution, the non-parametric Wilcoxon signed-rank test has been applied. On the other hand, the paired-samples t-test has been used for the data that show normal distribution. For the variables that display non-normal distribution, median differences have also been calculated because the median is a better indicator of central tendency than the mean when data is not normally distributed (Stent *et al.*, 2010; Lueg *et al.*, 2014). On the other hand, mean differences have been computed to support the t-test results.

5. Interpretation of the results

Appendix 2 demonstrates the Wilcoxon signed-rank test and t-test results. According to the t-test results presented in Appendix 2, the mean value of total property, plant & equipment under IFRS is not statistically different from the mean value under PAS despite the fact that the average mean value under IFRS has decreased by 14% when compared to PAS. As has been proposed before, the IAS 40 and 36 are expected to lead to decreases in property, plant & equipment, while the IAS 17 is expected to lead to an increase. Apparently, the IAS 40 and IAS 17 do not contribute to this decrease because the investment property does not change as opposed to our expectations. Additionally, the hotels do not report any finance lease liability before and after IFRS adoption. This finding is not in line with the results of one of the very few studies (Mısırlıoğlu *et al.*, 2013) conducted in Turkey which shows that financial lease liabilities increased significantly as a result of transition to IAS 17. In fact, coming up with this difference is not surprising because Mısırlıoğlu *et al.* (2013) state that manufacturing firms are dominant in the leasing group. As a result, the decrease in property, plant & equipment (which is not statistically significant) can be attributed to the first-time impairment test applied in line with the IAS 36.

In regard to the total intangible assets, the median value under IFRS has decreased by 42% when compared to the median under PAS. According to the Wilcoxon signed-rank test results, this decrease is also statistically significant at $p<0.05$. Since total intangible assets have fallen down, it seems that these assets have not been revaluated at higher fair values in compliance with IAS 38. Additionally, the detailed analysis of the statements of financial position of the case hotels reveals that there is no reclassification from the intangible assets to goodwill. The analysis of the statements of financial position also demonstrates that there is no research costs in the statements of financial position prepared under PAS. In fact, this can be due to the fact that service companies such as hotels do not engage in new product development activities as manufacturing firms do. In this case, it is obvious that the intangible assets have not been changed by any reclassification effect. Thus, the decrease in the intangible assets could be attributed to the application of impairment test according to IAS 36. This finding is also consistent with the findings of the other studies conducted in Turkey (e.g. Mısırlıoğlu *et al.*, 2013).

Concerning the impact of IAS 24, the Wilcoxon signed-rank test results demonstrate a statistically significant increase in the current payables to related parties at $p<0.10$. This finding is consistent with the findings of Mısırlıoğlu *et al.* (2013). Similar to this, the current receivables from related parties have also increased under IFRS. However, this increase is not statistically significant. In line with increases in current related accounts, there are decreases in other current receivables and other current payables. While the decrease in other current payables is significant at $p<0.05$, the decrease in other current receivables is not. On the other hand, the results do not reveal any change in trade receivables and payables. This means that, the increase in receivables and payables from/to related parties results from reclassification of some of the other receivables and other payables rather than trade receivables and trade payables. However, the IAS 21 has not reflected its expected impact because the results do not demonstrate any change in trade payables.

The results also reveal that the transition to IFRS does not have any statistically significant impact on financial assets and liabilities. The IAS 39 is expected to have mixed effects on the financial assets and liabilities, while IAS 21 is supposed to decrease financial liabilities. For non-current financial liabilities, median differences under PAS and IFRS are zero. On the other hand, although the current/non-current financial assets and current financial liabilities decreased under IFRS, these decreases are statistically not significant. Obviously, the impairment application in compliance with IAS 39 is responsible for the decrease in the non-current financial assets. The current financial liabilities, on the other hand, seem to decrease in relation to IAS 39 and 21.

As Appendix 2 presents, the median value of inventories has increased under IFRS. However, this increase is not statistically significant. This finding is in line with the findings of Terzi *et al.* (2013) which reveal that inventories of manufacturing firms listed in ISE have significantly increased as a result of transition to IFRS. Given this finding, it is apparent that LCM adjustment has not been done by the hotels. In fact, this result might be due to the change in the inventory costing method from LIFO to FIFO or average-cost.

The results further show that the non-current deferred tax assets and current/non-current deferred tax liabilities have increased in relation to IAS 12. However, none of these increases is statistically significant. The analysis of the statements of financial position also reveals that the application of IAS 12 is not uniform across the listed hotels in Turkey.

As a result of transition to IFRS, the median value of total current assets has increased and this increase is significant at $p<0.05$. It seems that the increase in the inventories is responsible for the increase in total current assets. The mean value of total non-current assets has also increased due to the change in non-current deferred tax assets under IFRS. Similarly, the mean value of total assets has also gone up. However, the increases in total non-current assets and total assets are extremely small and they are statistically not significant. Thus, H9 is partly confirmed.

The median value of current provisions has increased under IFRS although there is no change in the value of non-current provisions. However, the increase in the median value of current provisions is not statistically significant.

In relation to the total current liabilities, the mean value has increased as a result of the move to IFRS. Moreover, this increase is significant at $p<0.10$. On the other hand, although the non-current liabilities have increased under IFRS, this increase is not statistically significant. The current liability accounts which have increased under IFRS are provisions, payables to related parties, and deferred tax liabilities. However, among these accounts, only payables to related parties have revealed statistically significant increase. Considering the fact that the increase in the payables to related parties has resulted from the reclassification effect, the IAS 37 and 12 seem to have overall increasing impact of total current liabilities although they do not show statistically significant impact individually. On the other hand, the increase in the non-current liabilities, although it is not statistically significant, can be attributed to the insignificant increase in deferred tax liabilities. Parallel to the increase in total current and non-current liabilities, the mean and median value of total liabilities have also gone up. The change in total liabilities, however, is not statistically significant. This outcome is parallel to the ones found by Mısırlıoğlu *et al.* (2013).

The results further reveal that there is a slight insignificant increase in total equity as a result of a move to IFRS. As stated above, the application of IAS 36 has resulted in a statistically significant decrease in the intangible assets. Transition to IAS 36 has also decreased property, plant & equipment although this decrease is not statistically significant. On the other hand, the IAS 39 seems to be responsible for the decrease in financial assets. In this case, it can be concluded that the IAS 36 and 39 have negatively influenced equity, though this overall effect is statistically not significant. The increase in current provisions as a result of application of IAS 37 can be seen as the other factor which has negatively affected equity. The IAS 39 is also responsible for the decrease in financial liabilities which is supposed to have the positive impact on equity. Obviously, the mixed effects of IFRS have not resulted in any statistically significant change in equity.

As explained before, both mean and median values of total current assets and total current liabilities have significantly increased under IFRS. As a result of this, the current ratio has slightly increased. This slight increase, however, is not statistically significant. On the other hand, the cash & cash equivalents is not influenced at all under IFRS. The results regarding these accounts are not reported in Appendix 2 because they are not among the research variables in this study. Since the cash & cash equivalents have not changed while the total current liabilities have gone up, the acid-test ratio has fallen down. However, this decrease is statistically not significant. While these findings are in line with the ones found by other studies conducted in Turkey (e.g. Alkan & Doğan, 2012; Mısırlıoğlu *et al.*, 2013), they are opposite to some others (see Terzi et al, 2013).

Although it is not statistically significant, percentage mean and median change in total equity is higher than percentage change in liabilities. Therefore, the ratio of shareholders' equity to total liabilities has increased. However, the change in this ratio is extremely insignificant. This result is not consistent with the findings of Çelik *et al.* (2007) and Terzi *et al.* (2013) who found that transition to IFRS has significantly changed total debt to equity ratio of listed manufacturing firms in Turkey. While the ratio of total current liabilities to total liabilities & equity has increased under IFRS, ratio of total non-current liabilities to total liabilities & equity has decreased. None of these changes, however, is statistically significant. This finding is in line with the results found by Agca and Aktaş (2007) who explored the impact of IFRS adoption on the financial ratios of listed firms (except financial institutions) in Turkey. The results additionally demonstrate no statistically significant change in stockholders' equity ratio which is in line with the findings of Mısırlıoğlu *et al.* (2013). The results further reveal that there is no statistically significant change in debt ratio under IFRS. To sum up, the transition to IFRS does not influence the financial ratios of the case hotels that are listed in ISE even though their institutional contexts (e.g. size, auditors) differ from each other.

6. Conclusions

In this study, we explored the impact of IFRS on the statements of financial position and selected financial ratios of the hotels listed in ISE. According to the results, the IAS 36 and 24 have displayed their expected impacts significantly. However, since the IAS 24 has a reclassification effect, it has not altered total figures of assets and/or liabilities. On the other hand, whereas the IAS 37, 39, 12, and 21 have reflected their expected impacts, the changes they have resulted in are not statistically significant. On the contrary, the other standards such as IAS 40 and 17 have not yielded any change in the accounts in the expected direction. The results also reveal the IAS 36 is responsible for the statistically significant decrease in intangible assets. This is similar to results found by Mısırloğlu *et al.* (2013) who investigated the impact of IFRS on the account numbers of the full sample of listed firms in ISE. This means that, the IAS 36 has a similar effect on intangible assets of the hotels as well as of the other firms operating in the other sectors in Turkey.

On the other hand, a move to IFRS has a significant impact on property, plant & equipment. This finding is in line with the ones found in the other studies conducted in Turkey in order to explore the impact of IFRS adoption either on the financial statements of the full sample of firms or the manufacturing firms listed in ISE (Mısırlıoğlu *et al.*, 2013; Terzi *et al.*, 2013). These important results suggest that transition to IAS 36 and 40 do not have any significant impact on property, plant & equipment of hotels. Another important conclusion that can be derived from the current study is that, while the IAS I7 influences the property, plant & equipment and finance lease liabilities of manufacturing firms (see Mısırlıoğlu *et al.*, 2013), it does not reflect its impact for the hotels. This is due to the fact that the service firms such as hotels do not engage in financial leases as manufacturing firms do.

The findings also reveal that the overall impact of the IAS 37 and 12 result in a statistically significant change in total current liabilities. According to the results, there is a statistically significant increase in total current assets as well. However, despite the statistically significant increase in total current assets and liabilities, IFRS in general do not have any statistically significant influence on total assets, total non-current liabilities, total liabilities, and equity of the hotels. This important conclusion coupled with the parallel findings of Mısırlıoğlu *et al.* (2013), who found the same results for the total sample of listed firms including hotels, conveys an important message to managers of the hotels as well as the other policy makers such as the standard-setters and users of financial information. This message implies that transition to IFRS results in a relatively little or no change in the financial information regarding financial position of the hotels. Parallel to these, the results do not demonstrate any statistically significant impact on the selected financial ratios of the hotels despite the fact these ratios have been changed slightly. Especially, the findings concerning the current ratio and stockholders equity ratio are parallel to the ones found by Mısırlıoğlu *et al.* (2013). This important finding suggests IFRS adoption does not change liquidity and solvency of the hotels. Based on these outcomes, the stakeholders such as investors and creditors should understand that their evaluations regarding the financial position and debt-paying ability of the hotels will not change after mandatory IFRS adoption when compared to pre-IFRS period. However, they should not ignore the fact that the adoption of universally accepted accounting principles such as IFRS can improve reliability of the financial statements although it yields limited benefits in terms of providing more useful information. In addition to these, the managers of the hotels should not come up with the conclusion that it is not necessary to use IFRS because their adoption provides limited benefits. Instead, they should keep in mind that the IFRS adoption can make the financial statements more comparable and understandable in the global arena.

Our results should be interpreted considering the following limitations: First, the current study focuses on a single country. Therefore, due to the specific characteristics of Turkish accounting tradition, the results cannot be generalized to the hospitality sector. Thus, it is recommended that future research focus on the hotels in the other tax-oriented emerging countries as well as the EU in order to find out comparable and generalizable results. Second, the current study does not evaluate the impact of IFRS on the income statement line items and financial ratios calculated using income statement figures. This is due to the fact that the listed firms in Turkey were not required to report the adjusted income statements in the transition period. Third, the current study focuses on the transition period in order to measure the impact of first-time mandatory IFRS adoption. This is, however, exposed to the adaptation problems in the transition period. Thus, future studies should take into account the financial statements prepared after 2005 in order to see whether the impacts of IFRS are different from the ones in the transition period.

Despite these limitations, this study provides insight into which particular standard affects the statements of financial position of the hotels. Additionally, it sheds light into whether or not transition to IFRS influences the statement of financial position items and selected financial ratios of hotels in an emerging country such as Turkey. The current study also provides useful information to the decision-makers such as hotel managers, owners and investors who are currently evaluating the merits of applying IFRS for the hotels.

References

Aharony, J., Barniv, R. & Falk, H. (2010) "The impact of mandatory IFRS adoption on equity valuation of accounting numbers for security investors in the EU", *European Accounting Review*, vol. 19, no. 3: 535-578

Agca, A. & Aktas, R. (2007) "First time application of IFRS and its impact on financial ratios: a study on Turkish listed firms", *Problems and Perspectives in Management*, vol. 5, no. 2: 99-112

Aisbitt, S. (2006) "Assessing the effect of the transition to IFRS on equity: the case of the FTSE 100", *Accounting in Europe*, vol. 3, no. 1: 117-133

Alkan, G.I. & Dogan, O. (2012) "Uluslararası finansal raporlama standartlarının finansal rasyolara kısa ve uzun dönemli etkileri: IMKB'de bir arastırma", *Muhasebe ve Finansman Dergisi*, vol. 54: 87-100

Aubert, F. & Grudnitski, G. (2011) "The impact and importance of mandatory adoption of International Financial Standards in Europe", *Journal of International Financial Management and Accounting*, vol. 22, no. 1: 1-26

Balanda, K.P. & MacGillivray, H. (1988) "Kurtosis: A critical review". *The American Statistician*, vol. 42, no. 2: 111-119

Balsari, K.C. & Varan, S. (2014) "IFRS implementation and studies in Turkey", *Accounting and Management Information Systems*, vol. 13, no. 2: 373-399

Bulmer, M.G. (1979) *Principles of Statistics*, Dover Publications, Mineola, New York

Callao, S., Jarne, J. I., & Lainez, J. A. (2007) "Adoption of IFRS in Spain: effect on the comparability and relevance of financial reporting", *Journal of International Accounting, Auditing and Taxation,* vol. 16, no. 2: 148-178

Callao, S., Ferrer, C., Jarne, J.I. & Lainez, J.A. (2007) "The impact of IFRS on the European Union: is it related to the accounting tradition of the countries?", *Journal of Applied Accounting Research*, vol. 10, no. 1: 33-55

Çelik, M., Aygören, H. & Uyar, S. (2007) "The impact of international financial reporting standards on financial statements and financial ratios", The Balkan Countries 1st Conference on Accounting and Auditing, 08-09 March, Edirne, Turkey

Çelik, O. & Ecer, A., (2009) "Efficiency in accounting education: evidence from Turkish Universities", *Critical Perspectives on Accounting*, vol. 20, no. 5: 614–634

Clarkson, P., Hanna, J. D., Richardson, G. D. & Thompson, R. (2011) "The impact of IFRS adoption on the value relevance of book value and earnings", *Journal of Contemporary Accounting & Economics*, vol. 7, no. 1: 1-17

CMB (1989, XI/1) Sermaye piyasasında mali tablo ve raporlara ilişkin ilke ve kurallar hakkında tebliğ XI/1, [Accounting Standards Act], Resmi Gazete 20064 (29.1.1989)

CMB (2003, XI/25) Sermaye piyasasında muhasebe standartları hakkında tebliğ XI/25, [Accounting Standards Act in compliance with IFRS], Resmi Gazete 25290 (15.11.2003)

Cordazzo, M. (2013) "The impact of IFRS on net income and equity: evidence from Italian listed companies", *Journal of Applied Accounting Research*, vol. 14, no.1: 54-73

Delvaille, P., Ebbers, G. & Saccon, C. (2005) "International financial reporting convergence: evidence from three continental European countries", *Accounting in Europe*, vol. 2, no. 1: 137-164

Ferrer, C., Callao, S., Jarne, J.I. & Laınez, J.A. (2008) "The impact of IFRS on the Europeanfinancial reporting", paper presented at the 31st Annual Congress European Accounting Association, 23-25 April 2008, Rotterdam

Fitóa, A.M., Moyab, S. & Orgazc, S. (2013) "Considering the effects of operating lease capitalization on key financial ratios", *Spanish Journal of Finance and Accounting*, vol. 42, no. 159: 341-369

Gaston, S.C., Garcia, C. F., Jarne, J.I. & Gadea, J.A. (2010) "IFRS adoption in Spain and the United Kingdom: effects on accounting numbers and relevance", *Advances in Accounting, Incorporating Advances in International Accounting*, vol. 26, no. 2: 304-313

Grabinskia, K., Kedziora, M., & Krasodomska, J. (2014) "The Polish accounting system and IFRS implementation process in the view of empirical research", *Accounting and Management Information Systems*, vol. 13, no. 2: 281–310

Haller, A. & Eierle, B. (2004) "The adaptation of German accounting rules to IFRS: A legislative balancing act", *Accounting in Europe*, vol. 1, no.1: 27-50

Haller, A., Ernstberger, J. & Froschhammer, M. (2009) "Implications of the mandatory transition from national GAAP to IFRS – empirical evidence from Germany", *Advances in Accounting, Incorporating Advances in International Accounting*, vol. 25, no. 2: 226-236

Haller, A. & Wehrfritz, M., (2013) "The impact of national GAAP and accounting traditions on IFRS policy selection: Evidence from Germany and the UK", *Journal of International Accounting, Auditing and Taxation*, vol. 22, no. 1: 39-56

Hellman, N. (2011) "Soft adoption and reporting incentives: a study of the impact of IFRS on financial statements in Sweden", *Journal of International Accounting Research*, vol. 10, no. 1: 61-83

Istrate, C. (2014) "Impact of IFRS on the accounting numbers of Romanian listed companies", *Accounting and Management Information Systems*, vol. 13, no. 3: 466-491

Jermakowicz, E.K. (2004) "Effects of adoption international financial reporting standards in Belgium: the evidence from BEL-20 companies", *Accounting in Europe*, vol. 1, no. 1: 51-70

Kabir, M.H., Laswad, F. & Islam, M.A. (2010) "Impact of IFRS in New Zealand on accounts and earnings quality", *Australian Accounting Review*, vol. 20, no. 55: 343-357

Kim, O. (2013) "Russian accounting system: value relevance of reported information and the IFRS adoption perspective", *The International Journal of Accounting*, vol. 48, no. 4: 525-547

Lin, S., Ricardi, W. & Wang, C. (2012) "Does accounting quality change following a switch from U.S. GAAP to IFRS? Evidence from Germany", *Journal of Accounting and Public Policy*, vol. 31, no. 6: 641–657

Lowry, R. (2010) Concepts & Applications of Inferential Statistics. Poughkeepsie, New York

Lueg, R., Punda, P. & Burkert, M. (2014) "Does transition to IFRS substantially affect key financial ratios in shareholder-oriented common law regimes? Evidence from the UK", *Advances in Accounting, Incorporating Advances in International Accounting*, vol. 30, no. 1: 241-250

Mısırlıoğlu, İ.U., Tucker J. & Yükseltürk, O. (2013) "Does mandatory adoption of IFRS guarantee compliance?", *The International Journal of Accounting*, vol. 48, no. 3: 327-363

Moscarielloa, N., Skerrattb, L. & Pizzoa, M. (2014) "Mandatory IFRS adoption and the cost of debt in Italy and UK", *Accounting and Business Research*, vol. 44, no. 1: 63-82

Regulation, EC. (2002) Regulation (EC) No 1606/2002 of the European Parliament and of the Council of 19 July 2002 on the application of international accounting standards, available at: http://eur-lex.europa.eu/legal-content/EN/ALL/?uri=CELEX:32002R1606/ (accessed 7 April 2014)

Sahut, J.M., Boulerne, S. & Teulon, F. (2011) "Do IFRS provide better information about intangibles in Europe?", *Review of Accounting and Finance*, vol. 10, no. 3: 267-290

Şenyiğit, Y.B. (2014) "Determinants of voluntary IFRS adoption in an emerging market: Evidence from Turkey", *Accounting and Management Information Systems*, vol. 13, no. 3: 449-465

Simga-Mugan, C. & Hosal-Akman, N. (2005) "Convergence to international financial reporting standards: the case of Turkey", *International Journal of Accounting, Auditing and Performance Evaluation*, vol. 2, no. 1/2: 127-139

Soderstrom, N.S. & Sun, K.J. (2007) "IFRS adoption and accounting quality: a review", *European Accounting Review*, vol. 16, no. 4: 675-702

Stent, W., Bradbury, M. & Hooks, J. (2010) "IFRS in New Zealand: effects on financial statements and ratios", *Pacific Accounting Review*, vol. 22, no. 2: 92-107

Terzi, S., Oktem, R. & Sen, I.K. (2013) "Impact of adopting international financial reporting standards: empirical evidence from Turkey", *International Business Research*, vol. 6, no. 4: 55-66

Trewavas, K., Redmayne, N.B. & Laswad, F. (2012) "The impact of IFRS adoption on public sector financial statements", *Australian Accounting Review*, vol. 22, no. 1: 86-102

Wan Ismail, W.A., Kamarudin, K.A., Van Zijl, T. & Dunstan, K. L. (2013) "Earnings quality and the adoption of IFRS based accounting standards: Evidence from an emerging market", *Asian Review of Accounting*, vol. 21, no. 1: 53-73

http://www.borsaistanbul.com/sirketler/islem-goren-sirketler (on-line access: May 1st 2013)

Appendix 1. Distribution of the data pertinent to the variables

Variable	Panel A: Distribution of data related to the variables under PAS				Panel B: Distribution of data related to the variables under IFRS			
	Skewness	Kurtosis	P value (Sig.)		Skewness	Kurtosis	P value (sig.)	
			Kolgomarov-Smirnov	Shapiro-Wilk			Kolgomarov-Smirnov	Shapiro-Wilk
Inventories	2.636	6.958	0.000	0.000	2.636	6.960	0.000	0.000
Current deferred tax liabilities	1.757	2.342	0.000	0.000	2.646	7.000	0.000	0.000
Non-current deferred tax liabilities	2.646	7.000	0.000	0.000	1.542	1.164	0.004	0.003
Current financial liabilities	1.118	0.067	0.200	0.083	2.406	5.951	0.014	0.000
Non-current financial liabilities	2.560	6.632	0.001	0.000	2.560	6.632	0.001	0.000
Property. plant and equipment	0.126	-2.129	0.200	0.345	0.828	-0.635	0.200	0.387
Intangible assets	2.223	4.955	0.003	0.001	1.072	-0.904	0.039	0.018
Current trade receivables	2.244	5.464	0.004	0.004	2.243	5.462	0.004	0.004
Non-current trade receivables	2.579	6.724	0.000	0.000	2.577	6.718	0.000	0.000
Current trade payables	-0.375	-2.483	0.136	0.040	-0.373	-2.482	0.139	0.040
Current receivables from related parties	1.135	0.155	0.162	0.074	2.558	6.636	0.000	0.000
Non-current receivables from related parties	2.646	7.000	0.000	0.000	2.646	7.000	0.000	0.000
Current and non-current payables to related parties	2.309	5.391	0.002	0.000	2.310	5.393	0.002	0.000
Investment properties	2.646	7.000	0.000	0.000	2.646	7.000	0.000	0.000
Current provisions	2.587	6.756	0.000	0.000	2.550	6.584	0.002	0.000
Non-current provisions	0.504	0.251	0.200	0.710	0.058	-2.312	0.200	0.136
Total current assets	2.501	6.382	0.003	0.000	2.502	6.392	0.003	0.000
Total non-current assets	1.123	0.646	0.200	0.325	1.079	0.389	0.200	0.286
Total assets	1.644	2.711	0.200	0.087	1.603	2.486	0.200	0.085
Total current liabilities	1.059	-0.225	0.200	0.168	1.065	-0.219	0.200	0.161
Total non-current liabilities	2.554	6.601	0.001	0.000	2.566	6.658	0.001	0.000
Other Current Receivables	2.630	6.932	0.000	0.000	2.035	4.415	0.193	0.013
Other current assets	2.375	5.819	0.024	0.001	0.357	-1.816	0.200	0.194

Variable	Panel A: Distribution of data related to the variables under PAS				Panel B: Distribution of data related to the variables under IFRS			
	Skewness	Kurtosis	P value (Sig.)		Skewness	Kurtosis	P value (sig.)	
			Kolgomarov-Smirnov	Shapiro-Wilk			Kolgomarov-Smirnov	Shapiro-Wilk
Non-current financial assets	2.645	6.998	0.000	0.000	2.646	6.999	0.000	0.000
Current deferred tax liability	1.757	2.342	0.000	0.001	2.646	7.000	0.000	0.000
Non-current deferred tax assets	2.646	7.000	0.000	0.000	1.298	-0.414	0.000	0.001
Other current liabilities	1.826	3.384	0.057	0.010	2.615	6.877	0.000	0.000
Other non-current liabilities	2.646	7.000	0.000	0.000	2.646	7.000	0.000	0.000
Total Shareholders' equity	-0.121	-1.527	0.200	0.642	0.005	-1.402	0.200	0.550
Other non-current assets	1.676	2.132	0.034	0.006	2.546	6.556	0.003	0.000
Total liabilities	2.345	5.593	0.000	0.000	2.359	5.668	0.000	0.000
Total liabilities and equity	1.644	2.711	0.200	0.087	1.603	2.486	0.200	0.085
Current ratio	2.369	5.767	0.034	0.001	1.430	1.250	0.090	0.042
Acid-test ratio	2.420	5.952	0.003	0.000	1.702	2.080	0.001	0.003
Cash flow liquidity ratio	1.587	1.348	0.001	0.002	1.379	0.104	0.001	0.002
Debt Ratio	0.377	-0.251	0.200	0.782	0.340	-0.529	0.200	0.805
Stockholders Equity Ratio	-1.414	2.610	0.193	0.186	-1.335	2.262	0.200	0.269
Ratio of Current Liabilities to Total Liabilities+Stockholders' Equity	0.960	0.781	0.200	0.375	1.265	1.809	0.200	0.219
Ratio of Long Term Liabilities to Total Liabilities+Stockholders' Equity	1.216	-0.008	0.101	0.039	1.337	0.546	0.093	0.035
Ratio of Stockholders' Equity to Total Liabilities	1.631	2.045	0.040	0.024	1.648	2.074	0.017	0.020

Appendix 2. Wilcoxon signed-rank test and paired-samples t-test results

Panel A: Variables for which the data do not demonstrate normal distribution

Variable	Median-PAS	Median-IFRS	Median difference (%)	Mean-PAS	Mean-IFRS	Mean difference (%)	t-value	Z-value
Current receivables from related parties	336521	380610	13.101	446158.14	2283983.43	411.922		-1.604
Current deferred tax liabilities	21026	125649	497.589	31442.14	125564.86	299.352		-1.447
Non-current deferred tax liabilities	0	496687	-	208149.57	349489.00	67.903		-0.180
Current financial liabilities	2803798	871332	-68.923	1773492.29	1037305.29	-41.511		-1.461
Total liabilities	6640618	7393303	5.888	25241755.43	25283337	0.164		-0.944
Non-current financial liabilities	540195	540195	0.000	14940067.71	14936978.14	-0.021		-1.000
Intangible assets	230253	133472	-42.032	51092168.29	43925689.14	-14.027		-2.023**
Current trade receivable	1619676	1619676	0.000	2105081.29	2105605.43	0.025		-1.604
Non-current trade receivable	2797	2797	0.000	9502.43	9475.29	-0.286		-0.447
Current payables to related parties	205350	207220	0.911	3050662.43	3080872.14	0.990		1.826*
Investment properties	47863140	47571766	-0.609	6837591.43	6795980.86	-0.609		-1.000
Current provisions	28015	80401	186.993	341693.71	375603.43	9.924		-0.338
Total current assets	6054968	6145209	1.490	14096621.43	14164970.57	0.485		-1.892**
Total non-current liabilities	2457916	2457917	0.000	15656203.86	15671008.29	0.095		-0.405
Other Current Receivables	35279	56233	59.395	1961918.14	113990.43	-94.190		-1.214
Non-current financial assets	26269	26269	0.000	11638578.86	11601254.86	-0.321		-0.447
Non-current deferred tax assets	1360161	3049901	124.231	388617.43	871400.43	124.231		0.317
Other current liabilities	392759	224222	-42.911	4101844.57	830867.57	-79.744		-1.992**
Current ratio	0.93200	0.94600	1.502	4.19743	2.53786	-39.538		-0.674
Acid-test ratio	0.66600	0.65900	-1.051	3.84843	2.17900	-43.380		-1.461
Cash flow liquidity ratio	0.05800	0.05800	0.000	1.38171	0.86057	-37.717		-1.342
Ratio of Stockholders' Equity to Total Liabilities	2.60300	2.78600	7.030	6.86857	6.78514	-1.215		-0.730
Ratio of property. plant and equipment to total assets	0.83500	0.84300	0.958	0.77071	1.97686	156.499		-0.734

Variable	Median-PAS	Median-IFRS	Median difference (%)	Mean-PAS	Mean-IFRS	Mean difference (%)	t-value	Z-value
Panel A: Variables for which the data do not demonstrate normal distribution								
Panel B: Variables for which the data demonstrate normal distribution								
Current financial liabilities	1104384.00	0.00	-100.000	1773492.29	1037305.29	-41.511	1.350	
Property. plant and equipment	48606232.00	34698196.00	-28.614	51092168.29	43925689.14	-14.027	1.062	
Current trade payables	3051746.00	3051746.00	0.000	2193548.43	2197290.29	0.171	-1.029	
Non-current provisions	411063.00	188064.00	-54.249	352547.86	236390.43	-32.948	1.196	
Total non-current assets	51563993.00	51563994.00	0.000	66439660	66635137.29	0.294	-0.257	
Total assets	58232919.00	58232919.00	0.000	80536281.43	80800107.86	0.328	-0.365	
Total current liabilities	6497759.00	6494943.00	-0.043	9585551.57	9612328.71	0.279	-1.999*	
Total Shareholders' equity	55790375.00	55790375.00	0.000	46967882	47187994.86	0.469	-0.274	
Total liabilities and equity	58232919.00	58232919.00	0.000	80536281.43	80800107.86	0.328	-0.365	
Debt Ratio	0.27400	0.26100	-4.745	0.24014	0.24529	2.145	-0.688	
Stockholders Equity Ratio	0.72200	0.73600	1.939	0.72171	0.71671	-0.693	0.658	
Ratio of current liabilities to Total Liabilities+Stockholders' Equity	0.11900	0.11900	0.000	0.12157	0.12700	4.467	-0.911	
Ratio of Long Term Liabilities to Total Liabilities+Stockholders' Equity	0.03300	0.03300	0.000	0.11729	0.11586	-1.219	0.329	

*p<0.1
**p<0.05
***p<0.01

4

An examination of the relationship between CSR disclosure and financial performance: The case of Polish banks

Łukasz Matuszak[a1] and Ewa Różańska[a]

[a]*Poznan University of Economics and Business, Poland*

Abstract: The purpose of this study is twofold. First, this study investigates the trends of corporate social responsibility (CSR) reporting and financial performance (FP) in commercial banks in Poland. Second, this study examines the impact of the CSR disclosure of the banks on their financial performance (ROA, ROE, NIM). Sample consists of 18 banks. The data from annual reports for the period of 8 years (2008 – 2015) were both hand collected and obtained from Notoria Servis Database. A content analysis is used to measure the level of CSR disclosures and a panel data analysis is employed to examine the CSR-FP relationship. Software: GRETL. Two key findings: (1) Positive relationship between banks' CSR disclosures and their profitability measured by ROA and ROE. However, the relationship between banks' CSR disclosures and NIM is negative. Statistical analysis did not report any significant effect of CSR activities on ROA, ROE and NIM ratios. (2) Banks' CSR activities are not dominant predictor of their profitability as compared with control variables. To our best knowledge this research is the first quantitative analysis regarding banking sector in Poland. Further, this study was conducted in emerging market with different socio-economic context and regulations compared to developed market. The findings contribute to and increase the understanding of the relationship between CSR disclosures and FP. Finally, this study has important implications for policy makers, managers, investors, and others.

---

[1] *Corresponding authors*: Department of Accounting, Poznan University of Economics and Business; Al. Niepodległości 10, 61-875Poznań; email addresses: lukasz.matuszak@ue.poznan.pl, ewa.rozanska@ue.poznan.pl

Key words: corporate social responsibility, financial performance, polish banks.

1. Introduction

The beginning of the 21st century brought several financial scandals due to managerial opportunism and large scale of accounting fraud, reducing stakeholders' confidence in business enterprises. The accounting scandal at Enron, the Wall Street's crisis occurred in 2008 and the Madoff scandal raised comments referred as ''a decay in business morality'' (Chih *et al.*, 2010). To a large extent, the social consequences of these crisis created reputational issue for organizations, limiting their competitiveness and profitability.

Above mentioned criticism could possibly explain why business representatives, general public leaders, governments, investors and other stakeholders become proponents of the postulate according to which the company cannot pursue a strategy to maximize the financial result at the expense of fulfilling its obligations towards its employees, the environment and society as a whole. In response to this claim, companies begin implementing social responsibility activities and other strategies that allow them to improve their reputation and restore stakeholders' confidence (Servaes & Tamayo, 2013).

In the light of the above corporate social responsibility (CSR) has gained recognition and acceptance among stakeholders of the company and company itself. CSR is the subject of standardization within the guidelines of various kinds (e.g. GRI, ISO, Integrated reporting) both in voluntary or mandatory variant. Moreover, in many countries CSR indices are developed, emerging companies operating in sustainable and responsible manner, such as Dow Jones Sustainability Index (DJSI), the Financial Times Stock Exchange's FTSE4Good, the Fortune 500, Johannesburg Securities Exchange (JSE) index and Warsaw Stock Exchange's RESPECT index. These indices assess companies based on various criteria such as human rights, protection of environment, working conditions, labour standards, supply chain management.

Despite the fact that Corporate Social Responsibility (CSR) is currently widely discussed in theory and practice there is no general agreement about its definition. Definitions presented in the literature stress different aspects of CSR concept, such as: sustainability, sustainable development, corporate responsibility, triple-bottom line, corporate ethics, corporate citizenship, social enterprise, and corporate governance (Bassen *et al.*, 2006). Each of definitions in varied way specify the scope of the concept. Moreover, as yet, no definition has won such an advantage over others, that it was reasonable to consider it as absolutely dominant. Inaccuracies in defining CSR can be considered as a manifestation of the unsatisfactory state of the theoretical development of the concept of CSR. Although the occurrence in the literature various definitions and terms of CSR could also be regarded as an expression of the evolution and expansion of the scope in research on CSR, which today has already some achievements.

A corporation is generally encouraged to adopt CSR because of its perceived benefits. In long-term perspective CSR should improve companies' competitiveness and reputation and positively affect relationship between CSR activities of a company and its financial performance (FP). Although vast research has been undertaken in CSR area, the related studies have focused on the existence of the relationship between CSR and FP (Ambec & Lanoie, 2008; Dixon-Fowler *et al.*, 2013; Orlitzky *et al.*, 2003; Sharma & Starik 2002). However, researchers analysing relationship between CSR and FP formulate mixed results. Much of research and literature on CSR has been focused on developed markets, where organizations and institutions are more efficient and effective while research in emerging markets on the subject is limited (Dumitrescu & Simionescu, 2015; Arli & Lasmono, 2010). Therefore, there is a need for critical CSR research agenda focusing on developing economies, especially in the Central and Eastern Europe (CEE) countries that do not have a long CSR tradition and practice. According to Albu *et al.* (2016) CSR has evolved differently depending on the economic, legal and social condition of each CEE country. Thus, various empirical CSR research is needed to understand the differences in CSR applications and effects and to explain the existing differences in certain countries. These research should lead to more relevant CSR-related concepts, frameworks or models that are more applicable to CEE countries.

This study was conducted in Poland that is perceived as a very important emerging market in CEE. In Poland CSR concept is relatively new. After many years of communist system in Poland that can be characterized by dispossession of private capital, CSR issues were under State's responsibility and were not subject of scientific discussion. After 1989 the communism fell and Polish market started to change in the direction of free market economy, following the model of the developed markets (Waniak-Michalak *et al.*, 2016).

Taking this into account Poland is under-researched country comparing with other European countries. Majority of studies on CSR in Poland is descriptive and focuses mainly on range of CSR disclosures leaving other important aspects completely unexplored. For example, to our best knowledge no existing study has explored empirically the impact of CSR practices on companies' financial performance (measured by return on assets [ROA] and return on equity [ROE] and net interest margin [NIM]). In authors opinion, this is an important issue worth investigating, taking into account the general argument that CSR benefits not only stakeholders but also the companies themselves.

This research was done in banking sector. Banks were selected for the study because of several reasons. First, banking industry is profit-orientated and managers of banks have a responsibility to maximize profits. Second, banks play an important role in social and economic development of a country. Molyneux *et al.* (2014) suggest that under some conditions, private banks should be treated as public utilities. Third, banks have been considered as public trust institutions for a long time, which imposes special obligations associated with social responsibility on them. Szpringer (2009) states, that values such as protection of the environment, safety working conditions, fairness, regional and local development in the context of global competiveness and retail banking have an increasing impact on the banking market. Fourth, although the number of studies concerning banks, both in the context of undertaking CSR-related activities as well as reporting about them, has increased in recent years, they are still insufficient. Previous studies on CSR reporting in banks employed rather descriptive methods. This research analyses the issue in more exhaustive way. Fifth, in many prior studies on the link between CSR and FP, banks were excluded from research sample as they have little direct environmental impact (Siregar & Bachtiar, 2010). This study contributes to the existing literature by extending previous studies of CSR reporting on banking sector.

The purpose of this study is twofold. First, this study investigates the trend of corporate social responsibility (CSR) reporting and financial performance (FP) in commercial banks in Poland. Second, this study examines the impact of the CSR disclosures of the banks on their financial performance (ROA, ROE, NIM).

The remainder of this paper is organized as follows. The next section reviews the existing literature and discusses the theoretical background of the study. Section 3 presents the research methodology: describes data collection process, illustrates the construction of our CSR index and others variables, and discusses the econometric models used in this study. Section 4 presents the empirical results and interpretation. Finally, section 6 summarizes the results presented and interpreted, leading to a discussion of their theoretical and practical implications. The article concludes with a recommendation regarding future research agendas.

2. Literature review and hypotheses development

A number of theoretical perspectives have been examined in the literature on the relation between CSR disclosure and firm's financial performance. There is generally expected to be a positive relationship between CSR disclosure and financial performance according to socio-political theories - stakeholder theory (Freeman, 1984) and legitimacy theory (Suchman, 1995). Both these theories employ a stakeholder perspective.

According to Freeman (1984) a stakeholder is a "group or individual who can affect or is affected by the achievement of the organization's objectives". From these perspective, stakeholder theory recognizes the important impact of stakeholders on enterprise sustainability and success. Therefore, enterprises must manage stakeholder relationships by meeting the needs and expectations of diverse stakeholder groups - including environmental, employee, and societal groups (Freeman & Evan, 1990) - to be successful. Stakeholders express specific expectations with regard to an enterprise CSR activity such as effective use of natural resources, limitation of waste of resources, prevention of pollution, providing workforce diversity, employing the disabled, elimination of discrimination, etc. (Adebayo, 2000). So, environmental and social disclosures are made because they are demanded by stakeholders to satisfy their needs and expectations (Gray *et al.*, 1995a).

Legitimacy theory (Suchman, 1995), associated with the concept of "social contract" (Patten, 1991, 1992), recognizes the importance of stakeholder expectations and has been widely used in accounting research (e.g., Branco & Rodrigues, 2006) as a mechanism for understanding voluntary CSR activities and disclosures. According to Suchman (1995) legitimacy is "a generalized perception or assumption that the actions of an entity are desirable, proper or appropriate within some socially constructed system of norms, values, beliefs and definitions". It is a process "by which an organisation seeks" approval of the society (Kaplan & Ruland, 1991) through ensuring "congruence between the social values associated with or implied by their activities and the norms of acceptable behaviour in the larger social system in which they are a part. In so far as these two value systems are congruent we can speak of organizational legitimacy" (Matthews, 1993). In a strong form of legitimacy, enterprises try to meet social expectations and behave in a way that society demands from them (Patten, 2000) through real socially responsible activities. While in a week form of legitimacy information is provided through CSR disclosure by management (Cho & Patten, 2007; Freedman & Patten, 2004; Patten, 2002) even if this information does not reflect actual CSR performance.

The stakeholder theory and the legitimacy theory have a lot in common. According to Deegan and Blomquist (2006) stakeholder and legitimacy theories state that companies use social and environmental disclosure to enhance their status, provide information to stakeholders regarding their activities and discharge the social contract between companies and social and environmental organizations. However, as Deegan (2002) points out, the legitimacy theory, refers in its deliberations to society understood as a whole and to general social expectations. On the contrary, the stakeholder theory assumes explicit existence of various groups, which have different expectations and different power or capacity to put pressure on the companies to communicate social and environmental information.

Busch and Hoffmann (2011) emphasize that stakeholder theory, referred to as good management theory, is about doing good to those that the firm interacts with in order to create the enabling environment for the business firm to gain competitive advantage and grow. This approach assumes that being a good corporate citizen can also make a firm more profitable.

Haniffa and Cooke (2005) suggest also that enterprises that operate under some system of norms, values, beliefs and definitions prevailing among their stakeholders, can reduce the legitimacy gap by communicating more social and environmental information and thus improve their profitability.

Meeting corporate social responsibilities created by stakeholders' expectations builds trust and legitimacy which improves stakeholder relationships and leads to many other benefits. CSR disclosures may affect corporate financial performance through several crucial aspects: increased employees' motivation and productivity, increased products' acceptance among customers, increased acceptance among investors who support social or environmental values. Overall, the expected benefits of CSR disclosures may largely exceed their costs implying higher corporate financial performance (Khlif *et al.*, 2015).

As a result of the financial performance, enterprises can also realize capital market benefits from superior CSR performance, which in turn lead to higher values for these enterprises. The capital market benefits include especially a lower cost of equity capital (Dhaliwal *et al.*, 2011), and a lower cost of debt (Husted, 2005).

Although, the empirical studies which consider corporate performance as a consequence of social and environmental disclosure started over 6 decades ago, the literature presents inconclusive findings.

In fact, a number of narrative and meta-analytic reviews in the recent literature (Ambec & Lanoie, 2008; Dixon-Fowler *et al.*, 2013; Orlitzky *et al.*, 2003; Sharma & Starik, 2002) suggest a positive relationship between corporate social performance and corporate financial performance.

But in many empirical studies the fundamental contextual condition of stakeholder theory is not recognized. Stakeholders' goals, objectives and aspirations tend to differ across the contexts of industrial and national boundaries (Baird *et al.*, 2012). Thus, combining the CSR ratings of different industries and different countries may lead to inconsistencies, even though such a strategy yields more of positive CSR and financial performance relation. A better approach is therefore to conduct the study in the context of each industry and each country (Baird *et al.*, 2012; Soana, 2011).

Many sectors of the economy are still under-researched. As for the banking sector, the effect of corporate social responsibility on financial performance has not been examined extensively, and the few existing studies offer conflicting evidence. For example, Chih *et al.* (2010) empirically investigate a total of 520 financial firms in 34 countries between the years 2003 and 2005, and conclude that CSR and financial performance are not related. In contrast, Wu & Shen (2013) analyse 162 banks in 22 countries over 2003-2009, and report that CSR is positively associated with financial performance in terms of return on assets, return on equity, net interest income, and noninterest income. They also find that CSR negatively associates with non-performing loans. Differences in the results could be related to measurement issues, differences in sample as well as sample period. To obtain the unbiased and full-blown CSR effect Shen *et al.* (2016) apply three novel estimation methods, namely, conventional propensity score matching method, nearestneighbor variance bias-corrected matching method (nn-VBC) and Heckman's two-step method in switching regression. They collect data about CSR and non-CSR banks from 18 countries. Regardless of the methods used, CSR banks significantly outperform non-CSR banks in terms of return on assets and return on equity.

With respect to banking sector, several studies have investigated the relation between corporate social responsibility and financial performance in different countries (Cornett *et al.*, 2016 in U.S., Adeyanju, 2012 in Nigeria, Ofiri *et al.*, 2014 in Ghana, Soana, 2011 in Italy, Tafti *et al.*, 2012 in Iran, Taskin, 2015 in Turkey and Weshah *et al.*, 2012 in Jordan). A greater number of these studies show a positive correlation between CSR and firms' financial performance (Cornett *et al.*, 2016 in U.S., Adeyanju, 2012; Ofiri *et al.*, 2014; Tafti *et al.*, 2012; Weshah *et al.*, 2012). Mixed relationships were found in Taskin (2015), while no relationship between CSR and financial performance was presented in Soana (2011).

The fact that none of these studies was focused specifically on the Polish banking sector is indicative of a gap that needs to be filled to enrich the literature. This may be done by empirical research that bring evidence of the measurable payoff of CSR activity to Polish banks.

To measure bank financial performance researchers, use two kinds of measurement approach which is accounting-based financial performance (e.g. Soana, 2011; Weshah *et al.*, 2012; Wu & Shen, 2013; Ofori *et al.*, 2014; Taskin, 2015, Cornett *et al.*, 2016 Shen *et al.* 2016) and market-based financial performance (e.g. Soana, 2011; Tafti *et al.*, 2012).

In our analysis, we consider financial performance from the accounting perspective and following the previous studies we use three measures of bank profitability, that are generally investigated: average Return on Assets (ROA), average Return on Equity (ROE) and Net Interest Margin (NIM).

Based on the above theoretical justifications and empirical literature, the following hypotheses are tested:

H_1: There is a positive relationship between Polish banks' CSR disclosure and their financial performance measured by ROA.

H_2: There is a positive relationship between Polish banks' CSR disclosure and their financial performance measured by ROE.

H_3: There is a positive relationship between Polish banks' CSR disclosure and their financial performance measured by NIM.

Even though in the previous studies correlation have been found, the strength of CSR disclosure contribution to banks' profitability has not been discussed widely. Thus, the next hypotheses are tested:

H_4: Polish banks' CSR disclosure significantly contribute to their profitability measured by ROA.

H_5: Polish banks' CSR disclosure significantly contribute to their profitability measured by ROE.

H_6: Polish banks' CSR disclosure significantly contribute to their profitability measured by NIM.

3. Research methodology

3.1. Sample and research data

Empirical studies have been conducted on the population of all commercial banks, which have operated in the years 2008 - 2015 in Poland and which have made available their financial statements on their websites. The study was excluded representative offices of foreign banks and credit institutions. These banks represent very small percentage in total market share and most of them have very few branches, hence they were ignored from the analysis. The final sample comprises 18 commercial banks presented in Table 1. Most of these banks are listed on the Warsaw Stock Exchange.

Table 1. **List of banks**

No.	Name	Listed on the Warsaw Stock Exchange as at 31 December 2015
1	Alior Bank SA	Yes
2	Bank BPH SA	Yes
3	Bank Gospodarki Żywnościowej SA	Yes
4	Bank Gospodarstwa Krajowego SA	No
5	Bank Handlowy w Warszawie SA	Yes
6	Bank Millennium SA	Yes
7	Bank Ochrony Środowiska SA	Yes
8	Bank Pekao SA	Yes

No.	Name	Listed on the Warsaw Stock Exchange as at 31 December 2015
9	Bank Pocztowy SA	No
10	Bank Zachodni WBK SA	Yes
11	Credit Agricole Bank Polska SA	No
12	Getin Noble Bank SA	Yes
13	ING Bank Śląski SA	Yes
14	mBank SA	Yes
15	Pekao Bank Hipoteczny SA	No
16	Powszechna Kasa Oszczędności Bank Polski SA	Yes
17	Raiffeisen Bank Polska SA	No
18	SGB-Bank SA	No

The data collected for the purpose of the study involves the examination of financial statements, management commentaries and corporate social responsibility reports for the years 2008-2015 of the population of the study. Therefore, the overall sample includes 144 bank-year observations. Table 2 lists the variables used in our models, required data and sources of information.

Table 2. **Variables, required data and data sources**

Variables	Data	Data source	Previous studies
Dependent variables			
Average Return on Assets (ROA)	Net profit Average of total assets	NSD, Financial statements	Soana (2011); Wu & Shen (2013); Ofori *et al.*, (2014);Taskin (2015); Cornett *et al.* (2016); Shen *et al.* (2016)
Average Return on Equity (ROE)	Net profit Average of total equity	NSD, Financial statements	Soana (2011); Wu & Shen (2013); Ofori *et al.*, (2014); Taskin (2015); Cornett *et al.* (2016); Shen *et al.* (2016)
Net Interest Margin (NIM)	Net profit on interests Average of total assets	NSD, Financial statements	Wu & Shen (2013); Taskin (2015); Shen *et al.* (2016)
Independent variable			
CSR disclosure index (CSR)	CSR disclosures listed in appendix A	Management commentaries CSR reports	
Control variables			
Net Log of Total Assets (LogTA)	Total assets	NSD, Financial statements	Wu & Shen (2013); Ofori *et al.*, 2014; Shen *et al.* (2016); Cornett *et al.* (2016)

Variables	Data	Data source	Previous studies
Dependent variables			
Income Growth (IncGrow)	Income	NSD, Financial statements	Ofori *et al.*, 2014; Cajias *et al.* (2014); Chen & Wang, 2011
Leverage ratio (Leverage)	Debt Total equity	NSD, Financial statements	Weshah *et al.* (2012); Wu & Shen (2013); Shen *et al.* (2016)

The data are in two categories: (1) the financial data comprising the absolute values and the constructed ratios for the banks that constitute the subjects of this study, and (2) the CSR disclosure data used to calculate CSR index. The financial data of publicly listed banks were obtained from Notoria Serwis Database (NSD)[i]. For not listed banks the financial data were hand-collected from publicly available financial statements. The ratios were computed by the authors based on the collected data. The CSR disclosure data were hand collected from management commentaries and corporate social responsibility reports, which were available on banks' websites. The absolute values were standardized using their natural logarithms to make them appropriate for the linear regression analysis.

3.2. Dependent variables - measures of bank financial performance

To measure bank financial performance researchers, use two kinds of measurement approach which is accounting-based financial performance (e.g. Soana, 2011; Weshah, 2012; Wu & Shen, 2013; Ofori *et al.*, 2014; Taskin, 2015; Cornett *et al.*, 2016; Shen *et al.* 2016) and market-based financial performance (e.g. Soana, 2011; Tafti *et al.*, 2012).

In our analysis we consider financial performance from the accounting perspective and following the previous studies we use three measures of bank profitability, that are generally investigated: average Return on Assets (ROA), average Return on Equity (ROE) and Net Interest Margin (NIM).

ROA is the major ratio that indicates the profitability of a bank, which is defined as net profit over average total assets (ROA = Net profit/Average of Total Assets). It measures the ability of the bank management to generate income by utilizing bank assets at their disposal. In other words, it shows how efficiently the resources of the bank are used to generate the income. According to Kohers & Simpson (2002) ROA "measures the ability of bank managers to acquire deposits at a reasonable cost, invest these funds in profitable loans and investments, and profitably perform the daily operations of the bank".

ROE is also another financial ratio that indicates the profitability of a bank, which is calculated as net profit divided by average Total Equity Capital (ROE = Net profit/Average of Total Equity Capital). It represents the rate of return earned on the funds invested in the bank by its stockholders. A bank that has a high return on equity is more likely to be one that is capable of generating cash internally. Thus, the higher the ROE the better the bank is in terms of profit generation.

NIM is a measure of the difference between the interest income generated by banks and the amount of interest paid on borrowed funds (for example, deposits), relative to the amount of their average assets. The NIM variable is defined as the net interest profit divided by average of total assets (NIM = Net profit on interest/Average of Total Assets). For most banks the largest amount of revenues comes from interest on loans. As a result, this kind of revenue affects net income and capital, which determine financial success (Kohers & Simpson, 2002). The higher the net interest margin, the higher the bank's profit and the more stable the bank is. Thus, it is one of the key measures of bank profitability.

3.3. Independent variable - measure of CSR

There is no generally accepted method of measuring CSR activity of banks. Researchers have measured the CSR in diverse ways including the use of questionnaire surveys (Tafti *et al.*, 2012), spending measures like sponsorships and donations (Adeyanju, 2012; Weshah *et al.*, 2012), content analysis of disclosed CSR information in CSR reports (Taskin, 2015), unidimensional, and multidimensional ratings based on some observable social responsibility indicators, such as KLD ratings (Becchetti *et al.*, 2012), EIRIS Index (Wu & Shen, 2013), AEI Index (Soana, 2011), and SGP Index (Torres *et al.*, 2012). In this study to measure CSR disclosures we used content analysis and we have developed aggregated CSR index.

International regulations related to CSR distinguish the different areas of social responsibility, for example, ISO 26000 norm (2012) stands 7 areas: organizational governance, human rights, labour practices, the environment, fair operating practices, consumer issues and community involvement and development. Global Compact Principles focuses on responsibility in the area of human rights, labour standards, the environment and anti-corruption activities. The GRI guidelines include specific indicators divided into three categories: economic, social and environmental. Categories are divided into aspects, and for example, social category includes employment, labelling of products and services, human rights.

In the banking sector the most important are relations with employees, customers, investors, the environment and the local community (Krasodomska, 2012). Prior empirical studies have categorized CSR into different sub themes, for instance, Gray *et al.* (1995b) have classified the CSR disclosure as human resource, environmental, community, and customer; Kiliç *et al.* (2015) as environment, energy, human resources, products and customers, and community involvement. Thus, CSR disclosure has been classified into sub four themes in this research as environment, human resources, products and customers, and community involvement (see Appendix A).

In line with earlier studies, to measure the level of CSR reporting in commercial banks, content analysis method has been applied. The study analysed the existence or absence of particular CSR disclosures in corporate reports, namely management commentary, annual report, CSR report, sustainability report, environmental report. The study used the approach of assigning a value of 1 if an item of CSR disclosures is reported and 0 if it is not, no matter the communication channel. For example, if the disclosure item was presented in two or more reports by some bank the presence of the item was treated once. The CSR reporting index for each bank is calculated as follows:

$$CSR\ reporting\ index = \frac{\sum_{i=1}^{n} x_i}{n}$$

where:
xi – 1 if the item i is disclosed, 0 if the item i is not disclosed,
n - number of items.

The overall level of CSR reporting has been measured for the four areas, namely Environment, Human Resources, Products and Customers, Community Involvement.

In order to improve the predictive capability of the regression models proposed in the research, the CSR reporting index was properly lagged which permitted the testing of the causal relationship between the CSR and the FP. The causality testing through the appropriate lagging of the CSR as independent variable is a growing feature of the current literature (Cajias *et al.* 2014; Sun & Cui, 2014; Nollet *et al.* 2016). This is in line with the assumption that CSR is an investment in intangible asset that takes some time to generate the expected returns (Jiao, 2010).

3.4. Control variables

In the most of recent studies researchers incorporated different control variables in their models, such as size, banking risk, management preference, firm growth, earnings, industry and year. In our study, we include three control variables that occurred most in the empirical literature and that have been hypothesized to be correlated with banks' financial performance: the size, the risk and the growth. In terms of operationalization, the size was measured as the absolute value of the total assets but standardized by natural logarithm. In order to control for risk, we used leverage ratio defined as the debts to total equity (Leverage ratio = Debts/Total Equity). The growth was measured as the income growth.

Consistent with the current literature, we expect that banks' financial performance is positively associated with total assets (Ofori *et al.*, 2014) and income growth (Chen & Wang, 2011), while it is negatively associated with leverage ratio (Wu & Shen, 2013).

3.5. The models - effects of CSR disclosures on banks financial performance

To examine the effect of CSR disclosure on banks' financial performance, we estimate a panel data models.

Panel data typically refers to a particular type of multilevel data. Measurement at over time (T1, T2, T3...) is nested within subjects, for example firms. Each time is referred to as a "wave", so panel datasets are described in terms of the number of individual cases (N), and the number of waves (T). Panel data analysis is a useful method of research in contemporary social and economic studies. Panel data have several advantages over the one-dimensional data. First, find use in the testing of causality. Besides, based on this data it is easier to verify hypotheses, to eliminate the bias and reduce the problems associated with multicollinearity (Kopczewska *et al.*, 2009).

The proposed models are given as:

$$ROA_{it} = ß_0 + ß_1 LogTA_{it} + ß_2 IncGrow_{it} + ß_3 Leverage_{it} + ß_4 CSR_{it-1} + \varepsilon_{it}$$

$$ROE_{it} = ß_0 + ß_1 LogTA_{it} + ß_2 IncGrow_{it} + ß_3 Leverage_{it} + ß_4 CSR_{it-1} + \varepsilon_{it}$$

$$NIM_{it} = ß_0 + ß_1 LogTA_{it} + ß_2 IncGrow_{it} + ß_3 Leverage_{it} + ß_4 CSR_{it-1} + \varepsilon_{it}$$

where,
ROA_{it} – average Return on Assets of Bank *i* at time *t*,
ROE_{it} – average Return on Equity of Bank *i* at time *t*,
NIM_{it} – Net Interest Margin of Bank *i* at time *t*,
$LogTA_{it}$ – natural logarithm of total assets of Bank *i* at time *t*,
$IncGrow_{it}$ – income growth of Bank *i* at time *t*,
$Leverage_{it}$ – leverage ratio of Bank *i* at time *t*,
CSR_{it-1} – lagged CSR index,
$ß_0$ – an intercept,
$ß_{1...4}$ – a vector of exogenous variables and observations,
ε - a random component (errors),
i = 1, 2, ..., N, index of bank,
t = 1, 2, ..., T, index of time.
Three basic types of models: pooled models (OLS), fixed effects models (FE) and

random effects models (RE) were used to model panel data in the study. First, F-test was applied to determine which method performed best one to choose between pooled OLS and fixed-effect. In addition, in the case of the FE model with time-fixed effects, the Wald test was conducted to examine the impact of temporary variables. In the next stage of the analysis, the Breusche and Pagan Lagrange multiplier test was employed to decide whether the pooled OLS model or the random effect model was appropriate for the study. In addition, the fixed-effects model and the random-effects model were compared by using the Hausman's test. This procedure was repeated for each dependent variable ROA, ROE or NIM.

The results of the analyses are presented and discussed below.

4. Results and interpretation

4.1. Trend analysis of CSR reporting level and FP of Banks

The overall level of CSR reporting has been measured for the four areas, namely Environment (ENV), Human Resources (HR), Products and Customers (P&C), Community Involvement (CI). The reporting level of each CSR area is illustrated in Figure 1. The CSR reporting level is increasing over the years in all areas. This is a positive trend in the Polish banking sector. The commercial banks strongly improve the reporting on CSR. According to the figure, Community Involvement level exceeds 60% in 2014 and is well above the other areas throughout 2007-2014. This demonstrates the strong commitment of the banks in charity, volunteer and sponsorship. Besides, HR and P&C are quite close to each other in terms of reporting level that increased from 15% to approximately 50% during the examined period. The banks also show concern for the environment. Although Environment is the least reported area, it shows an upward trend. From 2007 until 2014, this level increased from 13% to 31%. The banks have still much to do to improve the level of reporting especially in the area of Environment.

Figure 2 illustrates development of profitability ratios throughout 2008-2015. Level of ROE for the banking sector changed dramatically from above 8 in 2008 to below 4 in 2015. Level of ROA and NIM were stable over study period and become around 0.5 and 2 respectively. Taking into consideration world economic crisis in 2008, it should be stated that Polish banking system was not affected by the crisis as much as we should expect. This is presented in very stable development of ROA and NIM. This situation could affect the relation between CSR and profitability ratios.

Figure 1. **CSR reporting levels**

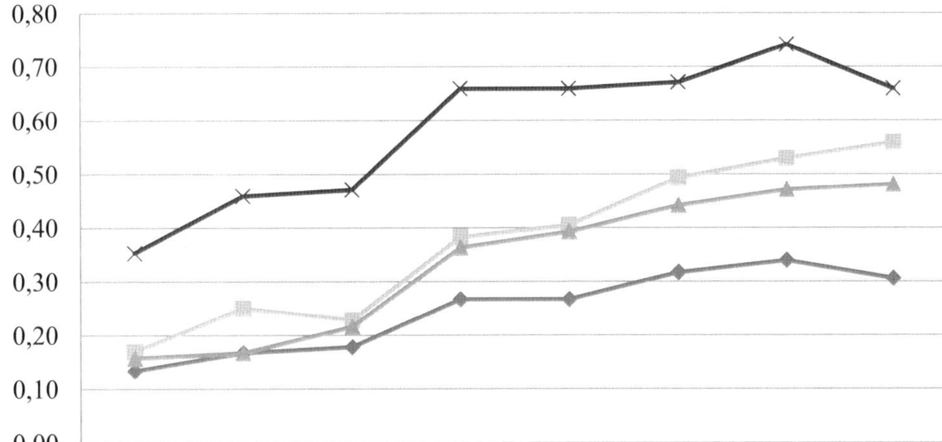

	2007	2008	2009	2010	2011	2012	2013	2014
ENV	0,13	0,17	0,18	0,27	0,27	0,32	0,34	0,31
HR	0,17	0,25	0,23	0,38	0,40	0,49	0,53	0,56
P&C	0,16	0,17	0,22	0,36	0,39	0,44	0,47	0,48
CI	0,35	0,46	0,47	0,66	0,66	0,67	0,74	0,66

Figure 2. **Development of performance measures**

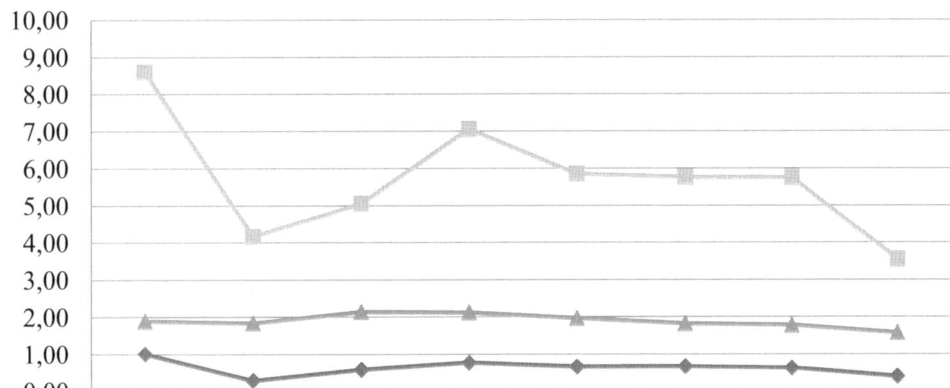

	2008	2009	2010	2011	2012	2013	2014	2015
ROA	1,00	0,28	0,58	0,76	0,65	0,66	0,62	0,39
ROE	8,60	4,16	5,05	7,05	5,85	5,76	5,75	3,55
NIM	1,89	1,83	2,14	2,12	1,96	1,82	1,78	1,57

4.2. Descriptive statistics

Table 3 presents descriptive statistics for dependent, independent and controlled variables used in regression analysis. The mean score for ROA is 0.96% and standard deviation of 1.04%. This suggests that over the study period ROA for the banks averages about 96% with individual yearly figures differing around 1.04%. Variations for ROA as indicated by the standard deviation are confirmed by the minimum and maximum values of -6.43% and 6.15% respectively. ROE registers a mean of 8.95% with very high standard deviation of 6.48%. This can be confirmed by high variability of ROE on figure 2. This suggest that banks are keen to generate about 885% return on for shareholders' investments. The mean score for NIM (2.94%) is higher than ROA and the variability over this value is also very high, as indicated by its standard deviation of (1.71%). The average growth in the banks during the analysed period was about 104.82% as indicated by the mean. This suggest incredible development in banking sector. Further, the average level of leverage suggests that an average bank has about 9.40% of equity as total liabilities. This confirms Saunders & Cornett's (2008) suggestion that banks are generally risky companies. The aggregated CSR mean (33.99%) suggests that banks rather do not regard their CSR activities as strategically oriented. High figure of standard deviation (27.77%) indicating significant differences in CSR activities among banks in Poland. This supports the thesis that CSR activities in banking industry in Poland are on early stage.

Table 3. **Descriptive statistics**

Variable	Minimum	Maximum	Mean	Median	Std. Deviation	Kurtosis	Skewness
ROA (%)	-6.43	6.15	0.96	0.915	1.04	20.37	-1.61
ROE (%)	-22.44	25.38	8.95	9.54	6.48	3.48	-0.73
NIM (%)	0,23	11.27	2.94	2.65	1.71	8.00	2.51
LogTA	0.56	5.59	3.41	3.61	1.20	-0.12	-0.64
IncGrow (%)	-0.06	593.66	104.82	95.52	46,67	82.31	8.15
Leverage (%)	0.31	20.21	9.46	8.82	4.04	0.44	0.87
CSR (%)	0.00	100.00	33,99	28.00	27.77	-0.72	0.57

4.3. Pearson correlation analysis

Table 4 presents correlation between variables. Correlation explores the bivariate relationships among the variables. Almost half of the correlation coefficients are less than 0.5 except for the value 0.799 between ROA and ROE. The results of the low correlations among selected independent variables may remove the problem multicollinearity in our model. As a rule of thumb, if the largest variance inflation factor (VIF) is greater than 10, there is evidence of collinearity. VIF figures depicted in table 2 are below 10, which confirm the absence of multicollinearity between variables in this study.

According to the results, there is a low positive insignificant correlation between ROA, ROE and CSR (0.079, p-value>0.05; 0.047, p-value>0,05) and negative insignificant correlation between NIM and CSR (-0,006; p-value>0,05). Significant positive correlation is observed between LogTA and ROA and ROE. IncGow is positively and insignificantly correlated with ROE and negatively correlated with ROA and NIM. Leverage is negatively significantly correlated with ROA and NIM.

Because of constraints of bivariate analysis in next step of the research we employed panel data analysis.

Table 4. **Correlation matrix of variables**

	VIF	ROA	ROE	NIM	LogTA	IncGrow	Leverage	CSR
ROA (%)		1						
ROE (%)		0.799**	1					
NIM (%)		0.109	0.092	1				
LogTA	1.304	0.239**	0.340**	-0.056	1			
IncGrow (%)	1.042	-0.075	0.146	-0.094	-0.128	1		
Leverage (%)	1.040	-0.293**	-0.012	-0.200**	-0.131	0.076	1	
CSR (%)	1.354	0.079	0.047	-0.006	0.480**	-0.194**	-0.185**	1

** Correlation significant at the 0.05 level

4.4. Panel data analysis

Table 5 depicts estimated coefficients from panel data analysis for ROA as dependant variable. First, we estimated OLS model and employed F-test in order to determine which model (the pooled OLS model or the fixed effects model) to employ. The estimated model has the form:

$$\widehat{ROA} = b_0 + b_1 LogTA + b_2 IncGrow + b_3 Leverage + b_4 CSR$$

The results of F-test indicated that (2.470; p-value<0.01) the fixed effects model was appropriate to use rather than the pooled OLS model. Among FE models, the least square dummy variable model (LSDV) was employed to understand the fixed effects. The effect of independent variables is mediated by the differences between banks. The pure effect of independent variables was estimated by adding a dummy for each bank. Each dummy absorbs the effects peculiar to each bank. In addition, it is worth noting that in the case of the FE model with time-fixed effects, the impact of temporary variables was observed, which confirms the Wald test (15.400; p-value<0.05). In addition, the Breusch and Pagan Lagrangian multiplier test for random effects indicated which model to choose between a random effects regression and a simple OLS regression. According to the Breush-Pagan test result

(0.881, p-value>0.10), the simple OLS regression was not preferable than the random effect model. In addition, we employed the Hausman's test statistics (17.395; p-value<0.01) to confirm that the fixed effects model was preferable compared with random-effects model. After running the necessary tests for choosing the right model, the fixed effect model with time-fixed effects was the most appropriate model for this research study. Therefore, the results of the fixed effect model with time-fixed effects were taken into consideration for further discussion.

According to the results presented in table 5, CSR coefficient (b4=0,0048) was positive implying that greater efforts aimed at improving CSR index might lead to some improvement in the ROA ratio. Thus, the first hypothesis (H1) can be accepted. However, beta of CSR index did not appear to be tangible, because its p-value is not significant (p-value>0.05). Therefore, the fourth hypothesis (H4) is rejected.

Table 5. **Estimated coefficients from the panel data analysis, years 2008 – 2015**

	ROA (dependent variable)			
Independent variables	**Pooled model**	**Fixed effects models**		**Random effects model**
	OLS	**FE (LSDV)**	**FE model with time-fixed effects**	**RE**
CSR (%)	-0.004 (-1.067)	0.006 (1.213)	0.0048 (0.983)	-0.002 (-0.622)
LogTA	**0.211***** (2.716)	**-0.739***** (-3.041)	**-0.692**** (-2.162)	0.146 (1.534)
IncGrow (%)	0.0009 (-0.519)	-0.004 (-2.117)	-0.002 (-1.267)	-0.001 (-0.663)
Leverage (%)	**-0.071***** (-3.424)	0.013 (0.303)	0.0004 (0.09)	**-0.072***** (-2.966)
Constant	**1.130***** (2.877)	**3.591***** (4.760)	**3.779***** (4.521)	**1.345***** (2.967)
T_2009			**-0.959***** (-3.120)	
T_2010			**-0.530*** (-1.700)	
T_2011			-0.071 (-0.218)	
T_2012			-0.299 (-0.845)	
T_2013			-0.222 (-0.601)	
T_2014			-0.255 (-0.646)	

	ROA (dependent variable)			
Independent variables	**Pooled model**	**Fixed effects models**		**Random effects model**
	OLS	**FE (LSDV)**	**FE model with time-fixed effects**	**RE**
T_2015			-0.582 (-1.411)	
N	144	144	144	144
R^2	0.135	0.356	0.432	0.145
Test Breusha-Pagana				0.881
F Test		2.470***	2.253***	
Test Hausmana				17.395***
Test Walda			15.400**	

t statistics in parentheses; * $p < 0.10$, ** $p < 0.05$, *** $p < 0.01$

LogTA (b1=-0.692) showed negative significant relationship with ROA, IncGrow (b2=-0.002) showed negative insignificant relationship and Leverage (b3=0.0004) showed positive insignificant relationship with ROA. This insignificant impact of variables implied that their beta values might be due to chances and might not be significantly different from 0. The provided independent variables explained almost 43.2% of the variation in the ROA variable.

Similar model selection procedure was undertaken for ROE and NIM. The estimated OLS models were as follows:

$$\widehat{ROE} = b_0 + b_1 LogTA + b_2 IncGrow + b_3 Leverage + b_4 CSR$$

$$\widehat{NIM} = b_0 + b_1 LogTA + b_2 IncGrow + b_3 Leverage + b_4 CSR$$

Table 6 depicts estimated coefficients from panel data analysis for ROE as dependant variable. After employed following tests F-test (4.148; p-value<0.01), Breush-Pagan test (17.98; p-value<0.01), Wald test (31.57; p-value<0.01), and Hausman test (13.95; p-value<0.1), the fixed effects model with time fixed effects was the most appropriate model for ROE. Therefore, the results of this model were taken into consideration for further discussion.

According to the results presented in table 6, CSR coefficient had a positive effect on ROE (b4=0,025), thus the second hypothesis (H2) can be accepted. However, there was not any statistical significance between CSR and ROE (p>0.05), therefore the fifth hypothesis (H5) is rejected. Control variables such as IncGrow (b2=0.023; p-value<0.05) had a positive and statistically insignificant effect on the dependent variable ROE. LogTA (b1=-0.985; p-value>0.05) had a negative and statistically insignificant effect on the dependent variable ROE. Leverage (b3=0.300; p-value>0.05) had a positive and statistically insignificant effect on the dependent variable ROE.

In addition, the results also indicate, that time had a significant impact on the ROE. The extent to which each year affected ROE show variables T_2009, T_2010, T_2011, T_2012, T_2013, T_2014, T_2015. The point of reference is the year 2008. For example, in 2009 banks on average reported lower level of ROE comparing with 2008 by -6.915% (p-value<0.01). In 2015, banks on average, reported lower level of ROE comparing with 2008 by -7.610% (p-value<0.01). These results can be confirmed visibly by the development of ROE ratio presented on figure 2. The provided independent variables explained almost 58.3% of the variation in the dependent variable.

Table 7 depicts estimated coefficients from panel data analysis for NIM as dependant variable. After employed following tests F-test (25.79; p-value<0.01), Breush-Pagan test (347.72; p-value<0.01), Wald test (21.83; p-value<0.05), and Hausman test (0.93; p-value>0.1), the random effect model was the most appropriate model for NIM. Therefore, the results of this model were taken into consideration for further discussion

According to the results presented in table 7, CSR had a negative effect on NIM (b4=-0.006), thus the third (H3) and must be rejected. However, the relation between CSR and NIM is statistically significant (p-value<0.05), therefore the sixth hypothesis (H6) is accepted. All the control variables: IncGrow (b2=-0.002), Leverage (b3=-0.071) and LogTA (b1=-0.168), showed negative relationship with NIM. Among control variables beta coefficients Leverage (p-value<0.05) was statistically significant whereas beta coefficients of IncGrow (p-value>0.1) and LogTA (p-value>0.1) were not significant. The provided independent variables explained only 7.4% of the variation in the dependent variable.

Table 6. **Estimated coefficients from the panel data analysis, years 2008 - 2015**

	ROE (dependent variable)			
Independent variables	**Pooled model**	**Fixed effects models**		**Random effects model**
	OLS	**FE (LSDV)**	**FE model with time-fixed effects**	**RE**
CSR	-0.028 (-1.329)	0.020 (0.748)	0.025 (0.943)	-0.014 (-0.615)
LogTA	**2.265***** (4.734)	**-3.010**** (-2.185)	-0.985 (-0.575)	**1.277*** (1.786)
IncGrow (in %)	**0.024**** (2.220)	0.009 (0.833)	**0.023**** (2.179)	**0.022**** (2.106)
Leverage	0.003 (0.022)	**0.569**** (2.322)	0.300 (1.171)	0.063 (0.377)
Constant	-0.417 (-0.173)	**12.234***** (2.285)	**10.626**** (2.375)	2.198 (0.703)
T_2009			**-7.610***** (-4.626)	
T_2010			**-5.308***** (-3.180)	
T_2011			-2.593 (-1.479)	
T_2012			**-3.898**** (-2.058)	
T_2013			**-4.173**** (-2.113)	
T_2014			**-4.012*** (-1.896)	
T_2015			**-7.488***** (-3.393)	
N	144	144	144	144
R^2	0.162	0.469	0.583	0.176
Test Breusha-Pagana				17.98***
F Test		4.148***	4.28***	
Test Hausmana				13.95***
Test Walda			31.57***	

t statistics in parentheses; * $p < 0.10$, ** $p < 0.05$, *** $p < 0.01$

Table 7. **Estimated coefficients from the panel data analysis, years 2008 - 2015**

	NIM (dependent variable)			
Independent variables	**Pooled model**	**Fixed effects models**		**Random effects model**
	OLS	**FE (LSDV)**	**FE model with time-fixed effects**	**RE**
CSR	-0.001 (-0.223)	**-0.007**** (-2.037)	0.002 (0.565)	**-0.006**** (-1.965)
LogTA	-0.121 (-0.901)	0.223 (1.228)	0.968*** (4.668)	-0.168 (-1.042)
IncGrow (in %)	-0.003 (-1.102)	-0.002 (-1.461)	**-0.002*** (-1.843)	-0.002 (-1.633)
Leverage	**-0.088**** (-2.469)	**-0.075**** (-2.338)	**-0.150***** (-4.819)	**-0.071**** (-2.375)
Constant	**4.590***** (6.762)	**3.349***** (5.942)	**1.717***** (3.167)	**3.500***** (7.595)
T_2009			-0.141 (0.706)	
T_2010			0.125 (0.620)	
T_2011			-0.012 (-0.057)	
T_2012			-0.545** (-2.377)	
T_2013			**-0.820***** (-3.430)	
T_2014			**-1.036***** (-4.041)	
T_2015			**-1.419***** (-5.310)	
N	144	144	144	144
R^2	0.055	0.913	0.866	0.074
Test Breusha-Pagana				347,72***
F Test		25.79***	29.21***	
Test Hausmana				0.93
Test Walda			21.83**	

t statistics in parentheses; * $p < 0.10$, ** $p < 0.05$, *** $p < 0.01$

5. Conclusions

5.1. Conclusions and recommendations

The purpose of this study is twofold. First, this study investigates the trend of corporate social responsibility (CSR) reporting and financial performance (FP) in commercial banks in Poland. Second, this study examines the impact of the CSR disclosures of the banks on their financial performance (ROA, ROE, NIM).

The CSR reporting level was increasing over the years in all areas. This is a positive trend in the Polish banking sector. Despite the fact that development of ROA and NIM were stable in analysed period, the level of ROE for the banking sector was changing dramatically. Taking into consideration world economic crisis in 2008, it should be stated that Polish banking system was not affected by the crisis as much as we should expect. This situation could affect the relation between CSR and profitability ratios.

Literature review conducted in section 2, revealed that previous studies reported divergent findings on the nature and the strength of the effects of the CSR activities on the financial performance of companies. The results of the prior studies include those with: strong positive effects, strong negative effects, neutral effects, and mixed effects. This study showed mixed effects of the CSR on the financial performance, depending on the particular model tested. The interpretations of the findings were also not consistent.

The study revealed a positive relationship between banks' CSR disclosures and their profitability measured by ROA and ROE. Similar results were reported by Dumitrescu and Simionescu (2015) who based on Romanian listed companies. However, the relationship between banks' CSR disclosures and NIM is negative. In this last case, the negative effect was interpreted in the literature as expressing either the shareholders' confidence in the firm and their preparedness to accept lower returns in the short run or in alignment with their private social responsibility values (Jenson, 2010) or as expressing the presence of managerial opportunism (Jiao, 2010).

Consistent, with the previous literature on the relation between the CSR and financial performance and the insights from the stakeholder theory, we hypothesized that the CSR index had significant positive effect on the accounting returns. In conflict with our hypotheses, we found that CSR did not significantly predict accounting returns.

Employed panel analysis did not report any significant effect of the banks' CSR activities on the accounting returns measured by ROA, ROE and NIM. This result was consistent with findings of Soana (2011), in which no significant effect was observed between the CSR and accounting returns. Conversely, our findings on the absence of significant relation between CSR and FP were at variance with Adeyanju, (2012), Ofiri *et al.* (2014), Tafti *et al.* (2012) and Weshah *et al.* (2012). In these studies, researchers found significant positive effects of the CSR on the accounting returns.

Moreover, the effect of the control variables on the accounting returns was observed but it was statistically insignificant. The regression results showed that CSR activities undertaken by banks are not dominant predictor of their profitability as compared with their control variables (LogTA, IncGrow, Leverage). Therefore, banks engaging in CSR practices should do so in conjunction with other factors which have a significant impact on financial performance.

The above-mentioned findings might have important theoretical and practical implications. This study has contributed to the existing literature in a number of ways. First, our findings of no significant effect of CSR disclosures on accounting returns did not support the stakeholder theory. Stakeholder theory is the perspective that business activities aimed at satisfying the stakeholders should help the business to create competitive advantage and improve the financial performance (Freeman & Evan, 1990). The results of the study align with Friedman's (1970) claim that business firms should not engage in social responsibility. Second, the research examines empirically the relation between CSR activities and financial performance in companies that perceive CSR activities as a tool for gaining and retaining legitimacy. Third, the research fills the gap in existing literature on CSR by adding Polish perspective on the phenomena, thereby enhancing our current understanding of the impact of CSR activities on FP in banking industry. Fourth, this study was conducted in Poland that is perceived as a very important emerging economy in Central and Eastern Europe. Thus, the findings regarding to relation between CSR and FP in Polish banks could have serious implications in other emerging economies in particular in Central and Eastern Europe region.

The findings of this study revealed also several practical implications and recommendations. First, the results of the study imply that, in order to be rewarded with legitimacy by stakeholders, managers should spend more resources and effort on their CSR activities and in longer perspective they might expect positive impact on financial performance. This therefore calls for increased shareholders' understanding of the managerial actions. The owners of shares would be better informed of actions taken by the management, if they were involved in organization's activity (OECD 2008). Therefore, the following recommendation for the management can be specified: (1) managers should ensure transparency of the managerial process, (2) the full disclosure of relevant information to all stakeholders is needed.

Second, according to Griffin and Prakash (2014), business sector (including banking sector) and government are obliged to effectively participate in CSR, if social conduct is to be sustainable. Governments and policy makers needs to encourage the companies to support the provision of public goods. Therefore, there is a need to call on the government to provide fiscal incentives and other stimulating factors to the business sector to encourage them to improve their CSR activities.

5.2. Limitations and future research

As with any empirical work, this study suffers from a number of limitations that may further constrain its generalizability and trustworthiness. First, this study is focused on the banking sector in Poland. Hence, the findings are biased and only applicable to that sector. Any attempt to generalize the results of the study beyond its context may render such generalized conclusions invalid.

Second, the sample size of 18 banks, arising from the small population of banks in the country and used for this study was another limitation. The limited number of banks included in the analysis could reduce the validity of the findings and conclusions. Nevertheless, a few empirical studies have used small sample sizes especially in emerging markets.

Third, the CSR disclosure data used for this study constitutes another limitation. The CSR disclosure data were hand collected from management commentaries and corporate social responsibility reports according to self-constructed disclosure checklist. It has the disadvantages to be difficult to replicate because the researcher may generally use his judgement during the coding process which can also bias the overall results.

Fourth, another major limitation to this study relates to the operationalization of both dependent and independent variables. We operationalized financial performance as ROA, ROE and NIM ratios so we use accounting-based approach. Alternative operationalization of the financial performance that exists in the empirical literature uses market-based ratios. To measure CSR disclosures, we used content analysis and we have developed aggregated CSR index, while researchers have measured the CSR in diverse ways including the use of questionnaire surveys, spending measures or third parties' ratings. Using any or a combination of these alternatives could produce different results. In the control variables, operationalization issues also arise. Therefore, differences in the operationalization of the variables may not permit a free generalization of the study or a perfect comparison with other studies.

Fifth, the limited number of control variables we used in this study is also a source of limitations of the study. If more control variables, which appear in the literature, had been included in the study models, we might have obtained different and, possibly, more accurate results.

Finally, the adopted quantitative design of the study has its inherent limitations and might limit the extent to which the findings may be generalized or replicated. Drawing conclusions merely from the analysis of numerical data to explain social interaction is risky. It is necessary to take into account also human nature, psychology and irrational behaviour of stakeholders.

In this regard, further research is recommended to expand the scope of the study so that It could be possible to determine, how did the relation CSR-FP change over time, especially before and after financial crisis. Such study can compare the impact of CSR disclosures on banks' financial performance in the pre-crisis and post-crisis periods. Apart from the above proposal, other future researches might extend the study by performing in-depth qualitative research to explore the exact meanings the stakeholders attach to the bank CSR activities and disclosures based on them.

Another future research could address the empirical linkage between CSR disclosures and financial performance in the banking sector of other emerging countries. Researchers may want to replicate the study, using content analysis and aggregated CSR index to measure the CSR as was done in this study or using some other forms of methodology to measure both dependent and independent variables. Lastly, some elements of the methodology could be adapted in further research, which examine the influence of CSR disclosure on financial performance in many other sectors. Such comparative studies could be done within the oil and gas, food and manufacturing or production sectors in order to obtain more understanding about the differences amongst them.

Acknowledgements

We wish to thank Prof. Luc Paugam, Prof. Nadia Albu, and anonymous referee and participants of the AMIS 2017 Conference at the Bucharest University of Economic Studies for their helpful comments.

References

Adebayo, E. (2000) "Corporate Social Responsibility Disclosure, Corporate Financial and Social Performance: An Empirical Analysis", Nova Southeastern University: Fort Lauderdale, FL.

Adeyanju, O.D. (2012) "An assessment of the impact of corporate social responsibility on Nigerian society: The examples of banking and communication industries", *Universal Journal of Marketing and Business Research*, vol. 1(1): 17-43.

Albu, C.N., Balsari, C. & Krasodomska, J. (2016) "Introduction to the Special issue on Corporate Social Reporting in Central and Eastern Europe", *Accounting and Management Information Systems*, vol. 15, no. 2: 193-205

Ambec, S. and Lanoie, P. (2008) "Does it pay to be green? A systematic overview", *Academy of Management Perspectives*, vol. 22(4): 45-62

Arli, D. & Lasmono, K. H. (2009) "Consumers' perception of corporate social responsibility in a developing country", *International Journal of Consumer Studies*, vol. 34: 46-51

Baird, P., L., Geylani, P.C. & Roberts, J.A. (2012) "Corporate social and financial performance re-examined: Industry effects in linear mixed model analysis", *Journal of Business Ethics*, vol. 109: 367-388

Bassen, A., Meyer, K. & Schlange, J. (2006) "The Influence of Corporate Responsibility on the Cost of Capital", *SSRN Electronic Journal* available on-line at https://ssrn.com/abstract=984406 (10.05.2017)

Becchetti, L., Ciciretti, R., Hassan, I. & Kobeissi, N. (2012) "Corporate social responsibility and share value", *Journal of Business Research*, vol. 65: 1628-1635

Branco, M.C. & Rodrigues, L.L. (2006) "Communication of corporate social responsibility by Portuguese banks: A legitimacy theory perspective", *Corporate Communications: An International Journal*, vol. 11 (3): 1356-3289

Busch, T. & Hoffmann, V.H. (2011) "How hot is your bottom line? Linking carbon and financial performance", *Business and Society*, vol. 50(2): 233-265

Cajias, M., Fuerst, F., & Bienert, S. (2014) "Can investing in corporate social responsibility lower a company's cost of capital?", *Studies in Economics and Finance*, vol. 31(2): 202-222

Chen, H. & Wang, X. (2011) "Corporate social responsibility and corporate financial performance in China: An empirical research from Chinese firms", *Corporate Governance*, vol. 11 (4): 361-370

Chih, H.L., Chih, H. & Chen, T. (2010) "On the determinants of corporate social responsibility: International evidence on the financial industry", *Journal of Business Ethics*, vol. 93: 115-135

Cho, H. & Patten, D. (2007) "The role of environmental disclosures as tools of legitimacy: A research note", *Accounting, Organizations and Society*, vol. 32: 639-647

Cornett, M.M., Erhemjamts, O. & Tehranian, H. (2016) "Greed or good deeds: An examination of the relation between corporate social responsibility and the financial performance of U.S. commercial banks around the financial crisis", *Journal of Banking and Finance*, vol. 70: 137-159

Deegan, C.M. (2002) "Introduction. The legitimising effect of social and environmental disclosures - a theoretical foundation", *Accounting, Auditing & Accountability Journal*, vol. 15 (3): 282–311

Deegan, D. & Blomquist, C. (2006) "Stakeholder influence on corporate reporting: an exploration of the interaction between WWF-Australia and the Australian minerals industry", *Accounting, Organizations and Society*, vol. 31: 343-372

Dhaliwal, D.S., Li, O.Z., Tsang, A. & Yang, Y.G. (2011) "Voluntary nonfinancial disclosure and the cost of equity capital: The initiation of corporate social responsibility reporting", *The Accounting Review*, vol. 86(1): 59-100

Dixon-Fowler, H.R., Slater, D.J., Johnson, J.L., Ellstrand, A.E. & Romi, A.M. (2013) "Beyond "does it pay to be green?" A meta-analysis of moderators of the CEP-CFP relationship", *Journal of Business Ethics*, vol. 112: 353-366

Dumitrescu, D. & Simionescu, L. (2015) "Empirical research regarding the influence of corporate social responsibility (CSR) activities on companies' employees and financial performance", *Economic Computation & Economic Cybernetics Studies & Research*, vol. 49(3): 52-66

Freedman, M. & Patten, D. (2004) "Evidence on the pernicious effect of financial report environmental disclosure", *Accounting Forum*, vol. 28: 27-41

Freeman, R. & Evan, W. (1990) "Corporate governance: A stakeholder interpretation", *Journal of Behavioral Economics*, vol. 19(4): 337

Freeman, R.E. (1984) *Strategic management: A stakeholder approach*, Boston, MA: Pitman.

Gray, R., Kouhy, R. & Lavers, S. (1995a) "Corporate social and environmental reporting: A review of the literature and a longitudinal study of UK disclosure", *Accounting, Auditing & Accountability Journal*, vol. 8(2): 47-77

Gray, R., Kouhy, R. & Lavers, S. (1995b) "Methodological themes: Constructing a research database of social and environmental reporting by UK companies", *Accounting, Auditing & Accountability Journal*, 8 (2): 78-101

Griffin, J.J. & Prakash, A. (2014) "Corporate social responsibility: Initiatives and mechanism" *Business & Society*, vol. 53(4): 465-482

Haniffa, R.M. & Cooke, T.E. (2005) "The impact of culture and governance on corporate social reporting", *Journal of Accounting and Public Policy*, vol. 24: 391-430

Husted, B.W. (2005) "Risk management, real options, and corporate social responsibility", *Journal of Business Ethics*, vol. 60: 175-183

Jiao, Y. (2010) "Stakeholder welfare and firm value", *Journal of Banking and Finance*, vol. 34: 2549-2561

Kaplan, S.E. & Ruland, R.G. (1991) "Positive theory, rationality and accounting regulation", *Critical Perspectives on Accounting*, vol. 2(4): 361-374

Khlif, H., Guidara, A. & Souissi, M. (2015) "Corporate social and environmental disclosure and corporate performance", *Journal of Accounting in Emerging Economies*, vol. 5: 51-69

Kiliç, M., Kuzey, C. & Uyar, A. (2015) "The impact of ownership and board structure on Corporate Social Responsibility (CSR) reporting in the Turkish banking industry", *Corporate Governance*, vol. 15: 357- 374

Kohers, T. & Simpson, W.G. (2002) "The link between corporate social and financial performance: Evidence from the banking industry", *Journal of Business Ethics*, vol. 35: 97-109

Kopczewska, K., Kopczewski, T. & Wócik, P. (2009) "Metody ilościowe w R. Aplikacje ekonomiczne i finansowe" [*Quantitative methods in R. Economic and financial applications*] CeDeWu, Warszawa.

Krasodomska, J. (2012) "Znaczenie społecznej odpowiedzialności banków dla bezpieczeństwa systemu finansowego" [*Importance of social responsibility of banks for the safety of the financial system*], *Zeszyty Naukowe, Polskie Towarzystwo Ekonomiczne*, no. 12: 151-159

Matthews, M.R. (1993) *Socially responsible accounting*, London: Chapman & Hall.

Molyneux ,P., Schaeck, K. & Zhou, T. (2014) "Too systemically important to fail' in banking – Evidence from bank mergers and acquisitions'", *Journal of International Money and Finance*, vol. 49: 258-282

Nollet, J., Filis, G. & Mitrokostas, E. (2015) "Corporate social responsibility and financial performance: A non-linear and disaggregated approach", *Economic Modelling*, vol. 52: 400-407

Organization for Economic Co-operation and Development (2008) OECD principles of corporate governance, available on-line at http://www.oecd.org/dataoecd/32/18/31557724.pdf (2016-12-01)

Orlitzky, M., Schmidt, F.L. & Rynes, S.L. (2003) "Corporate social and financial performance: A meta-analysis", *Organization Studies*, vol. 24(3): 403-441

Patten, D. (1991) "Exposure, legitimacy, and social disclosure", *Journal of Accounting and Public Policy*, vol. 10: 297-308

Patten, D. (1992) "Intra-industry environmental disclosures in response to the Alaskan oil spill: A note on legitimacy theory", *Accounting, Organizations and Society*, vol. 17(5): 471-475

Patten, D. (2000) "Changing superfund disclosure and its relations to other environmental disclosure", *Advances in Environmental Accounting and Management*, vol. 1: 101-122

Servaes, H. & Tamayo, A. (2013) "The impact of corporate social responsibility on firm value: the role of customer awareness", *Management Science*, vol. 59: 1045-1061.

Sharma, S. & Starik, M. (Eds.) (2002) *Research in corporate sustainability: The evolving theory and practice of organizations in the natural environment*, Northampton: Edward Elgar Academic Publishing.

Shen, C.H., Wu, M.W., Chen, T.H. & Fange, H. (2016) "To engage or not to engage in corporate social responsibility: Empirical evidence from global banking sector", *Economic Modelling*, vol. 55: 207–225

Siregar, S.V. & Bachtiar, Y. (2010) "Corporate social reporting: Empirical evidence from Indonesia Stock Exchange", *International Journal of Islamic and Middle Eastern Finance and Management*, vol. 3 (3): 241-252

Soana, M. (2011) "The relationship between corporate social performance and corporate financial performance in the banking sector", *Journal of Business Ethics*, vol. 104: 133-148

Suchman, M.C. (1995) "Managing legitimacy: strategic and institutional approaches", *Academy of Management Review*, vol. 20 (3): 571–610

Szpringer, S. (2009) "Społeczna odpowiedzialność banków. Między ochroną konsumenta a osłoną socjalną" [*Social responsibility of banks. Between consumer protection and social protection*], *Oficyna a Wolters Kluwer business*, Warszawa.

Tafti, S.F., Hosseini, S.F. & Emami, S.A. (2012) "Assessment of the corporate social responsibility according to Islamic values (Case study: Sarmayeh Bank)", *Procedia – Social and Behavioral Sciences*, vol. 58: 1139-1148

Taskin, D. (2015) "The Relationship between CSR and Banks' Financial Performance: Evidence from Turkey", *Journal of Yaşar University*, vol. 10(39): 21-30

Torres, A., Bijmolt, T.H.A., Tribo, J.A. & Verhoef, P. (2012) "Generating global brand equity through corporate social responsibility to key stakeholders", *International Journal of Research in Marketing*, vol. 29: 13-24

Waniak-Michalak, H., Macuda, M. & Krasodomska, J. (2016) "Corporate Social Responsibility and accounting in Poland: a literature review", *Accounting and Management Information Systems*, vol. 15(2): 242-303

Weshah, S., R., Dahiyat, A.A., Awwad, M., R.A. & Hajjat, E.S. (2012) "The impact of adopting corporate social responsibility on corporate financial performance: Evidence from Jordanian banks", *Interdisciplinary Journal of Contemporary Research in Business*, vol. 4(5): 34-44

Wu, M.W. & Shen, C.H. (2013) "Corporate social responsibility in the banking industry: Motives and financial performance", *Journal of Banking and Finance*, vol. 37 (9): 3529-3547

Appendix A
CSR disclosure items

Environment		**References**
EN1	Statement on environmental protection policy	GRI Standards 2016 (GRI 301: Materials, GRI 302: Energy, GRI 303: Water, GRI 304: Biodiversity, GRI 306: Effluents and Waste); Kiliç et al. 2015.
EN2	Prevention of pollution (waste disposal and recycling)	
EN3	Actions aiming to limit consumption of energy, materials, water (sustainable use of resources)	
EN4	Sustainability (any mention of sustainable development)	
EN5	Aesthetic value of the environment (designing structures in harmony with the environment, landscape)	
EN6	Environmental protection, biodiversity and restoration of natural habitats	
EN7	Taking account of the environment in credit policy (environmentally-friendly products, "green products", funding "low-emission" investment projects …)	
EN8	Environmental training and certificates (ISO 14001 vs)	
EN9	Joint projects with other companies providing environmental management services	
EN10	Environmental awards	
Human Resources		**References**
HR1	Employment and labour relations	GRI Standards 2016 (GRI 401: Employment, GRI 402: Labor/ Management Relations, GRI 403: Occupational Health and Safety, GRI 404: Training and Education, GRI 405: Diversity and Equal Opportunity); Kiliç et al. 2015.
HR2	Occupational health and safety	
HR3	Employee development (training…)	
HR4	Employee benefits (insurance, healthcare, social assistance ...)	
HR5	Relationships with trade unions	
HR6	Information on employee turnover	
HR7	Information on support for daytime care, maternity and paternity leave	
HR8	Encouraging diversity (employment of minorities, disabled persons, women ...)	
Product and customers		**References**
PC1	Comprehensibility and transparency of products / services	GRI Standards 2016 (GRI 416: Customer

PC2	Bank products addressed to marginalised groups (the disabled, aged customers, non-profit organisations ...)	Health and Safety, GRI 417: Marketing and Labelling, GRI 418: Customer Privacy); Kiliç et al. 2015.
PC3	Examination of customer satisfaction / service quality	
PC4	Protection of customers' data and privacy	
PC5	Customer service (settlement of problems, complaints, disputes, renegotiation of contract terms ...)	
PC6	Consumer awards	
Community Involvement		**References**
CI1	Donations for social activities and public benefit organisations	GRI Standards 2016 (GRI 413: Local Communities); Kiliç et al. 2015.
CI2	Support for education (scholarships, conferences, seminars, student internships…)	
CI3	Sponsorship of various sport, artistic and cultural events	
CI4	Sponsorship of various public health initiatives, projects, campaigns	
CI5	Support for local activities, industry, agriculture	

[i] Notoria Serwis Database contains an updated, standardized format of financial statements for all companies listed on the Warsaw Stock Exchange – reporting both in accordance with Polish and international accounting standards.

5

The balanced scorecard logic in the management control and reporting of small business company networks

Selena Aureli[a], Andrea Cardoni[b], Mara Del Baldo[c] and Rosa Lombardi[d,1]

[a]University of Bologna, Italy; [b]University of Perugia, Italy; [c]University of Urbino Carlo Bo, Italy; [d]University of Rome La Sapienza, Italy

Abstract: The purpose of this paper is to assess and integrate the application of the balance scorecard (BSC) logic into business networks identifying functions and use that such performance measuring tool may undertake for SME's collaborative development. Thus, the paper analyses a successful case study regarding an Italian network of small companies, evaluating how the multidimensional perspective of BSC can support strategic and operational network management as well as communication of financial and extra financial performance to stakeholders. The study consists of a qualitative method, proposing the application of BSC model for business networks from international literature. Several meetings and interviews as well as triangulation with primary and secondary documents have been conducted. The case study allows to recognize how BSC network logic can play a fundamental role on defining network mission, supporting management control as well as measuring and reporting the intangible assets formation along the network development lifecycle. This is the first time application of a BSC integrated framework for business networks composed of SMEs. The case study demonstrates operational value of BSC for SME's collaborative development and success.

Keywords: management control, balanced scorecard, business networks.

---

[1] *Corresponding author*: Rosa Lombardi, University of Rome La Sapienza, Italy, e-mail address sa.lombardi@uniroma1.it

1. Introduction

The strategic importance of collaborations between companies is now broadly recognised under an operative, scientific and institutional perspective. Technological developments, social changes in consumer behaviour and deep interconnections deriving from globalisation arise growing complexities on the *business environment* (Håkansson *et al.*, 2009), asking for more intense business collaboration (Mancini, 2016) able to enhance strategic and operational performance, especially for small and medium sized enterprises (SMEs). Therefore, *policy makers,* all over the world and at all territorial levels, firmly attempt to support the diffusion of strategic alliances (Huggins, 2001) to create synergies and to form international value chains consistent with the new industrial paradigms.

In line with this trend, in 2009, the Italian government promoted an innovative legislative framework[i] represented by the *contractual network* - usually called *network contract* -, simplifying the formal arrangement to set-up and manage collaborative relationships (Cardoni, 2012; Lombardi, 2015). The intended aim of the Italian government was to promote more dynamic and flexible business aggregations, overcoming some weaknesses showed by the existing formal settings, such as consortiums, cooperatives and temporary business associations (Aureli & Del Baldo, 2016a). Its goal was also to foster the formation of stable alliances to increase the competitiveness and innovative capabilities of the national productive system, mainly composed of SMEs (Cerved, 2015). As a specific contractual agreement bringing together firms to share information, co-produce, co-market and/or co-purchase, the network contract may support SMEs in reaching the critical dimension to bear innovative business development processes (Verschoore *et al.*, 2015), accumulate experience, know-how, information and increase internationalization (Fernhaber & Li, 2013; Aureli & Del Baldo, 2016a).

Italian contractual networks represent a promising field of study for management control in network settings as they have a distinctive characteristics: there is the legal obligation to explicit the strategic objectives that partners intend to achieve in the contract, the contents of the network programme and the criteria used to measure the progress towards the achievement of such objectives. This obligation calls for the definition of proper instruments for programming network's activities and managing and measuring performance within a network context (Mancini, 2016). New solutions are needed to support interconnection mechanisms between the partners' different business models.

At the same time, such requirements contrast the traditional reluctance of smaller enterprises to adopt management control systems as they are characterized by poor strategic planning and informal decision-making processes (Brouthers *et al.*, 1998). SMEs weakly perceive the need for balanced strategic control models (Hudson *et al.*, 2001a) and adopt advanced control instruments only under specific conditions related to the governance structure and the management style (Hudson *et al.*, 2001a; Laitinen, 2002). In all other situations, SMEs adopt approaches easy to implement and consistent with SMEs' needs, notably, the need to focus on operational aspects that are critical for their success (Hudson *et al.*, 2001b). SMEs prefer using informal and unstructured performance measurement practices because of their lack of human and financial resources, the prevailing reactive approach, their short-term strategic orientation, the difficulty in developing and formalizing mission and values, and the wrong perception of the benefits deriving from the implementation of a performance measurement system (Ates *et al.*, 2013).

Starting from these premises, the aim of this study is to assess the application of a management control instrument based on the balanced scorecard logic (hereinafter referred to as the BSC logic) within a reticular frame and, more specifically, in the field of contractual networks. In addition, this study aims to identify the functions that such an advanced instrument for performance measurement may undertake.

The empirical analysis focuses on the GPT network, a successful example of business network created by 21 Italian SMEs. The case study proposed is directed to show results of the application of the BSC logic within contractual networks. Results support several research evidence and implications among which we highlight the capability of the BSC logic to reveal the alignment between the strategic decisions and the selection, measurement and control of financial and intangible performance, as well as the capability of this instrument to support network control, strategy implementation and the communication of results to stakeholders. In addition, the case of GPT network suggests that the BSC logic is devoted to monitor strategy implementation so far and not to challenge or revise the existing strategic direction. The structure of the paper is the following. After the introduction, section 2 presents the literature review and section 3 identifies the methodology. Sections 4 and 5 analyse the case study and findings. Section 6 discusses the results and ends with some concluding remarks and our future research plan on the topic analysed.

2. Application of the balanced scorecard in the field of small business company networks

Although SMEs seem to not require sophisticated management control systems to implement and monitor strategies, due to their organizational simplicity and lack of formalization (Jänkälä, 2007), they could draw important benefits from the implementation of management control and performance measurement systems (MCS and PMS), especially in innovative settings and environment. The integration between qualitative and quantitative metrics (Laitin, 2002) remains the best feature to allow the owner-managers to monitor a wide range of qualitative and quantitative goals (Jarvis *et al.*, 2000) even if recent literature demonstrates that the BSC logic does not assure *per se* a significant impact on decision-making performance (Strohhecker, 2016). In some cases, the use of strategy maps may have detrimental effects for organizations whose outcomes are influenced significantly by uncontrollable factors.

In the context of networks of SMEs the integration between qualitative and quantitative metrics is fundamental. They need different performance measures to capture network's objectives heterogeneity spanning from financial goals to the consolidation of the collaboration in terms of network's reputation, visibility, growth, members participation and relationships building. Financial indicators might not be able to capture the complexity of networks (Varamäki *et al.*, 2008; Ferreira *et al.*, 2012). Thus, the use of 'integrated' or 'balanced' metrics better support decision makers – the network manager *in primis* – to proactively and strategically manage the collaboration (Ferreira *et al.*, 2012). In addition, each small firm participating the network may benefit from the collection and reporting of network performance measures to assess the results achieved by joint operations (Parung & Bititci, 2008) or specific enabling factors (i.e., resources and competences, value and culture, and modes of interaction) (Varamäki *et al.*, 2008).

To this extent, the BSC developed by Kaplan and Norton (1996) represents a dynamic and flexible tool that can be adapted to company networks to favor activity planning and network coordination (Hudson *et al.*, 2001a; 2001b), increasing the SMEs awareness of the results achieved in relation to the network's objectives and reducing the risk of network's failure (Varamäki & Vesalainen, 2003).

The BSC was originally intended as performance measurement tool (CIMA, 2005) characterised by the following elements (Kaplan & Norton, 1996): the balanced use of financial and non-financial measures to monitor results; attention to both short and long term objectives; simultaneous control of internal (e.g., efficiency in processes) and external aspects (e.g., the satisfaction of customers or other stakeholders); the adoption of indicators that measure the drivers of success and therefore favour an indication on future company performance (*leading indicator*), together with indicators on past results (*lagging indicator*); stimulation towards continuous improvement; flexibility in its construction (perspectives and indicators should be created and modified according to company strategy) and its adaptability to every possible organizational context.

Cited characteristics make the BSC a managerial instrument effectively fitting in the field of company networks. The inclusion of non-financial measures regarding innovation, internal processes and customer satisfaction together with the flexibility and adaptability of the BSC (Atkinson, 2006) allow for implementation within a wide range of collaborative networks, as demonstrated by the following cases: consortiums created to develop new technologies and to carry out common R&D activities (Kim & Kim, 2009); public-private partnerships operating in the healthcare sector whose objective is to satisfy the service users requirements (Cepiku *et al.*, 2011); public service networks where *citizen satisfaction* represents the main perspective (Funk, 2007); tourism networks in which the private objective of creating shareholder valuc lives side by side with the public matrix objective of improving the image of the tourism destination (Aureli & Del Baldo, 2016b). In all of these cases, traditional accounting measures and management instruments risk to become useless to the network manager whereas the BSC can provide a valid support.

Furthermore, in network contexts, the ability of the BSC to push management towards identifying and measuring all the possible success drivers that contribute to value creation (Eccles, 1991), including those of an intangible nature, becomes very important. In reticular contexts, socialisation mechanisms and knowledge sharing between partners are more or less intentionally activated and the BSC can contribute to understanding the importance of these intangible resources in the creation of a sustainable competitive advantage (Edvinsson & Malone, 1997; Stewart, 1997; Sveby, 1997). Even though this is not a specific instrument of knowledge management, such as the Performance Prism (Neely *et al.*, 2001) or the Value Creation Map (Marr, 2004; Marr *et al.*, 2004), the BSC may still support management by identifying and monitoring knowledge, especially when strategic maps are used (Kaplan & Norton, 2004).

An additional useful feature of the BSC in the field of collaborative networks consists of its attention to external forces, specifically referring to the key stakeholders who transfer tangible and intangible resources to see their specific expectations satisfied (Ahn, 2001; Funk, 2007). Even if the main shareholder holds a predominant role in this framework (Neely *et al.*, 2001), the BSC can be used to communicate with all partners, suppliers, customers and network funders and serve to monitor the level of satisfaction that is necessary to maintain and stabilize the network. In fact, the BSC is able to describe how the resources of the companies involved contribute to the network strategy (Laihonen *et al.*, 2014), favouring partners' dialogue and socialisation along the value chain (Mahama, 2006) and balancing of the interests of various partners (Funk, 2007).

Summarising, theoretical literature suggests that the BSC is more than a simple management control tool. It is a framework that may have the following valuable functions (Busco & Quattrone, 2015), when used in reticular contexts (Pekkola, 2013):

- clarify and describe the vision and mission of the network as key elements to define the strategies and expected results (Neely *et al.*, 2000);
- implement the common network strategy, highlighting the causal links between strategy, activity and impacts on performance (Kaplan & Norton, 1996; Atkinson, 2006), translating the objectives into specific action to be implemented (Epstein & Manzoni, 1997) and acting as an operational standard to influence partners behaviour (Kulmala & Lönnqvist, 2006; Mooraj *et al.*, 1999; Lawrie & Cobbold, 2004);

- measure the network performance and monitor the achievement of the strategic goals (CIMA, 2005);
- improve managers' decision-making processes and contribute to the identification of new emerging strategies (Simons, 1995; Kaplan & Norton, 2001; Naro & Travaillé, 2011);
- communicate network performance to stakeholders and other third parties (e.g. public authorities), in line with the tendency of using performance measurement instruments as an accountability tool (Marchi, 2011).

Such functions can be analysed in light of the Simons' framework (1995) as implemented by Van Veen-Dirks and Wijn (2002) with specific reference to the Balanced Scorecard.

Simons' framework provided that organizations should set four different types (or levers) of controls: beliefs systems, boundary systems, feedback systems and measurement systems, which can be used in a diagnostic or interactive manner. This distinction relates to how the information is used rather than the technical design features of the control system. Diagnostic control systems (DCS) are used to set standards, monitor organizational outcomes and correct deviations. On the contrary, control systems are used interactively (ICS) when information outputs serve for communication within the organization and detecting strategic uncertainties that need to be addressed via informal dialogue and other forms of interactions. Thus, the first type of controls supports the implementation of the strategy while the second type favours flexibility and strategic renewal thanks to informal communications that demand attention from managers and confrontation with the lower management levels. The main differences between ICS and DCS are reported in Table 1.

Table 1. Simons' framework applied to the Balanced Scorecard

Diagnostic Control Systems (DCS)	Interactive control Systems (ICS)
- Facilitate the measurement of the outputs of a process - Provide standards against which actual results can be compared - Correct deviations from standards	- Define a sub-set of important information to focus on given the strategic uncertainties faced by an organisation - Favour frequent and regular attention from operating managers at all levels on these information - Gather superiors, subordinates and peers together to interpret and discuss the information in the light of future strategic initiatives

(Source: adapted from Van Veen-Dirks and Wijn, 2002)

In the attempt to apply Simons' framework to the usage of Balanced Scorecard within firms, Van Veen-Dirks and Wijn (2002) noted that this specific measurement system can be used interactively or diagnostically but cannot be adopted to perform the functions of a strategic control system, i.e. to review and reformulate the strategy. According to these authors, the BSC is a formal system designed for strategy implementation, thus when its data are used interactively, they can merely suggest strategy adjustments. The BSC does not really question the basis of strategic planning as strategic control systems do.

Simons' levers of control framework has been applied in many research over the last 20 years to interpret findings on empirical usage of management control systems and performance metrics (Martyn *et al.*, 2016). Although developed from the author's study of intra-organizational controls within large enterprises, it provided helpful insights in the investigation of inter-organisational controls within networks (Kominis & Dudau, 2012) and with reference to SMEs (Granlund & Taipaleenmaki, 2005). Past research has demonstrated that control systems can both measure results to align network participants' performance and support partners to solve problems and search for opportunities when used to create a communicative environment within alliances (Mahama, 2006; Massaro *et al.*, 2014).

Among the various performance measurement models for managing networks proposed in literature (Bititci *et al.*, 2005; Ferreira *et al.*, 2012), the Business Network Scorecard (BNS) is deemed rather interesting because of three distinctive elements (Lombardi *et al.*, 2015). Firstly, it focuses on common network objectives (and not that of the leader or focal company), implying the adoption of a general shared vision of the network. Secondly, it adopts the network manager perspective, not considering the single company needs and tools to monitor the relations created with its suppliers (Kaplan *et al.*, 2010). In other terms, it is designed to be a management tool for the network and not a tool of network relations management. Lastly, it includes a fifth dimension of analysis, in addition to the four traditional dimensions (or perspectives) of the BSC, regarding the creation of value deriving from the reticular bonds created between the partners and the network towards the external environment. These bonds may not be quantified in monetary terms, but they may lead to the development of new ideas or be translated in the creation of social value for the local context that can be measured in quantitative and qualitative terms.

Therefore, this model adapts perfectly to the case of networks made by partners with equal decision power, where a focal company that guides collaboration does not actually exist, but there is a network manager who needs a governance instrument to simplify interactions and the exchange of information between partners and thanks to which he/she can monitor and report the results achieved, including those of an intangible nature.

Despite the growing interest on performance measurement system for networks and the diffusion of contractual networks in Italy (see Section 1) that need to be managed effectively and efficiently, to date no empirical application of BNS are available. To fill this gap we decided to investigate the possible application of the BNS model to the results achieved from a network of companies located in Central Italy used as a case study.

Based on the theoretical background described above, the research questions that have guided the empirical study are the following: 1) Can management control activities and reporting practices of a successful contractual network be interpreted to the multidimensional logic of the Business Network Scorecard model?; 2) Which functions and use can be recognised in the possible application of the BSC logic in the field of the contractual network investigated?

3. Methodological approach

To answer to above mentioned research questions, we adopted a qualitative research approach, basing the empirical study on the analysis of the GPT (Gruppo Poligrafico Tiberino) contractual network. Similar to previous studies (Camarinha-Matos *et al.*, 2009; Pekkola, 2013) one collaborative network forms the case study under investigation.

The case study method (single or multiple) has been widely used in the study of SMEs networks (Halinen & Törnroos 2005; Barnes *et al.*, 2012) and contractual networks (Aureli & Forlani, 2016; Del Baldo, 2016; Trequattrini *et al.*, 2012), also facing the problems of performance measuring and accounting in the reticular contexts (Cardoni, 2012; Aureli & Del Baldo, 2016b).

The analysis aims to check the possible application that the BSC logic ("the if") and the method of use ("the how") may have. The model can alternatively be used as a programming and control instrument, declined on a strategic and operative level (for the design of strategies and to identify the activities necessary to achieve the predefined objectives) and as a reporting and communication instrument of intangible strategic assets, aimed at reporting network performance with a multidimensional scope toward external stakeholders (Lombardi *et al.*, 2015).

Consistently with the research objectives the inductive approach, widely used in international managerial literature (Flick, 2009) and typical of the Italian academic tradition (Ferraris Franceschi, 1990), allows for a better understanding of real situations through an in-depth analysis of complex phenomenon characterised by a high level of non homogeneity, novelty and/or dynamism such as networks of SMEs. Coherently, the case study method is suitable for experimental research strategies (Eisenhardt, 1989; Yin, 1989) to investigate into a contemporary phenomenon such as the contractual network, through the use of several sources of information such as interviews, questionnaires, archive data, documental analysis, analysis of information contained in websites, direct and participating observation[ii] .

From a methodological point of view, we decided to focus on this new form of inter-firm collaboration because also relevant for EU policies (European Commission, 2008), which aim at creating the conditions for the sustainable growth and competitiveness of SMEs, representing more than 98% of businesses in the EU-27 countries, employing 67% of the workforce and clearly contributing to territorial and communities innovation (Dobbs & Hamilton, 2007; Fichter, 2009). The review of the 'Small Business Act' (European Commission, 2011) actually mentioned Italy and the network contract as a good practice to imitate, which is an absolute innovation and definitely of great interest and stimulus for European legislators since it fills a legal vacuum at the European level (see the chapter "Innovation and competence" of the 2011 'Small Business Act' review). Moreover, there is a widespread diffusion of this collaborative tool among Italian SMEs. Starting from the first network contract signed on March, 31st 2010 in Tuscany, latest national data (Unioncamere, 2016) indicate that the number of network contracts amounts to 3,243 and involve a total of 16,587 companies (respectively +28% and + 30% over the last year).

With reference to the GPT case, this has been selected on the basis of three main attributes: 1) the medium-large dimension of the network (according to UnionCamere, the average number of companies partnering a network is 5, while GPT counts 21 partners or "nodes") and its organisational complexity, presuming the adoption of formalised management systems (Ahn, 2001; Funk, 2007); 2) the stability of the collaboration (launched since 2005) that justifies the costs associated to the creation of a management control infrastructure (Ferreira *et al.*, 2012); 3) the dynamism and potential development of the network. Finally, the availability of the network's leader in collaborating has been taken into consideration, in particular the network manager, already involved in previous investigations (Saetta *et al.*, 2013).

The GPT network has several elements of interest and excellence related to: a) the strategic collaboration model that overcomes the typical logic of vertical coordination of the partnership along the supply chain (Saetta *et al.*, 2013); b) the organisational model of GTP as a collaborative networked organisation (Saetta *et al.*, 2013), also configured as a "hybrid" network (Zapata & Hall, 2012) whose "nodes" belong to the private and public sector; and 3) the development model, characterised by the increasing trend in economic-financial, social and environmental performance of the single partners and of the entire network. The dynamism, articulation and complexity of the network therefore make GPT a rather important context to understand if the currently adopted management control activities and performance measurement systems can be attributed to the multidimensional logic of the BNS model (Lombardi *et al.*, 2015).

The methodological process consists in verifying the possible application of the BNS model in three main steps. The first one includes the analysis of current management control systems and performance measurement systems adopted by GPT to show the performances that are kept under control. The second step involves the clarification of shared objectives that underlay these measures and their formalization into a matrix of objectives. The last phase refers to the design of a network-level performance measurement system, which takes the form of a multidimensional report, based on stated objectives and measures currently in use.

The use of the case study method as a strategy of investigation into a complex research area such us business networks requires paying attention to potential limits and some necessary precautions. As highlighted by Halinen and Törnroos (1998, 2005), four main problems has preliminarily to be analysed: the delimitation of the object of observation (*the problem of network boundaries*), network's complexity, the time factor and the comparison of cases.

The first critical aspect has been faced by favouring the *abductive approach* (Easton, 1995; Dubois & Gadde, 2002); we then identified the *business context* as a number of actors and relations between companies of the GPT, the *network horizon* (the *horizon of perception*, the *macro-position* and the *relationscape*) in terms of joint operations (the entire network) and excluded actions at the individual level (single company) in this phase. The approach adopted is based on the perspective of the network manager, formally appointed as President of GPT's Board of Directors. This role represents the meta-manager in charge of the (organisational, strategic and operative) coordination of each single node and of the system. Therefore, he represents the *key informant* (Halinen & Törnroos, 2005: 1291) from which information can be extracted, as a depositary of an integrated vision, past, present and future perspective of the network.

The second critical aspect, connected with the multidimensional nature of the network and its performance, has been faced through the use of a mix (triangulation) of information sources, by combining the primary sources of data (questionnaire and interviews) with the secondary sources (documental analysis, consultation of the official website, analysis of previous publications related to the GPT case), aimed at acquiring cognitive elements in order to answer the research questions as illustrated in the following figure (Fig. 1).

Specifically, three interviews were carried out with the President of the network during planned company visits (each lasting 2 hours, subsequently transcribed, coded and validated), in which the following aspects were discussed: the current structure of the network; the resources and financial structure of the network; the network objectives; the presence (and the type) of performance measurement instruments; the presence (and the type) of key performance indicators used to assess the achievement of network's objectives.

The President of GPT was also given a semi-structured questionnaire (Alonso, 2010), divided up into two main sections (for a total of 30 questions); the first aimed at investigating into which accounting and managerial control systems are used on a network level and which reporting model has been adopted; the second (divided up into 5 groups of questions) aimed at checking if the logic incorporated in the theoretical model of the BNS can be found in the control systems currently in use.

The documental analysis was applied to both public documents (network's annual reports and the contract signed) as well as private documents for internal use elaborated by the network manager (management reports or progress reports).

Figure 1. The research strategy and sources of information

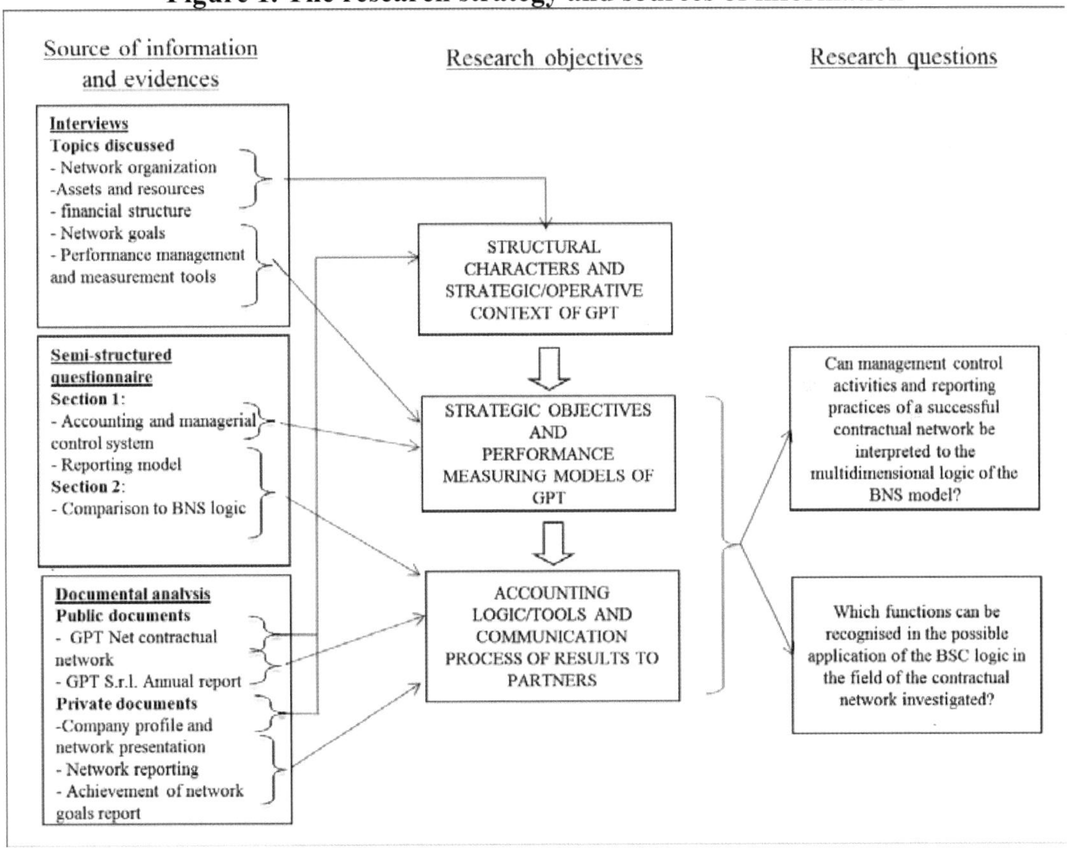

The third problem[iii], connected with the dynamism and flexibility of the network, has been faced by developing a longitudinal research in a process-related perspective (Pettigrew, 1997) to take into consideration changes from an operative, organisational and strategic point of view (Halinen & Törnroos, 1998). The period of time that the analysis refers covers several years, from 2005 to 2015.

4. The case study

The selected case study is GPT network, an innovative network of companies operating in Umbria (Central Italy) and established ten years ago as experimental outcome of a research project developed by the University of Perugia. The network was implemented by Net Value, an academic spin-off of the University, which is also an associate of the network. The objective of the network is to provide integrated and innovative solutions in the field of communication, printing, packaging and related services. It serves as the sole representative for the customer by benefitting from the joint skills and competences suitable for every solution and it is capable to fully support customer's product and service management.

To date, the network includes 21 partner companies and records a total turnover exceeding 130 million euro, more than 700 employees (approximately 8% of which dedicated to Research and Development) and 24 production plants. The network was officially set-up in 2005 following the strategic intuitions of three entrepreneurs operating in the print and packaging district of Città di Castello, who decided to set up a limited company (GPT S.r.l.) to share their skills and competences, enlarge their product portfolio, acquire new customers and provide the global market with innovative products. To reinforce the mutual commitment on assets and competences sharing, a "collaboration agreement" was formally signed to strengthen the collaboration towards strategic common goals and objectives.

The role planned for GPT overcomes a pure trading company of paper products, being designed as a collaborative network strategically aimed at product and process innovation. The model was designed on the theoretical model of Virtual Development Office (VDO), acting as a network collector and pointing to the market as a single organisation whose goal is: i) to identify the competitive position of the companies participating the network; ii) to promote several business opportunities within the network; iii) to define cooperation models and instruments; iv) to monitor performance; v) to favour product innovation and business model innovation.

The current legal structure includes the presence of a limited company, GPT S.r.l., whose shareholders are the 21 partner companies, and the formalization of a contractual network called "GPT Net" in 2012, replacing and reinforcing the original "collaboration agreement".

The section of the contract dedicated to the definition of the strategic objectives contemplates the following objectives:

> *"(a) to identify new market opportunities and increase the national and international market penetration of the network and of its participants; (b) to encourage research and development of new products and/or services and the innovation of technological and management processes; (c) to share and develop transversal services in order to optimise quality and reduce costs; (d) to identify opportunities for access to credit, private and public funding (e) to increase and diffuse technical and management skills within the network".*

The network programme considered in the contract includes:

> *"identification of new projects and/or specific market opportunities; development of coordinated forms of promotion of the products and services of the network participants, in Italy and abroad, also in the form of integrated solutions that include the products and services of two or more participant companies of the network; management and coordination of the negotiation, acquisition and execution phases of projects to be carried out in the network; identification, coordination and management of research, development and innovation activities useful for the network and its participants; identification of possible financial opportunities and public grants and management of request phases; identification, coordination and management of business opportunities to reinforce the technical and management skills of the network and of its participants".*

With reference to the measuring models of progress towards the strategic objectives, the following was considered:

> *"in each calendar year the Management Authority will check progress towards the strategic objectives in the final annual report, to be presented by 30th June of the following year to all network participants".*

With regards to governance, the contract includes the creation of a common Management Authority in charge of executing the network programme, to whom a mandate with representation was entrusted. For the entire duration of the contract, the company GPT S.r.l. was nominated to carry out this role, thus, its pro tempore legal representatives are the key managers in charge of making decisions on relevant issues.

5. The balanced scorecard for company networks: the first research findings

The literature analysis of BSC (Kaplan & Norton, 1996) as programming and control tool, or network performance reporting for external purposes (Marchi, 2011), allows for a control of the strategic-operative relevance of such tool for companies network. In other words, the use of a tool aimed at identifying the financial and non-financial performance of the network is proposed, enhancing the mutual activities carried out by the companies' network.

The Business Network Scorecard was applied ex-post to GPT network (Lombardi *et al.*, 2015) through the following operative instruments: i) matrix of the network objectives; ii) multidimensional report that indicates network performance through financial and non-financial measures; iii) comparison chart between network performance and the totalled performance of the partnering companies.

The BNS was applied according to data provided by GPT documents (network programme report; management annual report, joint balance sheet data, etc.) as well as by interviews carried out in order to test the relevance of this tool for network management control and for the network performance reporting to stakeholders.

When the project started, GPT network was adopting traditional control tools, mainly deriving from a calculation of the financial statement indicators and from forecasts on network performance according to the objectives to be pursued in the network. The individual appointed for network strategic control was the network manager, an expression of the academic element of the Net Value spin-off. Starting with the matrix of the network objectives, the main strategic objectives of the GPT network are summarised in the following table (Table 2).

Table 2. Objectives/Measures of the GPT network

OBJECTIVES		MEASURES
MARKET	*	Marketing action
	*	Business development
	*	Contacts with customers
	*	Participation in tenders
PRODUCT INNOVATION	*	Internal coordination activities in order to understand and handle the activities aimed at creating a new product (for example, printing of degree certificates)
INTERBUSINESS AND COLLABORATIVE PROCUREMENT	*	Synergy research through primary processes (mutual purchases) or support (mutual certification)
RESEARCH AND DEVELOPMENT AND INNOVATION PROJECTS	*	Research activities (degree thesis) to understand the opportunities of supplies from abroad

The matrix of objectives of BNS model is composed of five profiles or key perspectives, in order to measure and report network performance from a multidimensional point of view. The five main profiles for performance measuring, included in the multidimensional logic in which the GPT network is created, are divided up into the following perspectives: economic-financial; customers; internal processes; development and growth; value creation.

In the economic-financial perspective, the general objectives of the GPT network can be discovered, for example, in business development and in economic-financial returns of the joint activities by network. The customer perspective results in an objective of the added value creation for this category of stakeholders. The perspective of internal processes refers to the objectives of product creation and/or the supply of services. The perspective of development and growth of the network is based on the adoption of innovative processes, including investments in intellectual capital. The perspective of value creation measures the added value of network activities of a social, environmental and intellectual capital nature.

The BNS multidimensional report applied to GPT consists in the presentation of a network balanced assessment form, with the five perspectives as indicated above. The report includes a set of key indicators measuring GPT performance, which can be used as a network management control tool (e.g. to monitor partners' activities), a communication instrument to the network stakeholders and a tool to identify and disclose the amount and type of strategic intangible assets acquired or developed. Some examples include the indicators proposed to measure the network development, generated from an analysis of the innovations and investments in R&D and the metrics used to assess network's value creation with reference to social and environmental initiatives.

The data indicated in the multidimensional report applied to the GPT case refers to a time period of approximately 10 years, starting from the year in which the network was created in 2005. By analysing the perspectives of the multidimensional network report, performance indicators measured by the GPT network in the management annual report can be found as well as a set of useful information in order to define the combined operative strategy. Starting with the economic-financial perspective, the indicators attributed and established for GPT illustrate the ones proposed by the BNS model through four main categories of performance indexes and a good level of sub-indicators: GPT share capital, GPT profit/loss, proceeds of the network, network activity value. The combined ROE can be found among the additional indicators. The indicators of the customer perspective have been applied through the five categories indicated in the model, including a good level of sub-indicators: number of customers/contracts from the network; customer satisfaction level, number of complaints (production non-compliances), reputation of the network, additional indicators. Among these, the additional indicators are very original (*Large Accounts, Wide Markets, Special Markets*), as they aim to segment the GPT market. The internal processes are represented by the application of four categories of indicators and sub-indicators: the number of research projects launched by the network, production costs of goods and/or the supply of services, the number of employees in the network, equal opportunities. Additional indicators have not been defined. Network development and its indicators represent a very important analysis perspective for the GPT network, within which the following indicators are classified: investments in training of human capital, process and product innovations, network patents, R&D costs, additional indicators. The value creation perspective illustrates the most representative indicators of intangible performance of GPT (social, environmental and intellectual capital), through five categories of indicators: added value of the network and social initiatives, environmental impact and certifications, stakeholders, transfer of knowledge, additional indicators.

Table 3. GPT balanced assessment form examples

Economic-Financial		Customers		Internal processes		Network development		Value creation	
GPT share capital	- Legal form of limited company - Combined companies (19)	**Number of customers of the network (or number of contracts**	Contacts in market activities and contracts (152)	**Number of research projects launched by the network**	Large projects (5) and university spin off (1)	**Investment s in human capital training in the network**	Presence of training activities on quality system	**Added network value and social initiatives**	Presence of social initiatives
GPT performance	Years 2009-2014: Turnover of network orders (10 million euro)	**Customer satisfaction level**	Reduction in reply time to the market	**Production costs of goods and/or supply of services**	>300,000 euro	**Process and product innovation**	Categories of innovative products developed by the network (21)	**Environmental impact and certifications**	Environmental and quality certificates (UNI EN ISO 14001 and FSC; UNI EN ISO 9001)
GPT proceeds	Turnover (0.2 million euro) (2007 to 2008)	**Number of complaints (production non compliance)**	n. ½ per year	**Number of employee of the network**	More than 700 employees	**Network patents**	network patents (3)	**Stakeholders**	Participation in exhibitions
Value of network activities	Increase in member companies	**Reputation of the network**	A team of more than 300 companies	**Equal opportunities**	Women in the body that runs the network (2)	**R&D costs**	8% of employee working in R&D	**Transfer of knowledge**	Synergies on primary processes activated by the combined companies
Additional indicators	ROE 6.6%	**Additional indicators**	Large Accounts and Retail, Wide Markets Special Markets	**Additional indicators**		**Additional indicators**	Coordination activities of innovation process	**Additional indicators**	Screening activities for new business opportunities

The last element of the BNS model, the combined network- total companies performance form, has not been applied in this phase of the research.

6. Discussions and concluding remarks

Based on the GPT case, we can state that the Business Network Scorecard model is consistently fitting ex-post with the strategic, operative and reporting activities of the network, representing a useful managerial instrument that can be implemented into real life settings of collaborative processes.

With reference to the first research question, the case demonstrates how the strategic and operational goal setting as well as the managerial annual report contain the perspectives indicated by BNS, even in the absence of deliberate adoption of the BSC logic. Indeed the GPT case shows a significant coherence and integration between strategic objectives, short-term activities and results, measured by financial and non-financial indicators (Atkinson, 2006). Particularly strong is the alignment between the strategic decisions and the selection, measurement and control of financial and intangible performance (Glavan *et al.*, 2007). This integrated logic influences the whole set of reporting documents elaborated by the network manager to comply with institutional and managerial needs, from shareholders and partners meetings to quality assurance, and define a management control approach able to support the emergent and deliberate components of strategic management process.

However, an incomplete application of the multidimensional report of the GPT network can be found, as well as the need to extend analysis times of GPT data to be reclassified in the BNS. The objective is to propose a combined management control system to identify financial and non-financial network performance, to transfer useful information inside and outside of the network, with a view to programming and control and also for accounting of the intangible performance to network stakeholders.

Furthermore, the integration of sector-specific indicators is missing. In Table 3 we include some possible indicators whose validity must be checked with regards to the GPT case, through a sample of networks operating within the same sector.

Table 4. Sector indicators of the BNS-GPT model

Market segment Large Accounts and Retail	Network internationalisation plan
Market segment Wide Markets (market per sector)	Screening activities for new business opportunities
Market segment Special Markets (Universities, Health and public administration)	Development activities of integrated product-service systems
Coordination activities of the innovation process	

Moving onto the second research question, the paper suggests that since the network set-up the BSC logic has played a very important role in defining the network mission (Neely et al., 2000), communicating the project to potential partners (Marchi, 2011) and guiding the formalisation of the strategic objectives onto the network contract (Pekkola, 2013). The adoption of the multidimensional perspective on the management annual report presented at the meetings of partners called to approve the annual results indicate that the BSC logic has supported the control process and accounting of the network activities over the years (CIMA, 2015). Based on the report structure and contents an important training function can also be found, aimed at favouring learning and involvement of the partners whose trust and commitment was perceived as a fundamental asset by the network manager. Finally, thanks to the basic coherence between strategic objectives, progress achieved and new planned objectives, the BSC logic undertakes a vital role in the construction, analysis and communication of the intangible assets. This allows network manager to measure and report intangible performance that otherwise would not have been expressed, creating a general commitment on the validity of the strategic project for partners and the managerial team.

With specific reference to Simons' framework implemented as in Van Veen-Dirks and Wijn (2002) the GPT case showed a diagnostic use of the Balanced Scorecard logic. Analysing the form of the management report and the minutes of the meetings, the case showed a top-down flows of information from the network manager to partners with the specific aim to communicate results and create commitment. Even considering the collaborative and active role that partners play in the network context, which is not comparable to operating managers of a verticalized organization, the interactive use of management control system it is not visible. The report is elaborated to demonstrate the fulfilment of strategic objectives and to link the operational activities with long-term goals. A specific session of the report was always devoted to present new strategic initiatives and collaborative projects, but it was not conceived as an output of the discussion on information reported. To this extant, a stronger involvement of the partners on strategic and operational activities to the network should be necessary to put them in the condition to interactively interpret and discuss the information, creating the premises for strategy adjustments and possible revisions. A formal adoption of the Balanced Scorecard logic through BNS, followed by joint periodic discussion, could help in this way.

Summarising, the BSC logic adoption supported network development and stability. To this regard it cannot be ignored the important role played by the network manager and the academic spin-off Net Value in explicitly integrating the strategic perspective and performance measures as well as financial and non-financial indicators. To this respect, the managerial team succeeded in overcoming the typical weaknesses of SMEs, where owner-entrepreneurs intuitively integrate financial indicators with non-financial indicators but fail in the implementation of the needed routines and formalization to adopt the BSC logic successfully (Jarvis *et al.*, 2000).

We can conclude that the mandatory requirements established by the legislation on contractual networks could represent a relevant opportunity for SMEs to improve their managerial practice in business planning and performance management, both at individual and collaborative level. Moreover, if SMEs adopt the BSC logic they can better overcome the difficulties in developing the network's mission and strategy formulation that hinder the implementation of a performance measurement system (Ates *et al.,* 2013). As stated by Garengo and Biazzo (2012), the BSC approach can help network partners to unveil the strategy, improving the managerial culture of the whole network and every single partner.

References

Ahn, H. (2001) "Applying the balanced scorecard concept: an experience report", *Long Range Planning*, vol. 34(4): 441-461.

Alonso, A.D. (2010) "Importance of relationships among small accommodation operations around the city of Perth", *Tourism and Hospitality Research*, vol. 10(1): 14-24.

Anderson, E.W., Fornell C. & Lehmann. D.R. (1994a) "Customer satisfaction, market share, and profitability: findings from Sweden", *Journal of Marketing*, vol. 58(3): 53–66.

Anderson, J.C., Håkansson, H. & Johanson, J. (1994b) "Dyadic relationships within a business network context", *Journal of Marketing*, vol. 58(4): 1-15.

Ates, A., Garengo, P., Cocca, P. & Bititci, U. (2013) "The development of SME managerial practice for effective performance management", *Journal of Small Business and Enterprise Development*, vol. 20(1): 28-54.

Atkinson, H. (2006) "Strategy implementation: a role for the balanced scorecard?", *Management Decision*, vol. 44(10): 1441-1460.

Aureli, S. & Del Baldo, M. (2016a) *Formal Inter-firm Cooperation and International Expansion: How Italian SMEs are Using the Network Contract*, in Etemad. H., Denicolai, S., Hagen, B. & Zucchella A (ed) The Changing Global Economy and its Impact on International Entrepreneurship. The McGill International Entrepreneurship series, Cheltenham, UK: Edward Elgar Publishing, 157-182.

Aureli, S., Del Baldo, M. (2016b) "Performance appraisal of business networks. how small and medium enterprises define and monitor network objectives", *Management Control*, vol. 1: 35-58.

Aureli, S. & Forlani, F. (2016) "The importance of brand architecture in business networks: The case of tourist network contracts in Italy", *Qualitative Market Research: An International Journal*, vol. 19(2): 133-155.

Barnes, D., Clear, F., Dyerson, R., Harindranath, G., Harris, L. & Rae, A. (2012) "Web 2.0 and micro-businesses: an exploratory investigation", *Journal of Small Business and Enterprise Development*, vol. 19(4): 687-711.

Bititci, U., Mendibil, K., Martinez, V. & Albores, P. (2005) "Measuring and managing performance in extended enterprises", *International Journal of Operations & Production Management*, vol. 25(4): 333-353.

Bourne, M., Mills, J., Wilcox, J., Neely, A. & Platts, K. (2000) "Designing, implementing and updating performance measurement systems", *International Journal of Operations & Production Management*, vol. 20(7): 754-771.

Brouthers, K., Andriessen, F. & Nicolaes, I. (1998) "Driving blind: strategic decision-making in small companies", *Long Range Planning*, vol. 31(1): 130-138.

Busco, C. & Quattrone, P. (2015) "Exploring How the Balanced Scorecard Engages and Unfolds: Articulating the Visual Power of Accounting Inscriptions", *Contemporary Accounting Research*, vol. 32(3): 1236-1262.

Camarinha-Matos, L.M., Afsarmanesh, H., Galeano, N. & Molina, A. (2009) "Collaborative networked organizations – concepts and practice in manufacturing enterprises", *Computers & Industrial Engineering*, vol. 57(1): 46-60.

Cardoni, A. (2012) "Business planning and management accounting in strategic networks: theoretical development and empirical evidence from enterprises' network agreement", *Management Control*, vol. 3: 91-116.

Cepiku. D., Bianchi, A., Capaccioli, C., Costanzo, G. & Spandonaro, F. (2011) "Un modello per la misurazione delle performance delle reti: il caso studio del network antimalaria Tigray", *Politiche Sanitarie*, vol. 12(3): 101-115.

Cerved (2015) Rapporto Cerved PMI 2015. Milano: New Copy Service.

CIMA (2005) Effective Performance Management with the Balanced Scorecard. The Chartered Institute of Management Accountants, London.

Del Baldo, M. (2016) "Formal Cooperation for Developing Sustainability and Corporate Social Responsibility Among Tourism SMEs in Italy: Insights, Limits and Potentialities of the Network Contract", in Idowu, S.O. (ed.) *Key Initiatives in Corporate Social Responsibility. Global Dimension of CSR in Corporate Entities*, Vienna: Springer Series CSR Sustainability, 103-129.

Dobbs, M. & Hamilton, R.T. (2007) "Small business growth: recent evidence and new directions", *International Journal of Entrepreneurial Behaviour and Research*, vol. 13(5): 296-322.

Dubois, A. & Gadde, L.E. (2002) "Systematic combining. An abductive approach to case studies", *Journal of Business Research*, vol. 55(7): 553-560.

Easton, G. (1995) "Methodology and industrial networks", in Möller, K, Wilson, D.T. (ed), *Business marketing: an interaction and network perspective*, Norwell, MA: Kluwer Academic Publishing, 411-491.

Eccles, R.G. (1991) "The performance measurement manifesto", *Harvard Business Review*, vol. 69(1):131- 137.

Edvinsson, L. & Malone, M. (1997) *Intellectual capital: Realising your company's true value by finding its hidden brain-power*, New York: Harper Collins.

Eisenhardt, K.M. (1989) "Building theories from case study research", *Academy of Management Review*, vol. 14(4): 532-550.

Epstein, M.J. & Manzoni, J.F. (1997) "The balanced scorecard and tableau de board: translating strategy into action", *Management Accounting* (USA), vol. 79(2): 28-37.

European Commission (2008) Think Small First. A Small Business Act for Europe. http://eur-lex.europa.eu/

European Commission (2011) Review of the Small Business Act for Europe. http://eur-lex.europa.eu/

Ferraris Franceschi, R. (1990) *Il modello della ricerca*, Milano: Giuffrè.

Fernhaber, S. & Li, D. (2013) "International exposure through network relationship: implication for new venture internationalization", *Journal of Business Venturing*, vol. 28(2): 316-334.

Ferreira, P., Shamsuzzoha, A.H.M., Toscano, C. & Cunha, P. (2012) "Framework for performance measurement and management in a collaborative business environment", *International Journal of Productivity and Performance Management*, vol. 61(6): 672-690.

Fichter, K. (2009) "Innovation communities: the role of networks of promoters in Open Innovation", *R&D Management*, vol. 39(4): 357-371.

Flick, U. (2009), *An Introduction to Qualitative Research*, Sage, London, UK.

Funk, E. (2007) "The balanced scorecard equates interest in healthcare organizations", *Journal of Accounting & Organizational Change*, vol. 3(2): 88-103.

Garengo, P. & Biazzo, S. (2012) "Unveiling strategy in SMEs through balanced scorecard implementation: A circular methodology", *Quality Management and Business Excellence*, vol. 23(1): 79-102.

Glavan, M.E., Braescu, M., Dumitru, V., Jinga, G. & Laptes, R. (2007) "The relevance and quality of the accounting information in the managerial decisions", *Accounting and Management Information Systems*, Supplement, 103-115.

Håkansson, H., Ford, D., Gadde, L.E., Shenota, I. & Waluszewski, A. (2009). Business in Network, New York: John Wiley & Son Ltd.

Halinen, A., Törnroos, J.A. (1998) "The role of embeddedness in the evolution of business networks", *Scandinavian Journal of Management*, vol. 14(3): 87-205.

Halinen, A. & Törnroos, J.A. (2005) "Using case methods in the study of contemporary business networks", *Journal of Business Research*, vol. 58(9): 1285-1297.

Hudson. M., Smart, P.A. & Bourne, M. (2001a) "Theory and practice in SME performance measurement systems", *International Journal of Operations and Production Management*, vol. 21(8):1096-1116.

Hudson, M., Lean, J. & Smart, P.A. (2001b) "Improving control through effective performance measurement in SMEs", *Production Planning and Control*, vol. 12(8): 804-813.

Huggins, R. (2001) Inter-firm network policies and firm performance: evaluating the impact of initiatives in the United Kingdom", *Research Policy*, vol. 30(3): 443-458.

Jänkälä, S. (2007) *Management Control Systems (MCS) in the Small Business Context. Linking effects of contextual factors with MCS and financial performance of small firms*, Acta Universitatis Oulu, Ouluensis, G Oeconomica, 30.

Jarvis, R., Curran, J., Kitching, J. & Lightfoot, J. (2000) "The use of quantitative and qualitative criteria in the measurement of performance in small firms", *Journal of Small Business and Enterprise Development*, vol. 7(2): 123-134.

Kaplan, R.S. & Norton, D.P. (1996) "Using the Balanced Scorecard as a Strategic Management System", *Harvard Business Review*, January-February, 75-85.

Kaplan, R.S. & Norton, D.P. (2001) "Transforming the balanced scorecard from performance measurement to strategic management: part II.", *Accounting Horizons*, vol. 15(2): 147-160.

Kaplan, R.S. & Norton, D.P. (2004), *Strategy Maps Converting Intangible Assets into Tangible Outcomes,* Boston, M: Harvard Business School Press.

Kaplan, R.S., Norton, D.P. & Rugelsjoen, B. (2010) "Managing alliances with the balanced scorecard", *Harvard Business Review*, vol. 88(1/2): 114-121.

Kim, D.H. & Kim, C. (2009), *A Generic Framework of Performance Measurement in Networked Enterprises*, in Camarinha-Matos L.M., Paraskakis I., Afsarmanesh H. (eds) Leveraging Knowledge for Innovation in Collaborative Networks, Berlin: Springer, 259-265.

Kulmala, H.I. & Lönnqvist, A. (2006) "Performance measurement of networks: towards a non-financial approach", *International Journal of Networking and Virtual Organizations*, vol. 3(3): 299-316.

Laihonen, H., Jääskeläinen, A. & Pekkola, S. (2014) "Measuring performance of a service system – from organizations to customer-perceived performance", *Measuring Business Excellence*, vol. 18(3): 73-86.

Laitinen, E.K. (2002) "A dynamic performance measurement system: evidence from small Finnish technology companies", *Scandinavian Journal of Management*, vol. 18(1): 65-99.

Lawrie, G. & Cobbold, I. (2004) "Third-generation balanced scorecard: evolution of an effective strategic control tool", *International Journal of Productivity and Performance Management*, vol. 53(7); 611-623.

Lin, F. & Lin, Y. (2016) "The effect of network relationship on the performance of SMEs", *Journal of Business Research*, vol. 69(5): 1780-1784.

Lombardi, R. (2015), *Le reti d'impresa in economia aziendale. Profili critici e interpretativi*, Torino: Giappichelli.

Lombardi, R., Caputo, A., Russo, G. & Formisano, V. (2015) "Management control of contractual networks: the business network scorecard", *International Journal of Applied Management Science*, vol. 7(4): 269-286.

Mahama, H. (2006) "Management control systems, cooperation and performance in strategic supply relationships: a survey in the mines", *Management Accounting Research*, vol. 17(3): 315-339.

Mancini, D. (2016) "Accounting Information Systems in an Open Society. Emerging Trends and Issues", *Management Control*, vol. 1: 5-16.

Marchi, L. (2011) "L'evoluzione del controllo di gestione nella prospettiva informativa e gestionale esterna", *Management Control*, vol. 3: 5-16.

Marr, B. (2004) "Mapping the dynamics of how intangibles create value", *International Journal of Learning and Intellectual Capital*, vol. 1(3): 358-369.

Marr, B., Schiuma, G. & Neely, A. (2004) "The dynamics of value creation – mapping your intellectual performance drivers", *Journal of Intellectual Capital*, vol. 5(2): 312-325

Mastilak, C., Matuszewski, L., Miller, F. & Woods, A. (2012) "Evaluating conflicting performance on driver and outcome measures: the effect of strategy maps", *Journal of Management Control*, vol. 23(2): 97-114.

Mooraj, S., Oton, D. & Hostettler, D. (1999) "The balanced scorecard: a necessary good or an unnecessary evil?", *European Management Journal*, vol. 17(5): 481-491.

Naro, G. & Travaillé, D. (2011) "The role of the balanced scorecard in the formulation and control of strategic processes", *Journal of Applied Accounting Research*, vol. 12(3): 212-233.

Neely, A., Mills, J., Platts, K., Richards, H., Gregory, M., Bourne, M. & Kennerley, M. (2000) "Performance measurement system design: developing and testing a process-based approach", *International Journal of Operations & Production Management*, vol. 20(10): 1119-145.

Neely, A., Adams, C. & Crowe, P. (2001) "The performance prism in practice", *Measuring Business Excellence*, vol. 5(2): 6-13.

Parung, J. & Bititci, U. (2008) "A metric for collaborative networks, business process", *Management Journal*, Vol. 14(5): 654-674.

Pekkola, S. (2013) "Managing a network by utilizing performance measurement information", *Measuring Business Excellence*, vol. 17(1): 72-79.

Pettigrew, A. (1997), "What is processual analysis?", *Scandinavian Journal of Management*, vol. 13(4): 337-348.

Ryan, B., Scapens, R.W. & Theoblad, M. (2007), *Research Method and Methodology in Finance and Accounting*, London: Thomson.

Saetta, S., Tiacci, L. & Cagnazzo, L. (2013) "The innovative model of the Virtual Development Office for collaborative networked enterprises: the GPT network case study", *International Journal of Computer Integrated Manufacturing*, vol. 26(1-2): 41-54.

Simons, R. (1995), *Levers of Control. How Managers Use Innovative Control System to Drive Strategic Renewal*, Boston, MA: Harvard Business School Press.

Stewart, T.A. (1997), *Intellectual capital. The new wealth of organization*, New York, NY: Doubleday.

Strohhecker, J. (2016) "Factors influencing strategy implementation decisions: an evaluation of a balanced scorecard cockpit, intelligence, and knowledge", *Journal of Management Control*, vol. 27(1): 89-119.

Sveby, K.E. (1997), *The new organizational wealth. Managing and measuring knowledge-based assets*, San Francisco, CA: Berret-Koehler Publishers.

Trequattrini, R., Russo, G. & Lombardi, R. (2012) "Network governance: organizational and legal profiles", *Corporate Ownership & Control*, vol. 9(4): 346-350.

UnionCamere, (2016), "Statistiche dei contratti di rete". Retrieved from: http://www.infocamere.it/contratti-di-rete. Accessed: December, 3, 2016.

van en Veen-Dirks, P. & M. Wijn (2002) "Strategic control: meshing critical success factors with the balanced scorecard", *Long Range Planning*, vol. 35(4): 407-427.

Varamäki, E. & Vesalainen, J. (2003) "Modelling Different Types of Multilateral Co-operation between SMEs", *Entrepreneurship and Regional Development*, vol. 15(1): 27-47.

Varamäki, E., Kohtamaki, M., Jarvenpaa, M., Vuorinen, T. & Laitinen, E. (2008) "A framework for a network-level performance measurement system in SME networks", *International Journal of Networking and Virtual Organisations*, vol. 5(3-4): 415-435.

Verschoore, J.R., Wegner, D. & Balestrin, A. (2015) "The evolution of collaborative practices in small-firm networks: a qualitative analysis of four Brazilian cases", *International Journal of Management Practice*, vol. 8(2): 152-168.

Yin R.K. (1989) *Case study research-design and methods*, 2nd edn. Newbury Park, CA: Sage Publications.

Zapata, M.J. & Hall, C.M. (2012) "Public–private collaboration in the tourism sector: balancing legitimacy and effectiveness in local tourism partnerships. The Spanish case", *Journal of Policy Research in Tourism, Leisure & Events*, vol. 4(1): 61-83.

---

[i] Section 4-ter and following of LD no. 5 of 10th February 2009; Law 9 April 2009, No. 33 as amended by Law No. 122/2010.

[ii] An analysis of cases favours investigation into concrete experience or new areas of research (Yin, 1989), as well as the understanding of the nature of accounting practices and managerial and control systems (Bititci *et al.*, 2005; Ryan *et al.*, 2007).

[iii] The problem of comparability (with other *networks, industries and countries*, or their combination) does not apply as this study focuses on one single case.

6

The relationship between the risk management practices and financial performance of the Nigerian listed banks

Oyerogba Ezekiel Oluwagbemiga[a,1],
Ogungbade Oluyinka Isaiah[b] and Idode Patrick Esiemogie[c]

[a] *Bowen University, Iwo, Osun State, Nigeria*
[b]*Afe Babalola University, Ekiti State, Nigeria*
[c]*Bells University of Technology, Ogun State, Nigeria*

Abstract: We examine the relationship between the risk management practices and financial performance of the listed companies in Nigeria for the period of ten year from 2005 to 2014, with a particular attention on the 21 deposit money banks. Specifically, the study investigates how risk limit setting, risk adherence monitoring, risk policy review, credit risk management, operational risk management and market risk management has impacted the financial performance of listed banks in Nigeria. We employ both the primary (survey questionnaire) and secondary (audited financial statement) as sources of data. The overall results reveals that risk management practices have a statistically significant impact on financial performance. The results also reveals the trend in risk management practices in other developing economy such as Ghana, Pakistan, Kenya, Thailand, Tehran and the current global practices in Serbian and United state as presented in the literature review. This result leads to a recommendation that adequate risk management system should be put in place by the board of directors which should include the establishment of company's annual risk limit, risk appetite and risk strategy to curtail the excessive risk taking of the management. This system should be reviewed regularly to determine its adequacy, effectiveness and compliance level of the management with this risk management system..

---

[1] *Corresponding author*: Oyerogba Ezekiel Oluwagbemiga, Bowen University, Iwo, Osun State, Nigeria, E-mail: oyeezekiel2903@yahoo.com,

Keywords: Risk Management Practices, Market Risk Management, Operational Risk Management, Credit Risk Management, Return on Capital Employed, Earnings per Share.

1. Introduction

The main objective of this study is to examine the relationship between the risk management practices and financial performance. The study focused on the deposit money banks listed on the Nigeria stock exchange for a ten year period from 2005 to 2014. Three aspect of risk management practices which include risk limit setting, monitoring of adherence to risk limit and risk policy review were evaluated in addition to three inherent risks faced by the listed banks which includes the credit risk, operational risk and market risk. To evaluate financial performance, two measures of financial performance were considered, that is, return on capital employed and earnings per share.
Risk management according to Stanton (2012) refers to the process by which an organization identifies and analyses threats, examines alternatives, and accepts or mitigates those threats even before they begins to impede the activities of the organization. Similarly, Culp (2008) opined that risk management is viewed today as one of the key characteristics of successful companies which enable firms to view all risks facing them through some form of pre-planned activities. Also, risk management can be perceived as a management process that requires a firm's management to identify and assess the collective risks that affect firm value and apply an organizational wide strategy to manage those risks in order to attain higher level of efficiency (Meulbroek, 2002).

The primary goal of risk management is to maximize shareholder value (Beasley *et al.,* 2008; Hoyt & Liebenberg, 2011; Pagach & Warr, 2011). Banner *et al.* (2004) asserted that risk management is a value adding technique that is aimed at generating additional profit for a company by giving an overview of all risky activities, constructing recovery plans and constant monitoring of day-to-day operations. Thus, Hoyt and Liebenberg (2011) suggested that profit maximizing firms should consider implementing only an aspect of risk management that increases expected shareholder wealth. According to Vieira (2010), increase in risk complemented by risk concentration may confer vulnerability to corporate segment. Therefore, risk management strategies contribute in an essential manner to value creation of a business organization.

Furthermore, the global trend in company failures, corporate scandals, fraud and malpractices are among the reasons for companies to effectively implement risk management programs. These companies' failures have been linked to poor risk management and weak corporate governance (Manab *et al.*, 2010). Rosen and Zenios (2001) emphasize that corporate governance is vital for effective risk management and that none of the risk management activities can be achieved without corporate governance compliance. Thus, corporate governance and risk management are therefore interrelated and interdependent implying that stability and improvement of the company's performance are highly dependent on the effective role of both components (Sobel & Reding, 2004; Manab *et al.*, 2010).

On the relationship between the risk management system and banks' performance, listed banks serves as financial intermediaries, thus, risk management is of much concern to them, as it is to the other listed companies. In fact, listed banks face a greater number of risks than other sectors of the economy (Nocera, 2009). These additional risk exposure stems from the huge capital being kept in the custody of the bank officials (Khan & Ahmed, 2011). Therefore, in order to mitigate these greater risks, listed banks have been encouraged to allocate more resources to risk management (Ongore, 2011). Although, efficient risk management may draw resources and adversely affect profitability, it is crucial for their long term sustainability (Stanton, 2012).

Al-Tamimi and Al-Mazrooei, (2007) also noted that effective risk management is not only necessary for giving reasonably high returns to the shareholders but prudent risk management is also the signal to avoiding financial distress that could lead the organization to bankruptcy. Therefore, risk management in the banking industry is of necessity to the industry players, as well as for policy makers. In spite of the afore-mentioned role of risk management to the performance of banking institution, literatures on the relationship between the risk management practices and the financial performance of listed banks are very scarce. This gap necessitated the current study. The rest of the paper is as follow: Section 2 was dedicated to the review of relevant literatures. The research methodology was presented in section three. Presentation and analysis was done in section four while section five was committed to the conclusion and recommendations.

2. Risk management system and financial performance: an empirical review

In the aftermath of the financial crisis, there have been series of proposals from policy makers and international organizations regarding corporate governance reforms that need to manage the risks that financial institutions pose for the economy (Alexander, 2012). These proposals have been addressing either better risk management, by creating a risk management committee at the level of the board of directors, or by narrowing the incentives for compensation, or by altering the rules of limited liability (Mulbert & Citlau, 2011). The ideas that have been promoted regarded the expertise in risk management of the board members, the presence in the board meetings of the chief risk officer, or the creation of risk management committees at the level of the board. All the proposals targeted the creation of risk management procedures.

At the international level, the advanced ideas suggested that corporate governance procedures have to be used in improving the risk management and support the financial stability (Walker, 2009). The significance of risk management has been stressed by the Basel Committee on Banking Supervision in 2010 report, 'an effective internal controls system and a risk management function (including a chief risk officer or equivalent) with sufficient authority, stature, independence, resources and access to the board' (Basel Committee on Banking Supervision, Principles of Enhancing Corporate Governance, 2010). Similar position had OECD, which emphasized on the risk management at the firm level and on the presence of chief risk officer (OECD Steering Committee on corporate Governance, Corporate Governance and the Financial Crisis, 2010).

The question that is raised when it comes to risk management is how much risk is acceptable? International guidelines provide no practical procedures on the measurement of risk, besides the conceptual long-term value-based approach, which implies a continuous assessment of risky decisions (Dermine, 2011). The 2007-8 financial crises have raised awareness on the need for proper risk management mechanisms as part of the corporate governance. Initially, the literature on risk management was focused on isolated treatment of uncertainties (Miller, 1992) while excluding the other interrelated risks. Hence, in the 1990s the focus shifted to an integrated perspective of risk management, which allowed a more comprehensive evaluation of different aggregated risks (Miller, 1992; Sabato, 2010).

The risk identification is a necessary condition for a sound and safe financial environment. However, there has to be stressed on the differences between risk and uncertainty. Dermine (2011) outlines that risk is the situation when the probability distribution of losses can be identified with relevant data, while in the case of uncertainty, the distribution of losses cannot be measured, as the situation being new, no relevant data are available. Another aspect of the risk management that is gaining the attention of the scholar is the link between risk management and firm performance.

Cheruyot *et al.* (2014) conducted a study on the effect of Safari Card system as a revenue risk management practice on financial performance of Kenya wildlife service on a sample of 296 drawn from 1,286 employees in the National Parks where Safari card System is used to collect the Parks entry charges. The study relied on both primary and secondary data which was processed to answer the research objectives using a descriptive survey research design while data analysis was done using descriptive statistics and presented in frequency tables and charts. The relationship between Safari Card as a risk management practice and financial performance was tested using a regression model. The results show that introduction of Safari Card as a transactional risk reduction system by Kenya wildlife system increases its liquidity as a measure of financial performance. The idea of the study was properly conceptualized. However, the major deficiency of the study was that the study was not based on any theoretical framework. Also, the measurement of performance was limited to liquidity and working capital whereas other performance indicators were neglected.

Kittipat and Nopadol (2014) conducted a study of the relationship between a successful enterprise risk management system, a performance measurement system and the financial performance of Thai listed companies. The study was done by collecting data from persons directly involved with these two systems with a total of 101 respondents. The results of the study indicate that success of the enterprise risk management system and performance measurement system have a weak positive correlation with the financial performance of an organization as measured by return on assets (ROA), return on equity (ROE) and earnings per share (EPS). It does, however, prove to be essential that managers develop, improve and utilize both systems in order to gain a competitive advantage and sustain the growth of an organization. It was reported that out of 520 copies of questionnaire distributed, only 101 copies were retrieved which formed the basis for the analysis. The narrowness of research sample reduces the robustness of the study and also makes generalization questionable.

In a study by Junaidu and Sunusi (2014) on the effect of credit risk management (CRM) on the profitability of Nigerian banks with a view to discovering the extent to which default rate (*DR*), cost per loan asset (*CLA*), and capital adequacy ratio (*CAR*) influence return on asset (*ROA*) as a measure of banks' profitability. It was established that CRM has a significant positive effect on the profitability of Nigerian banks as indicated by the coefficient of determinations *R*2 value which shows the within and between values of 40.89% and 58.35% (which are impressive) while the overall *R*2 is 43.91%, indicating that the variables considered in the model accounts for about 44% change in the dependent variable, that is, profitability.

Furthermore, empirical evidence was also provided by Adeusi *et al.* (2013) through their study on the relationship between the risk management practices and financial performance of the listed banks in Nigeria with the use of a pooled secondary data over a period of 4 years where 10 banks were randomly selected from a total of 21 listed banks in Nigeria. The results revealed a statistically significant relationship between financial performance and risk management practices and thus recommends for an improvement in prudent risks management in order to protect the interests of investors and other stakeholders in the Nigeria listed banks.

In another study conducted in Ghana, Opoku (2011) documented a significant positive relationship between the risk management practices and financial performance of First Atlantic merchant Bank Ghana Limited (FAMBL). Also, the findings in Yahaya *et al.* (2015) on the analysis of risk management mechanisms and organizational performance in deposit money banks in Nigeria revealed that overall organizational performance was positively affected by the risk management mechanisms of the banks and its liquidity policies. However, a negative and insignificant relationship was found between the firm variables such as financial leverage, size and age of the bank and financial performance measure with return on equity and return on assets.

Also, on the global level, several empirical evidences have been documented on the relationship between the risk management practices and financial performance. For instance, Zubairi and Ahson (2015) examine the strength of linkage between current risk management practices and profitability of five Islamic Banks in Pakistan. In order to achieve the study objective, the risk management practices of five Islamic banks were studied and quantified over a period of seven years. The study uses both the primary (survey questionnaires) and secondary data (annual reports) to gather information. The link of these practices with the banks' financial performance after controlling for other internal and external determinants of profitability was analyzed by adopting an econometric framework. Estimating pooled regression and checking the reliability of the estimated model through Augmented Dickey-Fuller test, it was found that risk management framework had a statistically significant negative impact on profitability during the period under review.

In Serbia Pagach and Warr (2010) study the effect of adoption of enterprise risk management (ERM) principles on firms' long-term performance by examining how financial, asset and market characteristics change around the time of ERM adoption. With the use of a sample of 106 firms who announced the hiring of a Chief Risk Officer (an event frequently accompanied by adoption of Enterprise Risk Management) it was reported that some firms that adopted ERM experience a reduction in earnings volatility. However, their overall results fail to find support for the proposition that ERM is value creating because ERM adoption has no material change on a range of observable financial measures.

The United State study by Hussein and Karl (2013) investigated the impact of risk taking on bank financial performance during 2008 financial crisis. This study uses descriptive and inferential statistics to test the hypotheses over the four years,

2006-2009, that span the financial crisis. The sample consists of 74 bank holding companies (BHCs) in the United States with total assets near $5.8 trillion at the end of 2006. These large BHCs account for a substantial proportion (52%) of the total amount of banking assets in the United States. Each of these BHCs had total assets in excess of $3 billion at the end of 2006. However, the study found a significant relationship between BHCs' risk taking levels and their financial performance. BHCs with lower risk-taking levels were found to have higher average financial performance than BHCs with higher risk-taking levels from 2006 to 2009. The study's findings support the claim that risk affected the earnings of the BHCs during the financial crisis. The results suggest that risk taking contributed to the 2007-2008 financial crises, and that aggressive risk taking was an important contributor to the recent financial crisis. In this study, the financial performance of the banks was measured by the return on assets (ROA), calculated as the bank's total net income divided by its average total assets, and return on equity (ROE), calculated as the bank's total net income before extraordinary items divided by its average shareholders' equity but there was no clear documentation of the risk indicators in the study.

In a study conducted in Tehran, Ramazanali *et al.* (2014) examine the impact of financial pressures and risk management on financial performance of investment firms and banks using106 firms listed on Tehran Stock Exchange (TSE) for a 5-year period from 2006 to 2011 with both descriptive and inferential statistics. The results of their hypothesis testing showed that there is no significant correlation between risk and financial performance of investment firms. However, a significant correlation was found between financial constraints and financial performance of investment firms and banks. The short coming found in this study was that the study relied mainly on secondary data without considering the opinion of the stakeholders in the study. From the above, the following hypothesis emerges: Risk management systems have significant relationship with the firm financial performance in the Nigerian listed financial institutions.

3. Objectives and research methodology

The general objective of this study was to establish the relationship between the risk management practices and financial performance for the 21 listed banks in Nigeria leading to the specific objectives where the link between the risk limit setting, monitoring of adherence to the risk limit, review of risk policy, credit risk management, operational risk management, market risk management and financial performance (return on capital employed and earnings per share) were established. The study covered a period of ten year from 2005 to 2014. The ten year period was chosen primarily to cover the pre and post 2008 financial crises and the economic recession that followed. There are only 22 listed banks on the Nigeria stock exchange. Considering the relative small size of this population, the decision to cover the entire population was made. However, one bank declined participation because of the internal restructuring being embark on. Therefore, the population is also the sample size for the study.

The three dimension of risk management investigated in this study in line with the provision of CBN revised guidelines, NDIC guidelines were setting of risk limit by the directors, risk adherence monitoring and risk review by the board of directors. According to OECD, (2014) risk management practices is the process by which a company manages the risks that it faces which involves three dimensions or steps. The setting of risk limit and control before the commencement of business to avoid excessive risk taking by the management and monitoring of adherence to this limit must be undertaking by the board of directors as well as periodic review of the risk policy of the company.

Therefore, to undertake a survey research on those three aspects of risk management, a structured questionnaire that drew largely from the OECD risk management guideline was administered to the chief risk officers and internal auditors of the 21 banks to arrive at a total of 42 respondents for the study. This approach was perceived necessary due to the inherent ambiguity observed in the previous research instruments (questionnaires) generally and low level of research efforts on this crucial topic. It also allowed the acquisition of relevant data on risk management through a series of logical questions independent of the opinions of the respondent institutions.

In addition to the survey data, time series data was collected from the audited financial statement of the listed banks to measure the effectiveness of risk management practices under the general heading of credit risk management, operational risk management and market risk management. According to Fatemi and Foolad (2006) credit risk is the risk of loss originated by a debtor's failure to pay a loan or line of credit. Therefore, in line with IAS 39 and IFRS 9, this study adopted incurred loss approach and the expected loss approach in the measurement of credit risk in which credit risk was taken as the natural logarithm of total bad debit written off by the bank for the period. Basel (2007) defines operational risk as the risk of direct or indirect loss resulting from inadequate or failed internal processes, people and systems or from external events. In view of that, operational risk was measured using the natural logarithm of the sum total of both internal fraud and external fraud. Market risk on the other hand is the risk of asset valued change associated with systematic factor (Santomero, 1997). Thus, market risk was taken as the natural logarithm of the loss in cash flow or fair values of financial instruments.

To evaluate the financial performance, two measure of performance were considered in this study. They are return on capital employed and earnings per share. ROCE and EPS are accounting and market-based measures of financial performance which will provide a comprehensive check for the results (Hanison & Hudalis, 2012; Ntim, 2012). ROCE is used to measure how a firm's profitability is relative to their capital which is the efficiency of management in utilizing the company's capital to generate earnings (Hanison & Hudalis, 2006). Similarly, earnings per share ratio (EPS ratio) measure the amount of a company's net income that is available for payment to the holders of its common stock (Miller & Triana, 2009). A company with high earnings per share ratio is capable of generating a significant dividend for investors which is the ultimate aim of many investors (Mehrani, 1999). Second, earnings per common share are usually the first financial ratio investors look at when analyzing a stock (Ongore, 2011).

Furthermore, data analysis was conducted using both descriptive and inferential statistics. In an attempt to determine the risk management practices that impact the financial performance in the listed Nigerian banks using the descriptive statistics, 5-Likert scale approach was used in the questionnaire. The higher the score, the greater the strength of the respondent's agreement with the adequacy of risk management practices implemented by their respective banks. The descriptive statistics of the time series data was also presented using mean, median, maximum, minimum and standard deviation. Inferential statistics includes the correlation analysis and regression analysis which enables the study to relate the risk management practices to the financial performance of the listed banks. The multiple regression models defining the linear relationship between the risk management practices and financial performance has been stated as follows:

$$ROCE = \beta_0 + \beta_1 RLS_t + \beta_2 RAM_t + \beta_3 RPR_t + \beta_4 CRISK_t + \beta_5 ORISK_t + + \beta_6 MRISK_t + \varepsilon_t$$

$$EPS = \beta_0 + \beta_1 RLS_t + \beta_2 RAM_t + \beta_3 RPR_t + \beta_4 CRISK_t + \beta_5 ORISK_t + + \beta_6 MRISK_t + \varepsilon_t$$

Where:

ROCE= Return on Capital Employed in time t
EPS= Earnings per Share in time t
RLS= Risk Limit Setting in time t
RAM= Risk Adherence Monitoring in time t
RPR= Risk Policy Review in time t
CRISK= Credit Risk
ORISK= Operational Risk
MRISK= Market Risk
β_0 = Represents the Constant
ε_t= is the error term assumed to be normally distributed with zero mean and constant variance.
β_1- β_6= Represents the Coefficient of the Independent Variables

4. Results and discussion

The results of the diagnostic test, descriptive statistics and inferential analysis results were presented in this section. The detailed interpretations as well as the discussion of empirical findings were also carried out in this section. The diagnostic tests carried out for this study includes the reliability test, autocorrelation test (also known as test for independence) and homoscedasticity test.

4.1 Reliability Test

Reliability test is an indication of the stability and consistency with which the instrument measures a concept and helps to assess the goodness of a measure (Miller & Triana, 2009). Therefore, in this study, Cronbach's Alpha which is a reliability coefficient was used to indicate how well the items in the set are correlated with one other. According to Sekaran (2008) the closer a Cronbach's Alpha is to 1 the higher the reliability and thus, a value of 0.7 was recommended. The reliability analysis was conducted for dependent variable, return on capital employed and earnings per share, independent variables which includes, risk limit setting and control, monitoring of adherence to risk limit and risk programme review. The findings as presented in table 4.1 indicated that return on capital employed produced a coefficient of 0.901, earnings per share had a coefficient of 0.701, while risk limit setting, risk monitoring and risk programme review produce a coefficient of 0.704, 0.793, 0.710 respectively. Since, all the items produced a Cronbach's Alpha greater than the minimum acceptable coefficient, the data collected can be considered reliable and therefore accepted for further statistical analysis.

Table 1. Reliability Test

	Variables	Cronbach's Alpha	No. of Items
1	Return on Capital Employed	0.901	5
2	Earnings per Share	0.701	5
3	Risk Limit Setting	0.704	5
4	Risk Adherence Monitoring	0.793	5
5	Risk Policy Review	0.710	5

4.2 Test for Autocorrelation-Durbin Watson Statistic for Return on Capital Employed and Earnings per Share

Durbin Watson Statistic was conducted to test for autocorrelation in the data collected before accepting it for regression analysis. According to Kothari and

Garg, (2014), Autocorrelation occurs when the residuals are not independent from each other. In other words, when the value of y(x+1) is not independent from the value of y(x). Therefore, the null hypothesis that there was no autocorrelation in the data collected for this study was tested with use of Durbin Watson Statistics. The results as presented in table 2 revealed that the Durbin Watson Statistics for lag 1 was 1.835524 with a p-value of 0.245 while the Durbin Watson Statistics for lag 2 and 3 were 1.883643 and 1.843001 with a p-value of 0.386 and 0.130 respectively. Since the p-value was greater than 0.05, the null hypothesis which stated that there was no autocorrelation in the data was not rejected.

Similarly, the results of autocorrelation test for earnings per share presented in table 3 revealed that Durbin Watson Statistics for lag 1 was 2.201917 with a p-value of 0.062 while the Durbin Watson Statistics for lag 2 and 3 were 2.141619 and 1.987443 with a p-value of 0.132 and 0.946 respectively. Since the p-value was greater than 0.05, the null hypothesis which stated that there was no autocorrelation in the data was taken to hold. The result implies that the residuals were independent from each other. Similarly, the rule of thumb which states that values of $1.5 < d < 2.5$ show that there is no auto-correlation in the data was satisfied by this result (Barley, 2009). It can therefore be said that the return on capital employed for year 2006 was not a function of return on capital employed for the year 2005. Return on capital employed for 2007 was also not a function of return on capital employed for 2006 and soon. In like manner, earnings per share for year 2006 were totally independent from earnings per share for the year 2005. Earnings per share for 2007 was also totally independent from earnings per share for 2006 and soon.

Table 2. Durbin Watson Statistics for Autocorrelation

Lag	D.W Statistics	P-Value
1	1.835524	0.245
2	1.896343	0.386
3	1.843001	0.130

Table 3 Durbin Watson Statistics for Autocorrelation

Lag	D.W Statistics	P-Value
1	2.201917	0.062
2	2.141619	0.132
3	1.987443	0.946

4.3 Test for Homoscedasticity- Bruisch Pagan Statistics for Return on Capital employed and Earnings per Share

Another assumption of linear regression analysis tested in this study was homoscedasticity which implies that the error terms along the regression line were equal. According to Barley (2009), the violation of homoscedasticity which is otherwise known as heteroscedasticity make it difficult to gauge the true standard deviation of the forecast errors, usually resulting in confidence intervals that are too wide or too narrow. Particularly, if there is increase in the variance of the error term over time, confidence intervals for out-of-sample predictions will tend to be unrealistically narrow. In that case, heteroscedasticity may also have the effect of giving too much weight to a small subset of the data (namely the subset where the error variance was largest) when estimating coefficients. Thus, to prevent such scenario when conducting a research, it is expedient to test for homoscedasticity before carrying out a regression analysis.

Therefore, this study tested the null hypothesis that the data collected was homoscedastic in variance using Bruisch Pagan test. The result of the test presented in table 4for return on capital employed revealed that the test statistics was 205.9717 while the p-value was 1 indicating that the data collected was not heteroscedastic in variance and thus necessitating the acceptance of null hypothesis that the data collected was homoscedastic in variance and can be relied on for regression analysis. The result of the test for homoscedasticity for earnings per share presented in table 5 revealed that the test statistics was 162.6865 while the p-value was 0.98 indicating that the data collected was not heteroscedastic in variance and thus necessitating the acceptance of null hypothesis that the data collected was homoscedastic in variance and can be relied on for regression analysis.

Table 4.Bruisch Pagan Test for Homoscedasticity

Test Statistics	Degree of Freedom	P-Value
205.9717	5	1.000

Table 5.Bruisch Pagan Test for Homoscedasticity

Test Statistics	Degree of Freedom	P-Value
162.6865	5	0.98

4.4 Descriptive statistics

The descriptive statistics for the primary data, time series data and financial performance indicators were presented in table 6. This includes the mean, median, maximum, minimum and standard deviation for the variables. Based on the survey result, the risk limit setting and control in the 21 listed banks in Nigeria produced a mean score of 4.28 with a standard deviation of 0.22 over a period of ten years implying more or less little variation in the board approach to the risk limit setting and control. It can also be inferred that virtually all the listed banks in Nigeria have a pre-determine risk limit put in place by the board of directors in line with the mission, vision and philosophy of those banks which probably enable the management to avoid excessive risk taking. Although, the board of directors were able to communicate their risk acceptance level to the management, but this was limited to credit risk alone whereas other important risk aspect such as operational risk and market risk were given little or no attention.

Concerning the risk adherence monitoring, the mean score was 4.31 while the standard deviation was 0.19 suggesting high degree of monitoring of compliance levels with risk limit by the management of the limited banks in Nigeria with a little variation across the year and the industry. The monitoring exercise was carried out by the board via its committees as indicated by the respondent and the published financial statements. The Risk Committees at the board level monitors the Group's plans and progress towards meeting regulatory Risk-Based Supervision requirements and migration to Basel II compliance as well as the overall Regulatory and Economic Capital Adequacy. The Group's Board of Directors has delegated responsibility for the management of credit risk to the Board Credit Committee. The Board Credit Committee considers and approves all lending exposures, including treasury investment exposures, as well as insider-related credits in excess of limits assigned to the Management Credit Committee by the Board.

Management Credit Committee therefore, formulates credit policies in consultation with business units, covering credit assessment, risk grading and reporting, collateral, regulatory and statutory requirements. The committee also assesses and approves all credit exposures in excess of the Managing Director's limit as set by the Board. The Asset & Liability Management Committee monitors the Group's standards and policies covering the various components of Market Risk. These include issues on Interest Rate Risk, Liquidity Risk, Investment Risk and Trading Risk. It ensures that the authority delegated by the Board and Management Risk Committees with regard to Market Risk is exercised, and that Market Risk exposures are monitored and managed within the company's acceptable risk limit.

Risk policy review produced the lowest mean of 4.17 with a little standard deviation of 0.14. This little standard deviation implies that the listed banks been a highly regulated industry, the practices are more or less the same across the industry and years with a slight difference between the industry leader and others. Majority of the banks maintained an annual review of the risk policy. However, more frequent reviews were only conducted based on the opinion of the board, when changes in laws, market conditions or the group's activities are material enough to impact on the continued adoption of existing policies in the board level approach of providing a risk management framework to their respective banks

Table 6. Descriptive Statistics

	Mean	Median	Max.	Min.	Std. Dev.
RLS	4.28	4.30	4.50	4.10	0.22
RAM	4.31	4.38	4.48	3.50	0.19
RPR	4.17	4.09	4.00	3.65	0.14
ROCE	0.51	0.545	0.81	0.04	0.23
EPS	0.73	0.59	6.31	-0.23	0.12
CRISK	354526	138844	781184	112460	2346
ORISK	1117378	813447	2771980	755109	2246
MRISK	134667	442339	675000	73196	215

4.5 Inferential statistics

This section establishes the relationship between the risk management practices and financial performance of the listed banks in Nigeria using correlation and regression analysis. The essence of correlation analysis in this study was to ensure there is no multicolinearity in the data while regression analysis was used to determine the impact of each explanatory variable on the dependent variables. Two ordinary least square regressions were carried out. The first one linked the risk limit setting, risk adherence monitoring, risk policy review, credit risk, operational risk and market with return on capital employed while the second regression linked the risk limit setting, risk adherence monitoring, risk policy review, credit risk, operational risk and market with earnings per share.

4.5.1 Pearson Correlation Matrix for Dependent and Independent Variables

Correlation matrix is used to determine the extent to which changes in the value of an attribute is associated with changes in another attribute. The correlation coefficient according to Kothari and Garg (2014) can range from -1 to +1, with -1 indicating a perfect negative correlation, +1 indicating a perfect positive correlation, and 0 indicating no correlation at all. Table 7 revealed that there was a significant positive correlation between return on capital employed and risk limit setting at 0.672, there was also a strong positive correlation between the return on capital employed and risk adherence monitoring at 0.626. Similarly, there existed a significant positive correlation between return on capital employed and risk policy review at 697 as well as return on capital employed and marker risk at 0.660. The relationship between return on capital employed and operational risk on the hand was found to be negatively significant at -0.604. Finally, the correlation between return on capital employed and credit risk was0.234.

From table 7, all the independent variables were found to have a positive correlation with one another. The highest correlation was found between the risk limit setting and risk adherence monitoring at 0.661, followed by the correlation between risk policy review and credit risk at 0.656. The relationship between the risk adherence monitoring and market risk was moderate at 0.416. The lowest correlation existed between the market risk and other independent variables.

According to Wong and Hiew (2005), the correlation coefficient value (r) ranging from 0.10 to 0.29 can be considered weak. Also, the correlation coefficient from 0.30 to 0.49 can be considered moderate while the correlation from 0.50 to 1.0 can be considered strong. In like manner, Field (2005) stated that correlation coefficient should not go beyond 0.8 to avoid multicolinearity. Thus, it can be concluded that there was no multicolinearity problem in this research since the highest correlation coefficient was 0.661existing between the risk limit setting and risk policy review.

Table 7. Pearson correlation matrix for the variables

		ROCE	RLS	RAM	RPR	CRISK	ORISK	MRISK
ROCE	Pearson Correlation	1						
	Sig. (2-tailed)							
	N	285						
RLS	Pearson Correlation	.672**	1					
	Sig. (2-tailed)	.000						
	N	285	285					
RAM	Pearson Correlation	.626**	.661**	1				
	Sig. (2-tailed)	.000	.000					
	N	285	285	285				
PRP	Pearson Correlation	.604**	.613*	.629**	1			
	Sig. (2-tailed)	.000	.000	.000				
	N	285	285	285	285			
CRISK	Pearson Correlation	.697**	.649**	.656**	.619**	1		
	Sig. (2-tailed)	.000	.000	.000	.000			
	N	285	285	285	285	285		
ORISK	Pearson Correlation	.234**	.263**	.160**	.277**	.222**	1	
	Sig. (2-tailed)	.000	.000	.007	.000	.000		
	N	285	285	285	285	285	285	
MRISK	Pearson Correlation	.660**	.508**	.416**	.393**	.557**	.154**	1
	Sig. (2-tailed)	.000	.000	.000	.000	.000	.009	
	N	285	285	285	285	285	285	285

**Correlation is significant at the 0.01 level of significance (2-tailed).

* ROCE-Return on capital employed, EPS-Earnings per share, RLS- Risk limit setting, RAM- Risk adherence monitoring, CRISK-Credit risk, ORISK-Operational risk, MRISK-Market risk

4.5.2 Regression analysis

Using ordinary least square, regression analysis was carried out to determine whether risk limit setting, risk adherence monitoring, risk policy review, credit risk, operational risk and marker risk have significant explanatory effect on the return on capital employed and earnings per share of the listed banks in Nigeria. The results of the regression of ROCE on explanatory variables were reported in table 8 while those of EPS on explanatory variables were reported in table 9.

The coefficient of determination, R-Square as presented in table 8 was 0.867 suggesting that the variables considered in this study accounted for about 87% of the variation in financial performance of the listed banks in Nigeria measured by the return on capital employed while the remaining 13% can be attributed to the other variables not captured by this study model. The overall probability is positive and significant at 1% level of significance.

Table 8. Regression Results for ROCE and Explanatory Variables

	R		R Square		
	.931		.867		
	Sum of Squares	Df	Mean Square	F	Sig.
Regression	30255.981	6	6051.196	365.339	.000
Residual	4637.702	204	16.563		
Total	34893.683	210			

	Unstandardized Coefficients		Standardized Coefficients	T	Sig.
	B	Std. Error	Beta		
Risk Limit Setting	.248	.113	.287	2.196	.029
Risk Adherence Monitoring	.155	.064	.175	2.429	.016
Risk Policy Review	.089	.099	.093	0.903	.367
Credit Risk	-.069	.096	-.075	-0.719	.473
Operational Risk	.314	.119	.336	2.644	.009
Market Risk	.135	.066	.155	2.026	.044
Dependent Variable: ROCE					

Risk limit setting has a statistically significant and positive relationship with the return on capital employed and thus, necessitating the rejection of the null hypothesis that risk limit setting has no significant relationship with financial performance. The positive and significant relationship between risk limit setting and financial performance suggests that listed banks in Nigeria have put necessary safeguard in place to prevent excess risk taking by the management which positively impacted the financial performance. The findings agreed with those of

Nocco and Stulz (2006) that stress the importance of good risks management practices in maximizing the firms' value.

Similarly, the relationship between the risk adherence monitoring and return on capital employed produce a t-statistics of 2.429 and p-value of 0.016 which indicates a positive and significant relationship between the variables. This implies that adequate financial performance in the listed banks in Nigeria is associated with the management's ability to adhere to the company's acceptable risk limit. The results supports those of Ferguson *et al.* (2013) who argued that the failure of corporate organizations were caused by the excessive risk taking of the management without reference to the organization policy and culture on risk taking.

Consequently, an insignificant relationship was found between risk policy review, and return on capital employed. Also, credit risk has a negative and statistically insignificant relationship with return on capital employed. Although, the evidence is not strong enough for the rejection of the null hypothesis, the relationship implies that the management has not been prudent in the allocation of credit facilities to the bank customers that resulted in higher bad debt which adversely impacted the financial performance of the banks. This result is contrary to that of Boahene *et al.* (2012) who utilized regression analysis in an attempt to reveal the connection between credit risk and profitability of selected banks and established that credit risk components (non-performing loan rate, net charge-off rate, and the pre-provision profit as a percentage of net total loans and advances) have a positive and significant relationship with bank profitability.

Operational risk is significantly positively correlated with the return on capital employed, thus our hypothesis which predicts a significant relationship between the two variables can-not be rejected. This implies that a significant reduction has been recorded by the listed Nigerian banks in both internal and external fraud which contributed to an increased financial performance. The results corroborates that of Oyerogba (2014) who reported that the combined effect of the predictor variables (operational risk disclosure, financial risks disclosure and strategic risks disclosure) explains 65.5% of the variations in the performance of listed companies in Nigeria.

The relationship between the market risk and return on capital employed was positive and statistically significant producing a t-statistics of 2.026 and p-value of 0.044. The result suggests that market risk is closely related to financial performance. This result was in agreement with those of Costa-Rica, Epure and Lafuente (2012) that applied regression analysis to study the effect of market risk on bank performance and discovered that performance improvements led to regulatory changes and that market risk accounts for differences in bank performance, while non-performing loans inversely affect efficiency and return on assets (*ROA*) and the capital adequacy ratio (*CAR*) has a positive influence on the net interest margin.

To further confirm the relationship between the dependent variable and independent variables, regression analysis was carried out using another financial performance indicator (Earnings per Share). The results of regression analyses presented in table 9 revealed a significant relationship between earnings per share and most risk management practices. Specifically, five indicators of risk management practices were found to be statistically significant with earnings per share four of which were in positive direction while the fifth variable has a negative relationship with the financial performance indicator. R Squared of the regression model was 0.392 indicating that 39% of the changes in financial performance were explained by the changes in the variables considered in this study while the remaining 61% of the variations were caused by other variables not captured in this study. The value of R Squared was considered acceptable in comparison to the findings of previous corporate governance literatures which includes Halme and Huse (1997) as 21.2%, Peters and Romi (2011) as 25% and Post (2011) as 24%.

From the results of the beta coefficients, risk limit setting was positively correlated with earnings per share. The coefficient was 0.335 while the t-statistics and p-value were 27.917 and 0.000 respectively. This implies that an increase in risk limit setting by one unit leads to an increase in earnings per share of listed banks in Nigeria by 34%. The findings agreed with those of AL-Ahmidu and Tukur (2014), results on risk management and firm financial performance in Nigeria for a sample of 74 firms quoted on the Nigerian Stock Exchange for the period 2001–2005 where a significant relationship was found between risk management and return on asset.

Similarly, the beta coefficient on risk adherence monitoring was positive and significant at 1% level of significance. The coefficient was 0.094 while the t-statistics and p-value were 2.611and 0.000 respectively. Thus, risk adherence monitoring was associated with an increase in earnings per share of the listed banks in Nigeria by 9%. This result was in line with *Clay et al.* (2013) who posit that adherence to risk limit benefit firms through greater access to financing, lower cost of capital, better profitability and increase the confidence of all stakeholders in the management of an organization.

In like manner, the results of beta coefficient on operational risk management also revealed that a statistically significant relationship exists between earnings per share and operational risk management of listed banks in Nigeria. For instance, the beta coefficient was 0.079 indicating that 7% of the increase in financial performance of Nigerian listed banks can be attributed to the reduction in both internal and external fraud. This result was in affirmative with the postulation of Hackston and Milne (1992) that as investors look for emerging economies to diversify their investment portfolios to maximize returns, they are equally concerned about governance factors to minimize risks in these economies. Also, Clark theory of profitability link company's profitability to the management ability to prevent fraud through adequate internal control mechanism (Benson, 2005).

In addition, a significant negative relationship was found between earnings per share and credit risk management of listed banks in Nigeria as beta coefficient was -0.162 and t- statistic was -12.462 indicating management's inefficiency in the administration of banks credit facility. The result contradicts those of Ben-Naceur and Omran (2008) that reported that bank capitalization and credit risk have considerable and positive influence on net interest margin, cost efficiency, and profitability of banks. Similarly, a positive and significant relationship was found between the market risk management and earnings per share suggesting that listed banks in Nigeria are efficient in the cash flow management over the period of the study. Risk policy review revealed no significant relationship with financial performance.

Table 9. Regression Results for EPS and Explanatory Variables

R	R Square
.626	.392

	Sum of Squares	Df	Mean Square	F	Sig.
Regression	1373.322	6	1373.322	182.261	.000
Residual	2132.378	204	7.535		
Total	3505.700	210			

	Unstandardized Coefficients		Standardized Coefficients	T	Sig.
	B	Std. Error	Beta		
Risk Limit Setting	.355	.012	.269	27.917	.000
Risk Adherence Monitoring	.094	.036	.461	2.611	.000
Risk Policy Review	-8.503	.000	-.016	-0.310	.757
Credit Risk	-.162	.013	-.797	-12.462	.000
Operational Risk	.079	.017	.185	4.638	.000
Market Risk	.038	.013	.690	2.925	.004

a. Dependent Variable: EPS

5 Conclusion and recommendations

In this study, the strength of risk management practices by the 21 listed banks in Nigeria and their effects on the financial performance were investigated using descriptive and ordinary least square regression analysis. The study used both primary data generated with the use of a well-structured questionnaire and time series data for a period of ten years ranging from 2005-2014. While there were slight differences in the banks approach to risk management practices, majority of the sampled banks were found to have a strong risk management policy as disclosed in the financial statement. The result was not unexpected owing to the fact that the study used a highly regulated industry. Therefore, compliance with prudential guidelines and other regulatory guidelines was perceived to be responsible for the adequate risk management practices observed in the financial statement of the banks. Further study can focus on a less regulated industry to determine the firms approach to risk management.

Furthermore, the overall results of the regression analysis revealed that adequate risk management practices is essential for the long term survival of listed banks in Nigeria. The results also reveals the trend in risk management practices in other developing economy such as Ghana, Pakistan, Kenya, Thailand, Tehran and the current global practices in Serbian and United States as presented in the literature review. Generally, the strength of risk management practices has a positive and statistically significant impact on the financial performance. This result is somehow similar to that of Hussein and Karl (2013) that found a significant relationship between BHCs' risk taking levels and their financial performance. BHCs with lower risk-taking levels were found to have higher average financial performance than BHCs with higher risk-taking levels from 2006 to 2009. It however contradicts that of Ramazanali *et al.* (2014) whose hypothesis testing showed that there is no significant correlation between the management of risk and financial performance of investment firms.

Similarly, within the risk management practices, risk policy review has statistically insignificant relationship with the two measures of financial performance. Credit risk was negatively correlated with both return on capital employed and earnings per share. However, the relationship was insignificant for return on capital employed while a significant relationship was found for earnings per share. The remaining four independent variables have significant and positive relationship with financial performance and thereby lend support to Zubairi and Ahson (2015) who reported that risk management practices had a statistically significant positive impact on profitability. On the contrary, risk management does not matter to the firm performance in Thailand as Kittipat and Nopadol (2014) reported a weak correlation between the risk management practices and financial performance of an organization, measured by return on assets (ROA), return on equity (ROE) and earnings per share (EPS). Given the findings of this study, we recommends that adequate risk management system should be put in place by the board of directors which should include the establishment of company's annual risk limit, risk appetite and risk strategy to curtail the excessive risk taking of the management. The system should be reviewed regularly to determine its adequacy, effectiveness and compliance level of the management with the risk management system.

References

Alexander, J.M. (2012) "Leadership instability in hospitals: the influence of board-CEO relations and organization growth and decline", *Administrative Science Quarterly,* vol. 38: 74-99

Al-hhmidu, N.H. & Tukur, M. (2014) "Multi-country study of bank credit risk determinants", *International Journal of Banking and Finance,* vol. 5(1): 135-152

Al-Tamimi, H. & Al-Mazrooei, M., (2007) "Banks' risk management: A comparison study of UAE national and foreign banks", *The Journal of Risk Finance,* vol. 8(4): 394-409

Barley, S.B. (2009) "Corporate governance and firm performance", *Journal of Corporate Finance*, Vol. 14: 257-273

Basel Committee on Banking Supervision (2007) "Corporate Governance for Banking Organizations (Enhancing Corporate Governance for Banking Organizations)", Bank for International Settlements, Basel.

Beasley, M.S. & Frigo, M. (2007) "Strategic Risk Management: Creating and Protecting Value", *Strategic Finance,* vol. 29: 288-286

Benson, S. M. (2005) "The Effects of Bank Regulations, Competition and Financial Reforms on MENA Banks' Profitability", *Economic Research Forum Working Paper* No. 44

Berner, A. & Udell, G. (1994) "Did Risk-Based Capital Allocate Bank Credit and Cause a Credit Crunch in the U.S", *Journal of Money Credit and banking*, vol. 16(2): 788-804

Boahene, S. H., Dasah, J., &Agyei, S. K. (2012) "Credit risk and profitability of selected banks in Ghana", *Research Journal of Finance and Accounting,* vol. 3(7): 6-14

Culp, A. (2008) "Voluntary financial disclosure by Mexican corporations", *The Accounting Review*, vol. 62 (3): 533-541

Dermine, R. S. (2011) "Diversification, size, and risk at bank holding companies", *Journal of Money, Credit, and Banking,* vol. 29(3): 300-313

Fatemi, A. & Foolad, I. (2006) "Risk management practices in German firms", *Managerial Finance journal,* vol. 26: 1–17

Fatemi, A., & Foolad, I. (2006) "*Credit risk management: A survey of practices*", Retrieved from http://www.emeraldinsight.com

Ferguson, O. (2013) "The impact of credit risk management on financial performance of commercial banks in Kenya", *Africa Management Review* vol. 3(1): 244-253

Gordon, C. (2009) "An analysis of the challenges faced by banks in managing credit in Zimbabwe", *European Journal of Business and Management,* vol. 4(1): 38-46

Garg J. (2014) "The diversification and financial performance of Us Credit Unions", *Journal of Banking and Finance*, vol. 32(9): 1836-1849

Hoyt, D. & Lienberg, A. (2011) "Corporate governance and bank performance in Romanian banking system", *Fascicle of the Faculty of Economics and Public Administration*, vol. 1(13): 219-225

Hussein, R. G. & Karl, R. (2013) "Finance and growth: Schumpeter might be right", *Quarterly Journal of Economics* vol. 10(8): 717-737

Khan, T. & Ahmed, H., (2001) "Risk management: An analysis of issues in Islamic financial industry", *Occasional Paper,* vol. 5.(2): 207-214

Kittipat, D. D & Nopadol, Z.A. (2014) "Evaluation of credit risk management policies and practices in a vietnamese Joint-Stock commercial banks transaction office", *Business Economics and Tourism,* vol. 4(2): 556-566

Manab, N.A., Kassim, I, & Hussin, M.R., (2010) "Enterprise-wide risk management practices: between corporate governance compliance and value creation", *International Review of Business Research Papers*, vol. 6(2): 239-252

Meulbroek, L. A (2002) "Senior manager's guide to integrated risk management", *Journal of Applied Corporate Finance*, vol. 14(4): 56-70

Miller, K.D. (1992). "A framework for integrated risk management in international business", *Journal of International Business Studies,* vol. 2(3): 311-331

Miller, M.J. & Triana, R .W (1999) "Exploring the reliability of social and environmental disclosures: content analysis", *Accounting, Auditing and Accountability Journal*, vol. 12(2): 237-256

Mulbert, K. & Citlau, P.O (2011) "The impact of effective credit risk management on bank survival", *Annals of the University of Petroşani Economics,* vol. 9(2): 173-184

Ntim, C. S. (2012) "Survey of banks' corporate governance in Indonesia, republic of Korea, Malaysia and Thailand", *Asian Development Bank Institute,* Retrieved on 21, December, 2014 from www.adbi.org/files/2005.07.05 survey.corporate.governance.bank.ASIA.pdf

Nepal, Z.Y (2012) "Enterprise risk management: Theory and practice", *Journal of Applied Corporate Finance*, vol. 18(4): 1-13.

OECD (2014) "*Risk management and corporate governance*, OECD Publishing, *http://dx.doi.org/10.1787/9789264208636-en*

Ongore, V.O. (2011) "The relationship between ownership structure and firm performance: An empirical analysis of listed companies in Kenya", *African*

Journal of Business Management, vol. 5: 2120-2128

Oyerogba, E.O (2014) "Risk disclosure in the published financial statements and firm performance: Evidence from the Nigeria listed companies", *Journal of Economics and Sustainable Development,* vol. 5(8): 86-95

Pagach, D.P. & Warr, R.S. (2011) "An empirical investigation of the characteristics of firms adopting enterprise risk management", Available at SSRN, http://ssrn.com/abstract=1010200

Peter, J. V. & Romi, T. (2011) "A general approach to integrated risk management with skewed, fat-tailed risks", *Journal of Financial Economics,* vol. 79(3): 569-614

Post, R. (2011) "Assessing the risk and performance of the GCC banking sector", *International Research Journal of Finance and Economics,* vol. 6(5): 72-78

Rosen, S. & Zenois, W.H (2001) "Incorporating strategic risk into enterprise risk management: A survey of current corporate practice", *Journal of Applied Corporate Finance,* vol. 18(4) 81-90:

Sabato, G. (2009) "Financial crisis: Where did risk management fail", Royal Bank of Scotland, Group Credit Risk Working Paper.

Santomero, A. M. (1997) "Commercial banking risk management: An Analysis of the process. *The Wharton Financial Institutions Center.* USA. Available in www form <http://fic.wharton.upenn.edu/fic/papers/95/9511.pdf >, retrieved 20.06.2010

Sekaran, A. S. (2008) "Efficacy of credit risk management on the performance of banks in Nigeria: a Study of Union Bank Plc", *Global Journal of Management and Business Research Administration and Management,* vol. 13(4): 1-12

Sobel, A. & Reding, L. (2004) "The determinants of bank interest rate margins: an international study", *Journal of International Money and Finance,* vol. 19(4): 813-832

Staton, P. S. (2012) "The impact of credit risk management on financial performance of commercial banks in Nepal", *International Journal of Arts and Commerce,* vol. 1(5): 9-15

Vieira, R.S. (2010) "The relationship between liquidity and profitability: An exploratory study of airline companies between 2005 and 2008", *UMEA Universitet Journal,* vol. 5(8): 844-856

Walker, R. (2009). "Exploring the reliability of social and environmental disclosures: content analysis", *Accounting, Auditing and Accountability Journal*, vol. 12(2): 237-256

The impact of income tax over financial performance of companies listed on the Bucharest Stock Exchange

Aurelia Ştefănescu[a], Ileana Cosmina Pitulice[a1]
and Viorica Georgiana Mînzu[a]

[a]*Bucharest University of Economic Studies, Romania*

Abstract: By its multiple facets, income tax is a subject of great interest both for academic and professional environment, on a microeconomic and macroeconomic level. After analyzing the relevant literature in the field, in order to demonstrate the influence of income tax over a company's performance, two econometric models were designed, having as dependent variables return on equity and net profit's margin rate. For applying multiple regressions we used a sample of companies listed on Bucharest Stock Exchange and the analysed indicators were extracted from their annual financial statements. Econometric modelling used for return on equity and net profit's margin demonstrated that effective tax rate influences in a negative way a company's financial performance. Limits of research have been evidenced as being methodological, such as the small size of the sample.

Keyword: empirical research, income tax, financial performance, listed companies, Romania

1. Introduction

The aspects regarding companies' income tax are of great interest both for the European and national environment, considering the impact of this indicator on

[1] Corresponding author: Ileana Cosmina Pitulice, Bucharest University of Economic Studies, 6 Piata Romana, Bucharest, e-mail: ileana.pitulice@cig.ase.ro

budgeratry revenues and Gross Domestic Product. From the perspective of GDP per capita, there are studies that demonstrate a convergence trend at European Union level. Convergence is significant in new integrated member states and lower in existing EU's member states (Albu, 2012).

The divergences regarding the prevailing of EU's interest over the national one for what the income tax is concerned creat dissensions in the individual tax system and the European one. The divergences between tax systems in the EU's member states are also determined by the different economic and social structures as well as conceptual differences regarding the role of tax system in general and a certain tax in particular (Georgescu, 2009).

The disparity of tax systems in the EU's member states is validated by the results of the study performed on the average tax rate by Devereux and Loretz (2008). They have evidenced that there is a significant difference of the effective tax rate, form 26.3% in Bulgaria (the minimum value) and 40.1% in Malta (the maximum value), while the average value at Europen level is around 30%. Also, the authors have tested the hypothesis of implementing the common tax base, in the same circumstances and they found out that the value of this indicator would be significantly reduced, the maximum value being reached in the same country, Malta (29.9%) and the minimum one in Italy 18.3%. Devereux and Loretz (2008) argue that the fiscal systems in EU would converge to a common denominator, thus generating a neutral tax system.

In order to achieve the harmonization of the tax systems in EU, European Commission has presented in 2001 the difficulties generated by the disparity of taxing in EU member states: influencing (disstorsion) of resource allocation negatively impacting on valuing the advantages of a real unique market as well as the international repartition of income tax which can disadvantage certain member states; the embrittlement of budgetary cash flow inputs by losses associated to fical competition; the trend of increasing tax systems inequity by a privileged treatment of mobile tax bases; the double taxing risk (Matei & Pîrvu, 2010).

The purpose of European Commission of harmonizing the fiscal systems at a European level is known as the Common Consolidated Corporate Tax Base. It was elaborated in 2011 and it is focused on the partially harmonization of income taxes paid by companies that operate activites in the European space. The adoption of this common income tax framework would be a value-added generator for: the correlation of complexity and economic environment globalization to a correct, efficient and fair tax system; coherent tax systems at EU's member states lavel; the decreasing trend of income tax non-payment intention; the elimination of double taxation; social and economic effects by increasing investments and the decrease in the unemploymetn rate.

Several studies revealed that in Central and Eastern Europe, the average income tax rate is of approximately 17%. At EU's level, in 2013-2014, only three member states have reduced the income tax percentage: Denmark (from 25% to 24.5%), United Kingdom (from 23% to 21%) and Slovakia (from 23% to 22%). From the EU's member states, Romania has the lowest income tax percentage (16%) (Schöb & Geageac, 2014).

Romania has introduced the income tax percentage of 16% in 2010, three years after of achieving the full EU membership status, the same percentage being used up to present. On the opposite side, income tax regulations (Fiscal Code) have been modified very often. Among the changes in income tax regulations, operated in the past five years, we can enumerate: fiscal concepts, contributors typology, fiscal year, declaration and payment procedure, correlation between fiscal rules and accounting regulations, the content of non-taxable revenues, the content of non-deductible expenses, the limits of deductible expenses, criteria for deductible expenses, particular aspects for fiscal depreciation, specific documents for fiscal procedures, procedures for correction of income tax calculation errors, fiscal losses.

The research results performed by Pitulice *et al.* (2016) have validated the negative impact of income tax on financial position and performance of companies listed on Bucharest Stock Exchange (BVB). Thus, the two econometric models constructed for net profit and return on assets have validated the research hypotheses, that is the negative impact of income tax on financial position and performance.

In this context, we empirically investigated the tax on profit's impact over the company's financial performance. Based on literature review performed in the first part of the paper, our research is developed on two coordinates – return on equity and net profit's margin rate-, each one of them aiming to demonstrate and assess the tax impact over the selected indicators. For both econometric models, the effective tax rate has passed the significance test and it also has a negative influence ver performance indicators. This finding can represent a premise for future studies of a larger breadth, with results that can be generalized.

This paper includes four structural components. The first one is dedicated to literature review by analyzing ideas published on this particular subject. Literature review is followed by research methodology. The third component presents research results while the fourth one is dedicated to final conclusions limits of research and future research directions.

2. Literature review

From the literature review we might say that income tax is approached on different levels. Studies have revealed the fact that external financing is favoring companies by contrast to self-financing, considering the deductible interest expenses and the increased value of return on equity. Complementary, under the taxation context, the average cost of capital is dependent of three components: the discount rates used, tax percentage and the percentage of liabilities in the capital structure (Modigliani & Miller, 1963).

Wu and Yue (2009) have researched the relationship between income tax percentages and the financing decision of economic entities in China. The research has considered the special taxation of income tax, that is 15% (the general taxation percentage being of 33%), facility of which certain economic entities have benefited based the area they acted in, but which was repealed later on. Thus, on a sample of 2.182 entities that benefited from special taxation of income, authors have analysed the changes in financial leverage from two perspectives: the maintenance of liabilities at the samel level and the decrease in equity, and contracting new loans with the increase in liabilities value. The results of the study have proved that financial leverage of these companies has increased with 3.3% following the increase of 18% in the tax percentage, and the degree of access on bank financing could be seen as a significant factor of financial structure.

Sterdyniak (2015) approaches the relationship between tax income and social taxes. He considers that reducing social taxes can be compensated by an increase in income taxation of companies, effects being measured for short and medium term. On short term, companies' return is not changed as the increase on income tax is compensated by reducing the workforce taxation. On medium term, entities use more workforces and less capital. Therefore, the global cost, calculated based on workforce's cost and capital cost, does not change.

An interesting approach of income tax is represented by financial performance. Ngobo and Stefani (2001) validates that financial performance is correlated to the activity sector, diversity and heterogeneity of economic entities based on a model that includes return on assets (ROA), return on investment (ROI) and q Tobin indicators.

The results of the research performed by Njaya (2014) have evidenced that financial performance of economic entities is positively influenced by their social responsibility and adopting a responsible behavior does not involve a smaller profit.

Another approach of income tax is generated by the fiscal aspects. From this point of view, there are numerous states that, for the income taxation of companies have adopted the possibility of deducting losses from the future fiscal years' profits. However, this provision can impact on the performance of direct investments projects and implicitly on the investment decisions adopted by an economic entity. Several studies have evidenced that, although a certain investment project would be rejected based on the negative net present value determined by its adoption, the decision can radically change if the entity can recover a previous fiscal loss. In this respect, two entities have been analysed, one having a loss to recover while the other one didn't both of them analyzing the adoption of an investment project with identical costs and cash-flows. Although individually, the net present value of the project is negative, the influence of recovering the previous loss is reflected in generation of a potential cash flow due to the tax economy which would be materialized only if the project is adopted (Dragotă & Ţâţu, 2011). Consequently, if an investor has to choose between two options, that is, setting up a new company and the acquisition of an existing one with a right to recover a previous loss, the investor would choose the second one.

The research results performed by Buijink *et al.* (2002) concerning the effective tax rates applied during 1990-1996 by 15 companies – EU's residents – have evidenced the fact that certain incentives both permanent and temporary are substantially different in EU member states and their effect is not the equalisation of real tax burdens at EU level.

As to the fiscal competition, Gondor (2011) claims that it has a positive effect for integration on EU's market, and the goal of harmonizing direct taxes must be staged from total harmonization to structural harmonization. Masso *et al.* (2013) analyse the advantages and risks of cancellation of retained earnings and maintaining taxation only for distributed profits, based on Estonia's case. Among the advantages of this reform with a greater impact over small entities there are ennumerated the increase in assets with greater liquidity and the decrease in companies financing through loans/liabilities. The risk involved by this fiscal policy is that of the trend of keeping the liquidity surplus in assets with minimum risk instead of making investments in equipments or research&development activities.

Da Rin *et al.* (2011) analyse the impact of fiscal policies over the setting up of new companies, considering the proportionate relationship between economic growth and new companies' set up by entrepreneurs. The research results proved a significantly negative impact over the new companies setting up rate. As the effect is a concave one, reducing taxes would influence the companies setting up rate only if the taxation level is under a certain limit.

Devereux and Griffith (2002) research income tax from a multinational view. Considering the increase of capital mobility between countries, the authors analyse the impact of income tax on capital localization. They consider that income tax is fundamental for attraction and maintaining capital by states' governments. Thus, the tax percentage used by one country influence a company's decision to activate or invest in that country.

Another approach of income tax is that correlated to the accounting regulations. Da Rin *et al.* (2011) sustain that reducing income tax rate is more efficient in countries where accounting standards are of high quality. They argue the fact that the quality of accounting standards used influence the possibility of hiding profit from taxation by manipulation of income statement. Epps and Cleaveland (2009) identify the difficulties of income taxation that accounting regulations, standards' interpretations and FASB try to give pertinent solutions: the lack of transparency for particular fiscal transactions, the difficulty in reconciliating income statement to the income tax fiscal statement, low disclosure of information on fiscal contingencies inside financial statements, the impact of internal control over the reliability of income tax fiscal statement.

Reffering to the tax rates, the study conducted by Gondor (2011) has evidenced that România has the lowest percentage of direct taxation; among the arguments there can be enumerated the lower tax rates for income tax and the single tax rates that generally assume a powerful minimization of direct rates comparing to the indirect ones.

The revision of the presented approaches evidence the fact that income tax is an integrated concept, considering its correlation with financing of entities, financial performance, social responsibility, fiscal and social policies, accounting regulations, macroeconomic and multinational aspects.

3. Research methodology

The sample we used comprised of a number of 20 companies listed at Bucharest Stock Exchange, whose financial-accounting information were analysed for the period 2013-2015. Selection of companies inside the sample depended on the access to financial information therefore only quoted entities were included. The selection criteria were:

- the selection of a single industry in which companies operated, in order to minimize as much as possible the action of certain factors characteristic only to specific areas; manufacturing industry was considered;
- we included in the sample only companies registered for the first and the second category of Bucharest Stock Exchange;
- we eliminated from the sample those quoted companies whose financial statements were not available (their state was suspended) or they were only partially available, in order to collect enough information for the empirical study;
- we retained only companies disclosing profit for the analysed period – this adjustment was considered necessary so that no distortions were created inside the econometric model.

In order to quantify the impact that income tax has over financial performance, we used multiple regression analysis, using the Excel's Data Analysis module and

Eviews 9 program. Based on the results obtained, we performed significance tests, corrections of the model where necessary and interpretations of these, in order to be able to express pertinent conclusions at the end of the paper.

Literature review revealed several factors impacting on a company's results. In this respect, for the construction of the analysis model, the following variables were used:

- endogenous: return on equity (ROE), profit's net margin rate (RMN);
- exogenous: the effective tax rate (*RIE*), company's size *(DIM)*, assets' structure (STR_A), long-term debts rate ($RDat_{TL}$), financial leverage (*LEV*). The calculation formulas for the variables are listed in Appendix 1.

4. Research results

For each of the two endogenous variables, a multiple regression was performed, the obtained results being interpreted for each one of them.

The Econometric Model of Return on Equity (ROE)

$$ROE = \beta_1 + \beta_2 RIE + \beta_3 DIM + \beta_4 STR_A + \beta_5 RDat_{TL} + \beta_6 LEV + e_t$$

At first, we have to identify the possible correlations, if any, between variables, so that they can be treated or eliminated. Data obtained reflect the inexistence of collinearity between variables, the greatest value observed being of 0.49.

Table 1. Values for correlation coefficients from the ROE model

	ROE	**RIE**	**DIM**	**STR_A**	**LEV**	**$RDat_{TL}$**
ROE	1					
RIE	-0.327	1				
DIM	-0.230	-0.084	1			
STR_A	-0.467	-0.036	0.184	1		
LEV	-0.026	-0.140	0.311	-0.018	1	
$RDat_{TL}$	-0.000	0.191	0.492	-0.034	0.455	1

Based on multiple regression results for ROE, we could establish that not all estimated coefficients are statistically significant. The values of $t_{calculated}$ for company's dimensions, financial structure and long-term debts rate are situated outside the null hypothesis rejection area, and their presence in the econometric model would have determined an artificial increase of R Square. Following the elimination of the variables above mentioned, a new model was constructed whose estimated coefficients are presented below:

Table 2. Estimated values for ROE model's coefficients

	Coefficients	Standard Error	t Stat	P-value	Lower 95%	Upper 95%
Intercept	0.246	0.031	7.943	0.000	0.184	0.308
RIE	-0.313	0.099	-3.145	0.002	-0.513	-0.113
STR_A	-0.210	0.048	-4.375	0.000	-0.306	-0.114

The t test confirms the fact that there are also other factors influencing the dependent variables and P-value is lower than the significance level α, therefore the coefficient is statistically significant.

The effective tax rate has an unfavourable effect over the analysed variable, as an increase of it with 1% determines a decrease of ROE with 0.3135 percentage points, if the other variables are kept on a constant level. The value of $t_{calculated}$ is -3.1457, so RIE variable impacts over ROE.

The non-current assets percentage in total assets is the other independent variable and the estimated coefficient equals -0.2105. If assets structure is increasing by one percent, ROE will decrease by 0.2105 percentage points. The t test confirmed the fact that STR_A variable has an impact over ROE, and by interpreting P-value, the coefficient can be considered significant.

Following the substitution of estimated coefficients, the model becomes:

$$ROE = 0.246 - 0.313RIE - 0.210STR_A$$

Table 3. Estimated values for quality analysis coefficients of ROE model

Regression Statistics	
Multiple R	0.581
R Square	0.337
Adjusted R Square	0.313
Standard Error	0.058
Observations	58

Anova

	df	SS	MS	F	Significance F
Regression	2	0.094	0.047	14.038	
Residual	55	0.185086	0.003365		
Total	57	0.279573			

The connection between analysed variables can be established at a medium level, as a result of the 0.5813 value of Multiple R. Even more, a percentage of 33.79% of the ROE's variation is determined by the effective tax rate and assets' structure.

Considering that the econometric model we analysed is based only on these two independent variables, this value is appreciated as acceptable. As the role of the systematic factors is superior of the residual ones, the F statistics has a value that exceeds the critical one (3.164). Thus, ROE's variation is more determined by the action of the determinant factors than by the role of happening. The probability associated to the previous test is closing 0, which determines the econometric model to be included in the category of statistically relevant models.

➢ *Test of the normality of errors*

Figure 1. Histogram of errors in ROE model

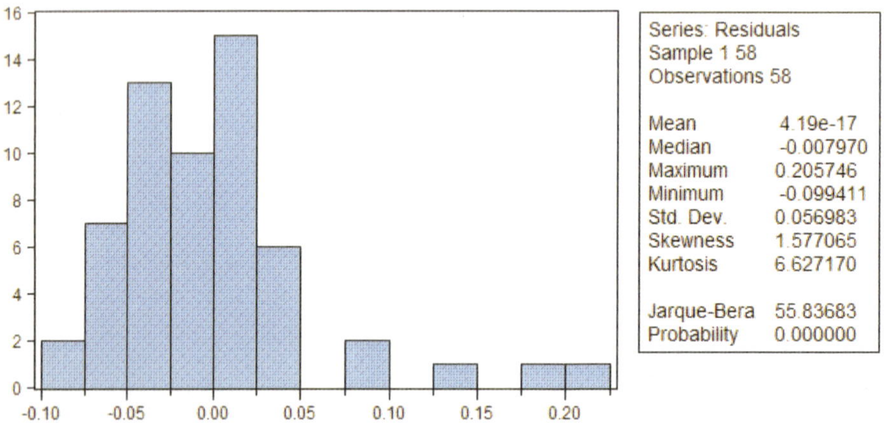

Histogram of errors reveals an abnormal situation, as their variation is very high. Also, the Jarque-Bera test has a high value that compared to the critical value selected from the χ^2 distribution with 2 freedom degrees, determines the hypothesis of a normal distribution of errors. The residues of the model do not reveal a normal distribution.

➢ *Autocorrelation of errors test*

Following the performance of initial regression, which was added the $\hat{e}_{t-1}$ regressor, the Lagrange Multiplier test determines the acceptance of alternative hypothesis, that of the existence of autocorrelation of errors. The decision was made based on P-value = 0.044 for the coefficient estimated for $\hat{e}_{t-1}$, probability which was lower than the significance level α. In this respect, econometric model correction is needed, so that we can obtain unbiased estimations of coefficients, as the following table reveals.

Table 4. Estimated values for ROE Model's coefficients in absence of autocorrelation

	Coefficients	Standard Error	t Stat	P-value	Lower 95%	Upper 95%
Intercept	0.241	0.035	6.859	0.000	0.170	-0.099
RIE	-0.295	0.098	-3.014	0.003	-0.491	-0.099
STR_A	-0.205	0.052	-3.895	0.000	-0.310	0.311

➤ *Test of heteroscedasticity of errors*

The White test statistics has registered a value of 15.15 and it is higher than the critical one selected from χ^2 = 11.07, which determines the rejection of homoscedasticity null hypothesis H_0. Therefore, the serie presents heteroscedasticity which will be presented as a limit of the research.

The Econometric Model of Profit's Net Margin Rate (RMN)

$$RMN = \beta_1 + \beta_2 RIE + \beta_3 DIM + \beta_4 STR_A + \beta_5 RDat_{TL} + \beta_6 LEV + e_t$$

In the table below, the obtained correlation coefficients are presented with relatively low values, fact that concludes the lack of multicollinearity. The highest identified value is 0.4921 that of the correlation coefficient established between company's dimension and long-term debts rate.

Table 5. Values of correlation coefficients from the RMN model

	RMN	RIE	DIM	STR_A	LEV	$RDat_{TL}$
RMN	1					
RIE	-0.355	1				
DIM	-0.047	-0.084	1			
STR_A	-0.466	-0.036	0.184	1		
LEV	-0.260	-0.140	0.311	-0.018	1	
$RDat_{TL}$	-0.046	0.191	0.492	-0.034	0.455	1

Following the performance of the initial regression, the output offers enough arguments for restriction of the model, as not all of the five coefficients are statistically significant. The unsignificant coefficients (company's dimension and long-term debts rate) will be excluded from the model. Variables that will be tested for their influence over the analysed RMN are effective tax rate, assets' structure and financial leverage. The interpretation of their action is based on the estimated coefficients presented below:

Table 6. Estimated values of RMN model's coefficients

	Coefficients	Standard Error	t Stat	P-value	Lower 95%	Upper 95%
Intercept	0.224	0.023	9.394	0.000	0.176	0.272
RIE	-0.286	0.068	-4.163	0.000	-0.424	-0.148
STR_A	-0.160	0.032	-4.883	0.000	-0.226	-0.094
LEV	-0.050	0.015	-3.260	0.001	-0.081	-0.019

The value of *Intercept* represents, as in ROE's model, the only estimation of regression that determines a positive influence over the analysed indicator. There can be concluded that there are other factors, not included in the model, determining the positive variation of profit's net margin rate.

The effective tax rate variable influences the endogenous variable in a decreasing direction. When effective tax rate increases by 1%, the RMN will count for a decrease of 0.2868 percentage points. The t test proved the fact that *RIE* has an effect on endogenous variable, its calculated value (-4.1632) being lower than the critical one. The coefficient can be considered as statistically significant, due to P-value lower than 0.05.

The estimated coefficient for STR_A variable has a negative value, indicating that the increase by 1% of assets' structure rate determines a decrease of RMN by 0.1608 percentage points. The t test (-4.8835) value being lower than the critical one, it can be concluded that the percentage of non-current assets in total assets has an effect over the dependent variable modifications. Even more, the estimated coefficient is statistically significant due to P-value being close to 0.

The financial leverage is the variable influencing the less RMN variable. However, this is the only model in which this variable is significant which determines its keeping in the final regression model. The estimated coefficient of *LEV* variable is -0.0507, therefore an increase in it with 1%, will determine a decrease of endogenous variable by the same value. By comparing the calculated value of the report ($t_{calculated} = -3.2605$) with the critical value ($t_{critical} = -2.3056$) it can be appreciated that part of the RMN's variation is due to *LEV* variation. Although, P-value equal to 0.0019 is under the significance level α, which means that the coefficient is statistically significant.

Following the substitution of estimated coefficients, the model becomes:

$$ROA = 0.224 - 0.286RIE - 0.160STR_A - 0.050LEV$$

The table below offers the information necessary for validating the model in its whole, so that a subsequent opinion over the quality of the estimations could be formulated. The variation of RMN is divided in two elements: the explained variance, provided by the effect of the factors included in the model, with the value of 0.073 and the unexplained variance provided by the model's errors, with the value of 0.085. As the role of the systematic factors is higher than that of the residual factors, that is 0.024>0.001, the F statistics value is higher than the critical one (F_{tabled}= 2.775) and thus, the rejection of the null hypothesis is evident. The action of determinant factors over the RMN is significantly different of the role of happening. The analysis of the probability associated to Fisher-Snedecor test reveals a favourable circumstance, the Significance F value being lower than the significance level α, thus confirming the statistical relevance of the model.

Table 7. Estimated values for quality analysis coefficients of RMN model

Regression Statistics	
Multiple R	0.680
R Square	0.462
Adjusted R Square	0.432
Standard Error	0.039
Observations	58

Anova

	df	**SS**	**MS**	**F**	**Significance F**
Regression	3	0.073	0.024	15.487	2.17E-07
Residual	54	0.085	0.001		
Total	57	0.158			

➢ *Test of the normality of errors*

The errors variation in RMN model is high, their histogram indicating an abnormal situation. Although, the analysis of the results in Jarque-Bera test confirms the conclusion based on graphic method, its calculated value of 110.808 being higher than the critical value of 5.991 (based on χ^2 distribution with 2 freedom degrees). Therefore, conclusion is that the residues of the model are not normally distributed.

Figure 2. Histogram of errors in RMN model

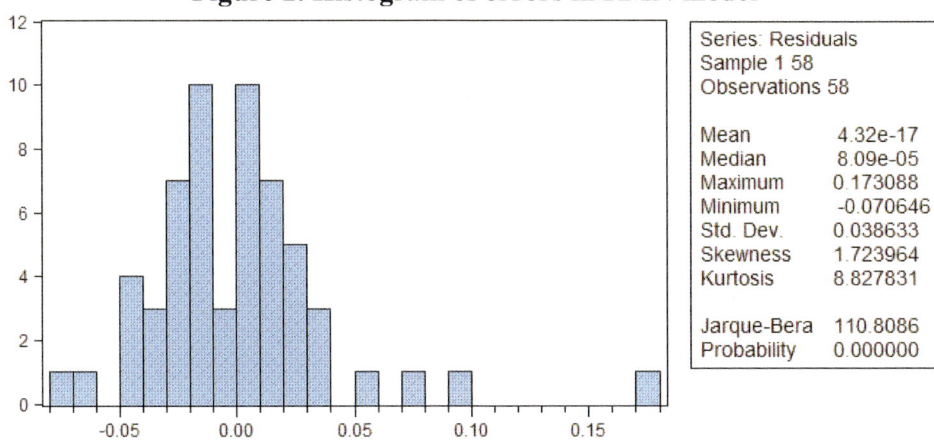

➢ *Autocorrelation of errors test*

Following the performance of initial regression, which was added the $\hat{e}_{t-1}$ regressor, the Lagrange Multiplier test determines the acceptance of null hypothesis, that of the inexistence of autocorrelation of errors. The decision was made based on P-value=0.082 for the estimated coefficient of $\hat{e}_{t-1}$, which is higher than the significance level α. It can be concluded that the results obtained are the best unbiased estimations of coefficients.

➢ *Test of heteroscedasticity of errors*

The White test represented the testing method for heteroscedasticity of RMN model. The test's statistics is 31.827, higher than the critical one selected from the repartition χ^2=16.918 (for α=0.05 and 9 degrees of freedom), so the null hypothesis H_0 of homoscedasticity will be rejected in favour of alternative H_1. The serie presents heteroscedasticity which is one limit of the research.

5. Conclusions

The research performed evidence that, on a conceptual level, income tax is approached in an integrated manner, based on its dimensions focused on fiscal policies, accounting regulations, performance, social responsibility, investors and macroeconomic policies.

The purpose of this research was that of identifiying a possible influence of income tax over company's financial performance and position. Following the analysis of performance concept, two representative indicators were selected in this respect that is ROE and RMN. For each one of these an econometric model was constructed in order to explain the variation of the performance indicator, also determined (more or less) by the effective tax rate variable. It was essential that tax impact is identified in its correlation with other factors and not on an individual basis, thus using multiple regressions.

For the Return on Equity model several insignificant variables were excluded as keeping them inside the model would have artificially increased the determination report. Model's coefficients, except the free term, were estimated as negative, reflecting the fact that none of the selected variables positively influences the sampled companies' performances. However, the purpose of analyzing the income tax effect was fulfilled, the estimated coefficient for this variable being significant. Performance indicator variation is generated in a 31.39% percentage by the determined factors, considered as significantly different from the role of happening.

The second model we have studied, that of net profit's margin, was different from the previous one by the appearance of financial leverage variable, its influence over the analysed indicator being a negative one. As to the effective tax rate, the same conclusion as for the previous model was reached: income tax negatively influences the net profit's margin rate. If looking at the whole of the econometric model, it can be assessed that the action of determinant factors over the net profit's margin model is significantly different from the role of happening.

As to the limits of the research, these are of methodological nature. First of all, the sample was formed of only 20 companies listed on Bucharest Stock Exchange, which can be appreciated as a low number. Also, considering the fact that analysis could not be performed over one single sector of the manufacturing industry due to the insufficiency of data, there could be particularities specific to each sector that are not taken into account. Even more, limits due to econometric modeling as well as those provided by the authors' analysis are inherent in an empirical research. As the research results provided, for the limits of the research we have to take into consideration the homoscedasticity tests results delivered for each of the two models.

References

Albu, L.L. (2012) "The Convergence Process in the EU Estimated by Gini Coefficients", *Journal of Economic Forecasting,* 15(4): 5-16

Buijink, W., Janssen, B. & Schols, Y. (2002) "Evidence of the effect of domicile on corporate average effective tax rates in the European Union", *Journal of International Accounting Auditing and Taxation,* 11(2):115-130

Devereux, M.P. & Loretz, S. (2008) "Increased efficiency through consolidation and formula apportionment in the European Union?", Oxford University Centre for Business Taxation Working Pape 08/12, http://www.sbs.ox.ac.uk /sites/default/files/Business_Taxation/Docs/Publications/Working_Papers/Series_08/WP0812.pdf [on-line access: September 1th 2016]

Devereux, M.P. & Griffith, R. (2002) "The impact of corporate taxation on the location of capital: A review", *Swedisch economic policy Review*, 9: 79-102

Dragotă, V. & Țâțu L. (2011) "Capital Budgeting: a Tax Shields' 'Mirage'"?, *Theoretical and Applied Economics*, 3(556): 29-38

Epps, K.K. & Cleaveland, M.K. (2009) "Insiders' perspectives of the effects of recent regulation on corporate taxation", *Research in Accounting Regulation*, 21(1): 34-47

Georgescu, M.A. (2009) "The tax burden in EU-27", *Studia Universitats Babes-Bolyai, Negotia*, LIV(1), available at ftp://ftp.repec.org/opt/R eDIF/RePEc/bbn/journl/2009_1_8_Georgescu.pdf [on-line access: September 1th 2016]

Gondor, M. (2011) "Reglemented harmonization vs fiscal competition in the field of direct European direct taxation, *Studia Universitatis Petru Maior, Series Oeconomica*, vol. 1, no. 1(13), http://www.annals. seap.usv.ro/index.php /annals/ article/ view File/393/403 [on-line access: September 1th 2016]

Masso, J., Meriküll, J. & Vahter, J. (2013) "Shift from gross profit taxation to distributed profit taxation: Are there effects on firms?, *Journal of Comparative Economics*, 41(4): 1092-1105

Marco, Da Rin, M., Di Giacomo, M. & Sembenelli, A. (2011) "Entrepreneurship, firm entry, and the taxation of corporate income: Evidence from Europe", *Journal of Public Economics*, vol. 95(9-10): 1048-1066

Matei, G. & Pîrvu, D. (2010) "Controversies regarding the corporate tax harmonization trend in the European Union", *Theoretical and Applied*

Economics, 8(549): 27-37

Modigliani, F. & Miller, M. (1963) "Corporate income taxes and the cost of capital: a correction", *American Economic Review*, 53(3): 433-443

Njaya, J.B. (2014) "L'impact de la responsabilité sociale (RSE) sur la performance financière des entreprises (PFE) au Cameroun", *Revue Congolaise de Gestion*, 1(19): 89-112

Ngobo, P.V. & Stefani, E. (2001) "Les différences de performance financière entre les entreprises: résultats du marché français", *Finance Contrôle Stratégie,* 4(1): 89-121

Romania's Parliament (2015) Legea nr. 227/2015 privind Codul Fiscal [Law no. 227/2015 regarding the Fiscal Code], published inthe Official Monitor of Romania no. 688/10.09.2015, updated with all modifications and subsequent completions

Pitulice, I.C., Ştefănescu, A., Mânzu, G., Popa, F., A., Niculescu (Diaconu), A. (2016) "Reserch of corporate tax impact on financial performance. Case of companies listed on Bucharest Stock Exchange", *Management and Economics Review,* 1(2): 203-261

Schöb, R. & Geageac, E. (2014) Studiu regional MAZARS Central Eastern European Tax Brochure 2014, http://rum.mazars.ro/Prima-pagina/Stiri/Presa /Comunicate-de-presa/Studiul-Fiscal-Regional-Mazars-2013-2014/ [on-line access: September 1th 2016]

Sterdyniak, H. (2015) "La grande réforme fiscale, un mythe français", *Revue de l'OFCE,* 3 (139): 327-397

Wu, L. & Yue, H. (2009) "Corporate tax, capital structure, and the accessibiliy of bank loans: Evidence from China", *Journal of Banking & Finance*, 33(1): 30-38

Appendix 1

Calculation formulas for variables

Variable	Calculation Formula
Return on Equity **(ROE)**	Net profit/Equity * 100
Effective Tax Rate **(RIE)**	Tax/Gross profit * 100
Assets' Structure **(STR_A)**	Non-curent assets/Total assets * 100
Financial Leverage **(LEV)**	Total liabilities/Equity * 100
Long-term Debts Rate **($RDat_{TL}$)**	Long-term liabilities/Total assets * 100
Profit's net Margin Rate **(RMN)**	Net profit/Turnover * 100

8

The impact of the implementations of the Sysrust's framework upon the quality of financial reporting: structural equation modelling approach

Ahmed Al-Dmour[a1], Maysem Abbod[a] and Rand Al-Dmour[b]

[a] *Brunel University, England*
[b] *University of Jordan, Jordan*

Abstract: The purpose of this research is to examine empirically, validate, and predict the reliability of the proposed relationship between the reliability of AIS process in the context of SysTrust' framework (principles and criteria) and the quality of financial reporting in shareholdings companies in Jordan. For this purpose, a primary data was used that was collected through a self-structured questionnaire from 239 of shareholdings companies. The extent of SysTrust's framework (principles and criteria) and the quality of financial reporting were also measured. The data were analyzed using structural equation modeling. The results showed that the magnitude and significance of the loading estimate and they indicated that all of the main five principles of SysTrust's framework are relevant in predicting the quality of financial reporting. Moreover, the reliability of AIS by the implementation of these five principles of SysTrust's framework were positively impacting the quality of financial reporting, as the structural coefficient for these paths are significant.

Keywords: SysTrust principles, internal control System, AIS, Jordan, shareholdings companies

[1] *Corresponding author*: England, London, Uxbridge, Brunel University, Department of Electronic and Computer Engineering, Brunel University; Post code UB8 3FG. Email: ahamedhanihamed.al-dmour@brunel.ac.uk

1. Introduction

According to Daneilia (2013), the quality of financial statements relies mainly on accounting information systems and internal controls that positively affect financial reporting. Potentiality of error in the reporting is related to the weaknesses of internal control, namely the supervision of accounting information system (Ricchiute, 2006). Further, the need of internal control is to produce reliable financial statements through supervising the relevant accounting system (Konrath, 2002). In terms of "quality", Toposh (2014) argues that maintaining characteristics of any accounting information system accounts on a well-designed internal control system which is applied to realize operational goals and performance. Romney and Steinbart (2009) pointed out that the AIS and good internal control structure can protect the system from problems such as fraud, error, equipment and software failures and problems due to political disaster. Another purpose of internal control, is to maintain the company's assets from theft, to make sure the information is reported accurately and implementation of laws and rules that apply (Warren *et al.*, 1996: 233). So it can be concluded that the internal controls used by management aims to control every activity in the company so that the company's operations (organization) will be implemented as planned, including producing of reliable financial reports.

Studies that emphasize the necessity and importance of the internal control system in the accounting system are increasingly being acknowledged (Zulkanian, 2009). Al-Qudah and Ahmed (2011) suggested a significant impact on the company's internal control AIS in creating accuracy, updated, comprehensive and comparative data. One of the internal control objectives in the IT environment is to obtain financial statements of high reliability and to provide an adequate and appropriate evidence to attain the goals of the organization (Al-Laith, 2012). Recently, the assessment of the effect of the internal control of AIS on the quality of financial reporting has received great attention by academic and professional accountants (Grant *et al.*, 2008; Canada *et al.*, 2009). They had much concern about answering the question whether the reliability of internal control will lead to systematic improvements in the quality of financial reporting. However, studies (that have examined the SysTrust's framework as an internal control method for assuring reliability in the professional accounting literature) are primarily devoted to explain the background and purpose of this service and its potential demand (Pugliese & Halse, 2000; Al-dmour *et al.*, 2018). Furthermore, several authors indicated that within organizations, attention must be given to the accounting standards and laws of each country because they affect accounting management (Davila *et al.*, 2004; Romney & Steinbart, 2017).

As in many other developing countries, financial reporting practices in Jordan are more of a result of "different sources of accounting influence" (Goitom, 2003) and the various legal requirements. The financial reporting in Jordan is regulated through the commercial laws. The Companies Law regulates all types of companies; the Banking Law regulates the banks, while the Insurance Law regulates the insurance companies. In the same context, the Securities Law regulates all companies' activities regarding listing and trading matters in the financial markets. According to the Companies Law No. 22 (1997), Jordanian companies are divided into General Partnership, Limited Partnership, Limited Liability Company, Limited Partnership in Shares, Public Shareholding Company. The securities of public shareholding companies can be listed and traded in Amman Stock Exchange and their minimum paid-in capital is 500,000 Jordanian Dinars (JD). According to the Companies Law No. 22 (1997), public shareholding companies are obligated to appoint an auditor. Duties are assigned to the Jordanian auditor according to the Companies Law - the major responsibility being to audit companies' accounts in accordance with the recognized auditing rules, the auditing profession's principles and its scientific and technical standards. Moreover, an auditor is to review the financial and administrative by-laws of the company and its internal financial controls, to ensure their suitability for the company's business and the safeguarding of its assets. Accordingly, auditors in Jordan are responsible for assessment of companies' internal controls, in addition to undertaking the appropriate substantive tests. In accordance with Companies Law No. 22 (1997), all public shareholding companies are required to prepare and issue their annual audited financial statements - their balance sheets, income statements, and cash flows statements - within three months from the end of the company's fiscal year. Further, each public company is to prepare and issue its semi-annual financial statements, certified by the company auditors within 60 days from the end of the half-year period.

The present study has, therefore, come to bridge this gap by assessing the impact of the implementation of the SysTrust's framework (principles and criteria) as internal control for assuring the AIS on the quality of financial reporting through an integrated approach. The study aims to overcome the limitations of the previous studies, and to improve understanding of the importance of the reliability of the AIS process in the environmental context of Jordanian organizational culture as a developing country and to empirically examine, validate and predict the viability of the study's proposed conceptual mod.

2. Theoretical background and literature review

2.1 The SysTrust's framework: definition and importance

According to the AICPA (2017), SysTrust's framework is an assurance service that independently tests and verifies a system's reliability. AICPA succinctly describes the overall purpose of SysTrust in the following way: "*Developments in information technology provide far greater power to companies at far lower costs.*" As business dependence on information technology increases, tolerance decreases for systems that are not secure, and these systems become unavailable when needed and unable to produce accurate information on a consistent basis. An unreliable system can cause a chain of events that negatively affect a company and its customers, suppliers, and business partners (Hunton, 2002).

The objective of a SysTrust engagement is to enable the practitioner to issue an attestation/assurance report on whether the management maintains appropriate reliability controls over its system(s). Potential users of a SysTrust report include: the entity itself as well as its shareholders, creditors, customers, suppliers, third-party users, including those who outsource to other entities and any other party who in some fashion relies on an information system. The term was intended to include auditing as a subcategory, as indicated in the following quote, which refers to the Special Committee's conceptual framework for assurance services: "The framework's primary objective is to provide a consistent view of assurance services. It provides guidelines that will enhance consistency and quality in the performance of services. It can also help establishing a common public perception of the CPA's function and value (AICPA, 2013). The AICPA Assurance Services Executive Committee (ASEC) has developed a set of principles and criteria (trust services principles and criteria) to be used in evaluating controls relevant to the security, availability, and processing integrity of a system, and the confidentiality and privacy of the information processed by the system. In this document, a *system* is designed, implemented, and operated to achieve specific business objectives (for example, delivery of services, production of goods) in accordance with management specified requirements. To check the reliability of a system; a set of principles and criteria are used for this purpose. This criteria is classified into five categories that they are relevant to systems reliability and to the reliability of financial statements of an organization as follows (ACIPA, 2017):

1. Availability: Agreed and committed system and information thereof that are used for operations (legal obligation).
2. Security: Protected systems against unauthorized access- physically and logically.
3. Confidentiality: Confidential information that is protected as committed to or agreed.
4. Processing Integrity: Processing data accurately, fully, in due timing and exclusively with proper authorization.

Privacy: Gathering, usage, disclosure, maintenance of personal information and its protection from unauthorized disclosure in accordance with internal policies and external regulatory requirements.

The main benefits of the use of SysTrust service include improved confidence in the systems of both business partners' and one's own internal systems, avoiding problems of system development (McPhie, 2000) and reducing the cost of business interruption insurance (Pugliese & Halse, 2000). The literature also suggests that

SysTrust provides a good framework for auditing internal systems (Al-Dmour *et al.*, 2018) and restructuring systems controls and procedures (Trabert & Mackler, 2001). While recognizing the potential benefits of trust services, Gray (2002) warns customers to investigate the relative value of the benefits against the associated cost before hiring a third party assurance provider. Accordingly, it is clear that system assurance has a positive impact on system users and their reliance and in turn on their decisions, especially when this assurance is provided on continuous basis, which is more suitable to the current changing environment. SysTrust developers also expect that the SysTrust report would be seen in the market as a sign of quality. According to this viewpoint, Trabert and Mackler (2001) imply that SysTrust opinions will function as a marketing tool and add value for the client. In the most recent version of the trust services guidelines, electronic seals or reports can be used with SysTrust engagements. Users may recognize that displaying the electronic seals or reports will help in their marketing efforts through improving their skill to distinguish themselves from other entities. This contention is supported by the results of the study of Arnold *et al.* (2000), which indicate that good-quality dealers are willing to pay for reports that differentiate along quality lines.

2.2 Literature review

In their study of electronic data interchange (EDI), Khazanchi and Sutton (2001) give evidence of the requirement for systems assurance, illustrating that numerous companies enforcing these systems do not use them to full benefit. This shows that entities authorizing EDI for their clients or customers should require assurance of suitable functioning. Results of these studies recommend a demand for trust services. It follows that there should be a positive effect on the business of clients that meet approved trust services standards. Moreover, a study by Havelka *et al.* (1998) argues that expression of agreement on measurement criteria for assurance services among providers and users will enable more effective and efficient production of those services. SysTrust is one of the models to update Internal Control Systems (ICS) of AIS through frame working the technological variables which affect designing AIS. Due to such nature, many of the practical studies have been implemented using the principles and criteria of SysTrust to examine performance of AIS. The term ICS has been used by COSO (1992) to refer to the risks associated with ineffectiveness management of public companies, both large and small. Integrated framework of COSO has long served as a blueprint for establishing internal controls that promote efficiency, minimize risks, and help check the reliability of financial statements, and comply with laws and regulations.

According to COSO's study, ICS is no longer an accounting concept. COSO"s report has outlined 26 fundamental principles associated with the five key components of ICS: (i) control environment, (ii) risk assessment, (iii) control activities, (iv) information and communication, and (v) monitoring. SACF (2001) considers the control objectives associated with use of IT. The study is widely known as COBIT. COBIT consists of three control groups: business objectives, IT resources, and IT-based process. The key feature of COBIT is coming from the fact that it developed 36 standards of control related to security of IT-based AIS. The study was conducted on more than 600 banks of the Italian banking industry. The study came with a conclusion that the intensive use of IT-based AIS has a reasonable impact on: (i) reduction in the cost of banking services, (ii) expansion of banking services package, and (iii) increasing banking profit. Another study was conducted by Raupeliene and Stabingis (2003) has considered the effectiveness of IT based AIS. The study has developed a quantitative model based on set of technological, economics, and social parameters.

Boritz (2005) conducts an extensive review of the literature to identify the key attributes of information integrity and related issues. He brought two focus groups of experienced practitioners to discuss the documented findings extracted from the literature review through a questionnaire that examining the core concepts of information integrity and it elements. Boritz (2005) considers information security as one of the core attributes to information integrity. This security should cover the following areas: Physical access controls and Logical access controls. The results indicated that the security has a lower impairment severity score than other severe practical aspects, such as availability and verifiability. Such findings of Boritz, pointed out the effective use of security controls in the organizations represented. In his study, Coe (2005) focuses on the fulfillment of Sarbanes-Oxley act 2002 that requires public companies to report about the effectiveness of their internal control systems Coe. The study explained also that the American companies are using COBIT for Sarbanes-Oxley act 2002 compliance, and this is because its objectives have been mapped to COSO in a publication entitled IT Control Objectives for Sarbanes-Oxley. COBIT also has been mapped to popular enterprise resource planning (ERP) systems, like SAP, Oracle and PeopleSoft.

This mapping and related guidance provides COBIT with framework references and methodologies for auditing and testing the major ERP systems. However, it is decided later to use SysTrust service to ensure the company's systems carry-out business processes reliably. Herein, Coe establishes five-step processes showing how the CPAs can use the trust service framework to evaluate a company's IT controls when the Entity primarily uses the COSO approach. These steps are: (i) Use COSO framework to identify the risks in each business cycle and the controls that mitigate them, (ii). Gather initial IT information, (iii) Identify all information systems that related to financial reporting. (iv) Use trust services framework to create one overall IT matrix, (v) Assess the controls identified in the matrixes created above. Martin (2005) mentioned the same steps in his study, in which he tried to explain how information system auditor can use the AICPA/CICA trust services framework to evaluate internal controls, particularly controls over information technology. The participants in the experiment were 481 middle and upper-level managers from a wide range of functional areas. The study concludes that auditor-provided assurances on information systems availability of security, integrity and maintainability will show significant key effects with respect to the probability of the participant entering into a contractual agreement with the ASP organization. In addition, the comfort level of the participant with the reliability of the ASP organization's ERP system will increase.

Also, Meharia (2011) aims to study the effects of assurance services and the trust in the mobile payment system on how users' use the system. To demonstrate this matter, the study depends on the Technology Acceptance Model (TAM). The study finds that the users' intention to use their attitude towards the system, determines their real use. Their attitude towards the system is decided by the apparent usefulness of the system and the simplicity of use. However, the study added that the assurance on the security, availability, confidentiality, privacy, and process integrity of the system will have a positive influence on the users' attitude towards the system, in combination with the apparent usefulness and simplicity of use. Also, from a security perspective, Siponen and Oinas-Kukkonen (2007) reconciled prior security research literature and emphasized the distinct importance of accessibility and availability as it relates to communication issues, like user authentication and appropriate maintenance of data retention. Strong *et al.* (1997) also segregated and highlighted the importance of accessibility as a determinant of data quality. In particular, they emphasized the importance of access security and timely availability to data. Likewise, Nelson *et al.* (2005) argued that accessibility that represents a system attribute, is distinct but similar in importance to the system's ability to produce reliable data, although they argued that this impact of accessibility is come in the second ranking in terms of influence on the system's processing reliability. Consequently, it is apparent that system assurance has a positive influence on system users, their reliance and, therefore, on their decisions, particularly when this assurance is provided constantly, which is more suitable according to the present inconstant environment. In reviewing the literature, it can be seen that Certified Public Accountants (CPAs) can provide assurance on RTA Information Systems. CPAs are accepted as independent parties that provide assurance concerning the accuracy and fairness of financial information. Also, CPAs are well-informed about the subject matter to be assured and the assurance matters, recognized for their independence, objectivity and reliability (Boritz & Hunton, 2002), and acquire advanced technical competencies (Burton *et al.*, 2012).

Experimental work indicates that there would be demand for both WebTrust (Hunton *et al.*, 2000; Lala *et al.*, 2002) and SysTrust (Boritz & Hunton, 2002) in the marketplace. Yet, as Bedard *et al.* (2005) note, there are a lot of issues, questions and risks in SysTrust engagements, and most auditors are leery about delving into the ill-defined arena of systems reliability assurance. Only limited researches to date has looked at ways in which to improve and deliver systems reliability assurance. Havelka *et al.* (1998) conducted a series of focus groups with systems development teams in order to establish criteria for assessing the quality of the information. Arnold *et al.* (2000) explore the market demand for graded reporting of systems quality versus use of a traditional auditor's binary reporting model. These studies represent the first incremental steps in understanding systems reliability assurance. The domain is wide, open, and in great need of additional research. While SysTrust provides some broad criteria that must be considered in assessing systems reliability, little is known about how to go about assessing these criteria effectively. Given the major role that IT systems play, particularly in enterprise systems environments, the profession must rapidly advance its ability to assess systems quality and academic researchers need to step forward to help in answering difficult questions that till to-date form barriers to widespread systems reliability assurance efforts.

Internal control weaknesses will lead to fragile accuracy and validity of financial data; and therefore; will weaken the quality of financial reporting. Weak financial data processed by the AIS will produce unreliable financial statements that cannot be relied on in making decisions by third parties, so that the later will use another reliable source for decision making (Costelo & Wittenberg, 2010). While Hall (2011) states internal control helped managers and accountants to prevent fraud and errors. Fraud occurs because of a violation of the rules and regulations. The error occurs due to lack of supervision including errors in financial reporting. Internal controls significantly affect investment decisions. Grant, *et al*., (2008) have examined the impact of IT deficiencies on financial reporting and determined significant differences between the companies that report IT deficiencies and the companies that do not report IT deficiencies. Four accounting errors: revenue recognition issues; receivables, investments and cash issues; inventory, vendor and cost of sales issues; and financial statement, footnote, US GAAP, and segment disclosures issues stand out as common financial reporting problems in companies found with weak IT controls. The study revealed that companies with IT control deficiencies report and high internal control (IC) deficiencies, are smaller, pay higher audit fees, and are typically audited by smaller accounting firms.

After reviewing the previous studies, in this specific area of research, relating to reliability of AIS control systems and the quality of financial reporting, it can be observed that there are not enough studies available, and this could be due to the fact that this area of research is reasonably new. In addition, many of the studies in this subject are administered on a small level and connected with combined studies from the fields of business management and, computer science. They are often in the form of reports or descriptive studies, and rarely experimental. To summarize, there is a lack of academic literature on the issues of trust services and its influence on the quality of financial reporting. It should also be noted that some of the investigations are conducted in isolation, without benefit from the findings of other studies.

3. Conceptual framework

Theoretical background and empirical studies on the SysTrust's framework as an internal control for assuring the reliability of AIS as well as the relevant theoretical literature on the quality of financial reporting were reviewed and integrated to develop a conceptual framework to guide this study. According to the existing frameworks on IS and accounting management (Dehning & Richardson 2002; DeLone & McLean 2003; Gable *et al.*, 2008), the quality of financial reporting is proposed to be influenced by the implementation of SysTrust's framework (principles and criteria) as an internal control of AIS process. Understanding the critical principles influencing financial quality reporting will assist organizations to improve the reliability of their financial data. Inadequate financial reporting quality will cause a lot of business operations to run inefficiently, and perform less in accordance with the demands and needs of the stakeholders. Supposedly, in order to anticipate these conditions, businesses must have reliable software and databases in generating quality information (Al-Dmour *et al.*, 2018). However, the effect of the reliability of AIS upon the quality of financial reporting has been given little attention in previous studies. The model proposed here is used to investigate whether better reliability of AIS control process by the implementation of SysTrust's framework (i.e., availability, security, processing integrity, confidentiality and privacy) would enhance the quality of financial reporting and to isolate those principles and criteria that are highly associated with the quality of financial reporting. The expected relationships of the implementation of the SysTrust principles and the quality of financial reporting are depicted in (Figure 1).

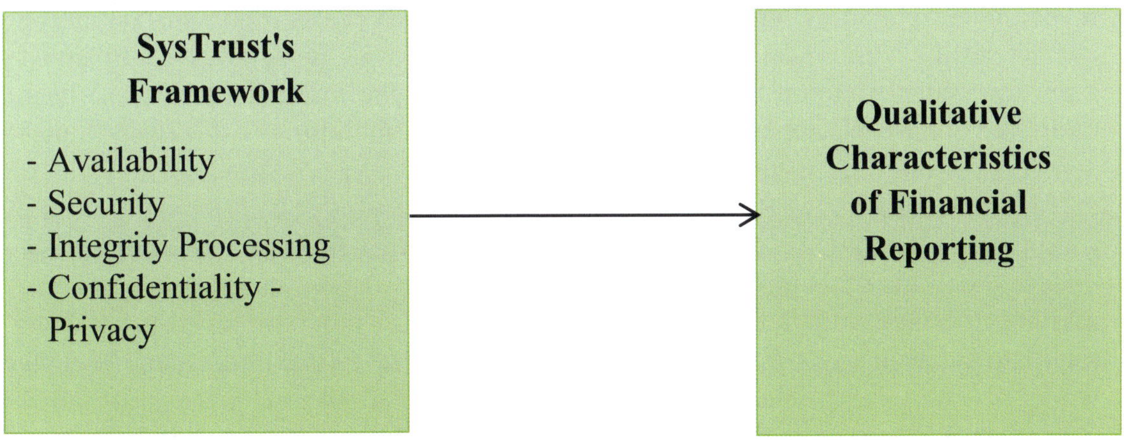

Figure 1. The Study's Proposed Conceptual Framework

The major constructs of the study's model are presented below with brief discussion. Furthermore, the expected relationship among these constructs are clearly defined and discussed throughout the presentation of each construct.

3.1 The quality of financial reporting

Kieso *et al.* (2016) defined the financial reporting as the process of presenting business financial statements in the form of financial report for both internal and external stakeholders of the company. Ramdany (2015) proposed the same concept by adding that it also includes initial recording and rating all business activities, especially financial transactions, then the reporting phase of these activities come up in order to present them to stakeholders. The primary objective of financial reporting is to provide high-quality financial reporting information concerning economic entities, primarily financial in nature, useful for economic decision making (FASB, 1999; IASB, 2008). Providing high quality financial reporting information is important because it will positively influence capital providers and other stakeholders in making investment, credit, and similar resource allocation decisions enhancing overall market efficiency (IASB, 2006; IASB, 2008). Many previous researches and literatures depended on using many measurement tools for examining financial reporting quality, ED (IASB, 2008), for example, stated that fundamental and qualitative characteristics such as relevance and faithful representation of information are one of the most important used tools, they depend on underling decision usefulness as a measuring tool for examining financial reporting quality. Other examples of these characteristics are comparability, verifiability, understandability, and timeliness, which also considered as critical tools for examining the content of financial reporting information, which in turn improves decision usefulness (IASB, 2010).

Many studies have been taken place in this field. Based on the above mentioned facts; the current study will depend on the seven point rating scales of qualitative characteristics mentioned on ED (IASB, 2008) to assess the quality of financial reporting except timeliness characteristic. To assure the internal validity of these items, the quality measures are built on prior empirical literature. Table (2) provides an overview of the 21 measured items used to operationalize the fundamental and to enhance the qualitative characteristics. The current study will depend on the following qualitative characteristics: relevance, faithful representation, understandability and comparability by totalize the scores on the related items and dividing it by the total number of items. These measures are employed in order to facilitate the comparison between the findings of using it and the findings of previous works in this field. Here are some brief explanations of these qualitative characteristics:

1. Relevance: IASB (2008) defines relevance as the capability of making a difference in decisions made by users on their capacity as capital providers. Relevance is usually operationalized in terms of predictive and confirmatory value (Beest *et al.*, 2009).

2. Faithful Representation: Faithful representation means that all information listed in financial report must be represented faithfully, IASB, (2006) stated that in order to accomplish this; all information and economic phenomena listed in annual reports must be complete, accurate, neutral, and free from bias and errors.
3. Understandability: Understandability is referred to the process of classifying, characterizing, categorizing, then presenting the financial information clearly and concisely, for (IASB, 2008) understandability means assuring financial information transparency and clearness, this process needs referring to some financial measures.
4. Comparability: Comparability means the ability the information has in explaining and identifying similarities in and differences between two common sets or transactions of economic phenomena (IASB, 2008: 39). According to the ED, comparability could be arrived by attaining consistent information by companies, this could happen by enforcing the company to use the same accounting policies and procedures, either from period to period within an entity or in a single period across entities (IASB, 2008: 39). Comparability refers to the users' ability to make comparisons over time between different financial statements of a certain entity and those of other entities (Alfredson *et al.*, 2007).
5. Timeliness: The last enhancing qualitative characteristic discussed in the IASB (2010) conceptual framework is timeliness. The framework defines timeliness as having information available to decision makers before it loses its capacity to influence decisions (IASB, 2010). In specific terms, timeliness relates to the decision usefulness of financial reports. It refers to the time it takes to reveal the information in annual reports. It is usually measured in terms of the number of days it takes for the auditor to sign the accounts after book-year end.

3.2 The SysTrust's principles

According to the AICPA, SysTrust's framework is an assurance service that independently tests and verifies a system's reliability. It is assumed that any system meets the SysTrust principles should be viewed as being more reliable and thus be trusted more than anyone that does not. In other words, trust in the system of specific provider is influenced by the extent to which the system meets the SysTrust principles. It is referred to as trust in system reliability in this study. According to the AICPA, SysTrust is an assurance service that independently tests and verifies a system's reliability. The five fundamental components (principles) that contribute to the overall objective of the system reliability and related measures are: availability, security, integrity processing, confidentiality and privacy. These SysTrust's principles and criteria are designed to be complete, relevant, objective, and measurable and to address all of the system components and the relationships among them. In some cases, for evidence-gathering purposes, the criteria may need to be broken down. For example, either to be broken down by system component to address infrastructure, software, people, procedures, and data or can be broken down by system development phase which includes investigation, acquisition, implementation, operation, and maintenance.

Based upon the study's conceptual framework, the study hypotheses are formulated and proposed as summarized below:

Ho1: The SysTrust's Framework (i.e. five principles: availability, security, integrity data processing, confidentiality, and privacy) are significantly implemented among business organizations.

Ho2: There is a significant relationship between the implementation of SysTrust's framework (i.e., availability, security, integrity data processing, confidentiality, and privacy) and the quality of financial reporting.

4. Research methodology

In order to obtain the empirical data needed to validate the study's conceptual model and examine the research hypotheses, a self –administrated questionnaire was used to collect the required data. The target respondents were the shareholding companies in Jordan and the single key respondents approach was used. The key respondents were financial or accounting managers and financial directors. The identification of the individual business organizations in the country (Jordan) could be done by obtaining names of all companies, as well as their addresses, from a variety of private and public sources in order to identify the type of business sector, and the range of the number of companies in each sector. Restrictions of time and financial resources could make the inclusion of all business companies impossible. Therefore, the target population is only limited to the shareholding companies listed in Amman Stock Exchange Market database. Table 1 gives the demographics of the population and number of respondents by sector.

Table 1. Study's Respondents

Type of Sector	No. of companies	No. of respondents	Percentages
Service	202	162	80
Industries	126	77	61
Total	328	239	73

Sources: ase.com.jo 2016

A total of 328 self-administered questionnaires were distributed to the respondents by e-mail, postal, and hand from and the response rate was 73% after a period of sixteen weeks and two follow-up reminders. 80% of the respondents were from service sector. Initially, research assistants called the companies to have appointments to distribute copies of the questionnaire to their companies. Researchers have gained support from several official bodies in collecting data and motivating companies to response and collaboration including University of Brunel, Chamber of Commerce, Jordanian bank Association, Ministry of Higher Education and Ministry of Industry and Commerce. After respondents answered the questions, the assistants collected te copies from them. In editing stage, the responses were reviewed for completeness and 16 questionnaires were eliminated because the respondents either failed to respond to all item measures for latent constructs used in this study or responded "no basis for answering" to some of the item measures. In this survey, some variables are factual (for example, companies' demographic information such as the type of sector), whereas others are perceptual (for instance, SysTrust principles, the quality of financial reporting). The dependent variables (i.e., the quality of financial reporting) and the independent variables (the extent of the implementation of SysTrust principles) were measured using a seven–point Likert scale.

5. Data results & discussion

5.1 Descriptive statistics

All the 95 items (70 items for SysTrust and 25 items for quality of financial reporting) were tested for their means, standard deviations, skewness, and kurtosis. The descriptive statistics presented below in Table 2 indicate a positive disposition towards the items. While the standard deviation (SD) values ranged from 0.99458 to 1.198, these values indicate a narrow spread around the mean. Also, the mean values of all items were greater than the midpoint (4) and ranged from 5.09 (A7) to 5.58 (S10). However, after careful assessment by using skewness and kurtosis, the data were found to be normally distributed. Indeed, skewness and kurtosis were normally distributed since most of the values were inside the adequate ranges for normality (i.e. -1.0 to +1.0) for skewness, and less than 10 for kurtosis (Byrne, 2010; Black *et al.*, 2010; Kline, 2010).

Table 2. Mean, Standard Deviation, and Normality of Scale Items

Construct /items		Mean	S.D	Skewness	Kurtosis
1	**The Quality of Financial Reporting**				
	1.Relevance				
R1	The annual reports disclose forward-looking information to help forming expectations and predictions concerning the future of the company	5.5260	1.18965	-0.930-	0.791
R2	The annual reports disclose information in terms of business opportunities and risks	5.4306	1.12267	-0.771-	0.338
R3	The company uses fair value instead of historical cost.	5.4566	1.18914	-0.973-	0.708
R4	Information helps you confirm profitability levels of the business	5.4162	1.19184	-0.559-	-0.402-
R5	Financial reports are presented annually as required by regulatory bodies of accounting	5.4075	1.08420	-0.755-	0.328
R6	No un due delays in the presentation of financial reports.	5.4942	1.11445	-0.813-	0.376

Construct /items		Mean	S.D	Skewness	Kurtosis
R7	The annual report provides feedback information on how various market events and significant transactions affected the company	5.4191	1.18717	-0.522-	-0.498-
	2. Faithful Representation				
F1	The annual report explains the assumptions and estimates made clearly; valid arguments provided to support the decision for certain assumptions and estimates in the annual report	5.1705	1.05904	-0.743-	0.734
F2	The annual report explains the choice of accounting principles clearly	5.0405	1.08405	-0.534-	0.040
F3	The annual report highlights the positive and negative events in a balanced way when discussing the annual results	5.0491	1.08503	-0.509-	-0.139-
F4	The annual report includes an unqualified auditor's report	5.2399	1.13072	-0.724-	0.446
F5	The annual report extensively discloses information on corporate governance issues	5.1590	1.09048	-0.495-	-0.264-
	3.Understandability				
U1	The annual report presented in a well-organized manner	5.3121	1.01623	-0.423-	-0.149-
U2	The notes to the balance sheet and the income statement are s sufficiently clear	5.3497	1.10949	-0.584-	-0.144-
U3	Sources and level of expenditure can easily be understood	5.3699	1.00815	-0.503-	0.586
U4	Business assets are easy to be identified in terms of value and nature	5.3410	1.08181	-0.573-	-0.044-
U5	the presence of graphs and tables clarifies the presented information	5.364	1.02167	-0.449-	0.462
U6	The use of language and technical jargon is easy to follow in the annual report	5.3491	1.08572	-0.593-	-0.059-
U7	The annual report include a comprehensive glossary	5.3035	1.04276	-0.432-	-0.080
	4.Comparability				
C1	The notes to changes in accounting policies explain the implications of the change	5.2023	1.10051	-0.473-	0.231
C2	The notes to revisions in accounting estimates and judgments explain the implications of the revision	5.2370	1.09089	-0.576-	-0.090-
C3	The company's previous accounting period's figures are adjusted for the effect of the implementation of a change in accounting policy or revisions in accounting estimates	5.2543	1.04897	-0.478-	0.135

Construct /items		Mean	S.D	Skewness	Kurtosis
C4	The results of current accounting period are compared with results in previous accounting periods	5.2341	1.13704	-0.624-	0.150
C5	Information in the annual report is comparable to information provided by other organizations	5.2688	1.15219	-0.517-	-0.138-
C6	The annual report presents financial index numbers and ratios.	5.2312	1.19843	-0.647-	0.130
2.	**SysTrust Principles**				
	1. Availability				
A1	The system availability requirements of authorized users, and system availability objectives, policies, and standards, are identified and documented.	5.1908	1.3741	-0.880-	0.272
A2	The entity's system availability are periodically reviewed and approved by authorized people.	5.1821	1.1641	-0.825-	0.852
A3	A formal process exists to identify and review contractual, legal, and other service-level agreements and applicable laws and regulations that could impact system availability objectives, policies, and standards.	5.1879	1.0991	-0.786-	0.800
A4	There are procedures to ensure that personnel responsible for the design, development, implementation, and operation of system availability features are qualified to fulfill their responsibilities.	5.2428	1.1262	-0.820-	1.124
A5	Management has assigned responsibilities for the maintenance and enforcement of the entity's availability policies to the CIO.	5.0000	1.1446	-0.560-	0.472
A6	The entity's user training program includes modules dealing with the identification and reporting of system availability issues, security breaches, and other incidents.	5.1705	1.2311	-0.863-	0.658
A7	Employees are trained to make substitute copies of the programs.	5.0145	1.1381	-0.752-	1.150
A8	Employees are trained on special procedures concerning reducing the time of system's stop as possible.	5.0983	1.1250	-0.674-	0.737
A9	There is a formal communication of system availability objectives, policies, and standards to authorized users through means such as memos, meetings, and manuals.	5.1879	1.0778	-0.743-	1.046
A10	The firm makes preventive maintenance to the computerized	5.1040	1.0717	-0.308-	-0.003-

Construct /items		Mean	S.D	Skewness	Kurtosis
	information system periodically and regularly.				
A11	The firm adopts policies and procedures for fast dealing with computerized accounting information system's mistakes to achieve a continuous availability to the system.	5.2110	1.0378	-0.385-	0.003
A12	Procedures are existed to provide backup, offsite storage, restoration, and disaster recovery consistent with the entity's defined system availability and related security policies	5.1329	1.0438	-0.530-	0.214
A13	Environmental protections, software, data backup processes, and recovery infrastructure are designed, developed, implemented, operated, monitored, and maintained to meet availability commitments and requirements	5.0954	1.0493	-0.570-	0.605
	2. Security				
S1	The firm's security policies have approved and documented the security requirements of authorized users.	5.6445	1.1128	-.0786-	0.383
S2	The entity's system security is periodically reviewed and compared with the defined system security policies	5.5462	1.0656	-0.620-	0.243
S3	The firm's has classified the data on the basis of its criticality and sensitivity and kept in the main devices.	5.6416	1.1491	-0.661-	0.055
S4	The firm uses appropriate procedures to separate duties, tools and functions of the system's administration from net administration	5.6705	1.1350	-0.774-	0.174
S5	A security awareness program has been implemented to communicate the entity's IT security policies to employees	5.5376	1.1844	-0.685-	0.089
S6	Personnel receive training and development in system security concepts and issues.	5.5145	1.1502	-0.708-	0.464
S7	Major computers are kept in closed place and the authorized people are allowed to access in to it.	5.5087	1.2092	-0.757-	0.420
S8	Physical access to the computer rooms, which house the entity's IT resources, servers, and related hardware such as firewalls and	5.6676	1.1556	-0.821-	0.339

Construct /items		Mean	S.D	Skewness	Kurtosis
	routers, is restricted to authorized individuals by card key systems and monitored by video surveillance.				
S9	Requests for physical access privileges to the entity's computer facilities require the approval of the manager of computer operations.	5.5867	1.1110	-0.583-	-0.161-
S10	Documented procedures are existed for the identification and escalation of potential physical security breaches.	5.5896	1.1160	-0.837-	0.489
S11	Firewall events are logged and reviewed daily by the security ad- Unneeded network services (for example, telnet, ftp, and http) are deactivated on the entity's servers...	5.5694	1.1380	-0.973-	0.972
S12	the firm uses physical selector as fingerprints or eyes' to access into data Firewalls are used and configured to prevent unauthorized access	5.5751	1.1300	1.109-	2.063
S13	The entity uses industry standard encryption technology, VPN software, or other secure communication systems (consistent with its periodic IT risk assessment) for the transmission of private or confidential information over public networks, including user IDs and passwords.	5.5376	1.1164	-0.836-	0.850
S14	The firm takes suitable steps to protect the main devices by keeping them away from danger and in fire resistant places	5.4191	1.2946	-0.897-	1.167
S15	Personal computers are programmed to be locked electronically after finishing work with a limited period of time.	5.5751	1.1948	1.040-	1.257
S16	The firm takes special control procedures to prevent transferring the computers outside	5.4595	1.1470	-1.048-	1.855
S17	Updating continuously the antivirus software used in the computerized systems.	5.4566	1.1291	-1.016-	1.892
S18	Logical access security measures have been implemented to protect against unauthorized	5.5058	1.1144	-0.741-	0.960
	3. Integrity Processing				
Ig1	The entity's processing integrity and related security policies are established and periodically reviewed and approved by a designated individual or group	5.3728	1.0562	-0.998-	1.492
Ig2	Firm's' administration develops procedures to make sure f the	5.2225	.98373	-0.973-	1.603

Construct /items		Mean	S.D	Skewness	Kurtosis
	completion and accuracy of documents that represent sources of data.				
Ig3	There are special tests to make sure of the integration of input data to check data validity before processing	5.1821	1.0921	-0.971-	1.395
Ig4	Fields' frequency and their capacity are reviewed, high and low limits are examined to check the reliability and accuracy of the inputs	5.1445	1.07781	-0.933-	1.042
Ig5	Data is inserted by authorized people	5.1532	1.0644	-0.875-	1.389
Ig6	Make sure of the computer's response to every item of the input	5.1734	1.0489	-0.807-	1.395
Ig7	Computerized accounting information systems include a pointer appeared as a message whenever something wrong happened in input process.	5.2428	1.0922	-0.695-	0.502
Ig8	Make periodically the settlements' procedures between sub accounts computerized information systems.	5.3208	1.0034	-0.435-	0.320
Ig9	Files of data are named with appropriate names.	5.2081	1.0591	-0.468-	0.160
Ig10	All the system's outputs are revised in terms of logic and formation accuracy	5.2399	1.0565	-0.521-	0.253
Ig11	The compatibility between inputs and outputs are reviewed daily	5.2919	1.0264	-0.722-	0.357
Ig12	Computer's reports are distributed into the appropriate users	5.1908	.97119	-0.543-	0.517
Ig13	The sensitive outputs are protected from unauthorized access	5.1936	1.0215	-0.789-	0.644
Ig14	Any mistake in the outputs is corrected when it is discovered.	5.1994	.97094	-0.428-	0.306
Ig15	There are control procedures for protecting information when they are transferred via nets as coding and checking of the transmission.	5.1965	.94583	-0.795-	0.730
Ig16	System output is complete, accurate, distributed, and retained in accordance with processing integrity commitments and requirements.	5.2283	.98828	-0.580-	0.362
Ig17	Procedures exist to prevent, detect, and correct processing errors to meet processing integrity commitments and requirements	5.2023	1.0437	-0.367-	-0.360-
	4. Confidentiality				
C1	The entity's system confidentiality and related requirements are established and periodically reviewed and approved by a designated individual or group.	5.2746	1.0368	-0.428-	-0.059-

Construct /items		Mean	S.D	Skewness	Kurtosis
C2	The system confidentiality and requirements are communicated to authorized users.	5.3092	1.0410	-0.693-	0.421
C3	The entity publishes its confidentiality and related security policies on its corporate intranet.	5.1474	1.0974	-0.838-	1.083
C4	The security administration team has custody of and is responsible for the day-to-day maintenance of the entity's confidentiality and related security policies and recommends changes to the CIO and the IT steering committee	5.2197	1.1860	-0.506-	-0.160-
C5	The process for informing the entity about breaches of confidentiality and system security and for submitting complaints is communicated to authorized users.	5.2168	1.1199	-0.759-	0.700
C6	Error messages are revealed to authorized personnel	5.1647	1.1339	-0.615-	-0.016-
C7	Confidentiality processes are existed to restrict the capability to input information to only authorized individuals.	5.2081	1.1125	-0.609-	0.081
C8	Management has developed a reporting strategy that includes the sensitivity and confidentiality of data and appropriateness of user access to output data	5.2572	1.0633	-0.659-	0.398
C9	Employees are required to sign a confidentiality oath as a routine part of their employment. This agreement prohibits any disclosures of information and other data to which the employee has been granted access to.	5.1272	1.1272	-0.887-	1.312
C10	Logical access controls are in place that limit access to confidential information based on job function and need.	5.2659	1.1053	-0.917-	1.496
C11	Requests for access privileges to confidential data require the approval of the data owner. Business partners are subject to nondisclosure agreements or other contractual confidentiality provisions.	5.2775	1.0650	-0.630-	.157
C12	Access to confidential information from outside the boundaries of the system and disclosure of confidential information is restricted to authorized parties in accordance with	5.2743	1.1368	-0.427-	-0.069-

Construct /items		Mean	S.D	Skewness	Kurtosis
	confidentiality commitments and requirements.				
	5. Privacy				
P1	The entity defines documents, communicates, and assigns accountability for its privacy policies and procedures.	5.2775	1.0650	-0.630-	0.157
P2	The entity provides notice about its privacy policies and procedures and identifies the purposes for which personal information is collected, used, retained, and disclosed	5.2283	1.0940	-0.730-	0.581
P3	The entity describes the choices available to the individual and obtains implicit or explicit consent with respect to the collection, use, and disclosure of personal information.	5.2457	1.1243	-0.791-	0.526
P4	The entity collects personal information only for the purposes identified in the notice	5.1792	1.1432	-0.754-	0.337
P5	The entity limits the use of personal information to the purposes identified in the notice and for which the individual has provided implicit or explicit consent. The entity retains personal information for only as long as necessary to fulfill the stated purpose	5.2659	1.1053	-0.917-	1.496
P6	The entity provides individuals with access to their personal information for review and update.	5.2572	1.0982	-0.960-	1.477
P7	The entity discloses personal information to third parties only for the purposes identified in the notice and with the implicit or explicit consent of the individual	5.2225	1.1744	-1.023-	1.279
P8	The entity protects personal information against unauthorized access (both physical and logical).	5.1850	1.1166	-0.609-	0.170
P9	The entity maintains accurate, complete, and relevant personal information for the purposes identified in the notice.	5.2659	1.1001	-0.910-	1.100
P10	The entity monitors compliance with its privacy policies and procedures and has procedures to address privacy-related complaints and disputes	5.1272	1.1272	-0.887-	1.312

5.2 Measurement model validation

This study is applying the Structural Equation Modelling (SEM) technique in order to test and validate the proposed relations among the constructs in the study's conceptual framework. A two-stage approach of the SEM (measurement model and structural model) was employed to analyses the empirical data. By running AMOS21, the model fitness and constructs' reliability and validity were assessed in stage one (the measurement model) by means of the confirmatory factor analyses (CFA). This is followed by a structural model assessment which related to the validation of the conceptual model proposed and the testing of the causal paths between the main independent (exogenous) and dependent factors (endogenous). The main independent constructs (exogenous) is the components of SysTrust's framework: (1) availability, (2) security (3) processing integrity, (4) confidentiality, and (5) privacy, while the independent factor is the quality of financial reporting (endogenous) in the conceptual model. All of these constructs were subjected together to both the measurement model and the structural model analysis and the results are presented under the following subsections.

5.2.1 Measurement model: confirmatory factor analysis

The confirmatory factor analyses (CFA) was employed to initially evaluate the measurement model's fitness (unidimensionality), and then measure the constructs' reliability and validity. It is also worth mentioning that the quality financial reporting was considered as a second-order construct. In this regard, relevance, faithful representation, comparability, and understandability as the main constructs for the quality financial reporting and these dimensions represent first-order factors measured through their own observed factors (items). The second-order of the confirmatory factor analyses (CFA) model fit was tested firstly for quality of financial reporting and noticed that it does not have adequate level of model fitness due to the fact that all some of indices do not capture values within their threshold levels ($\chi2 = 2767.336$, df = 204; and $\chi2/df = 13.565$),comparative fit index [CFI] = 0.756, goodness-of-fit index [GFI] = 0.678, incremental fit index [IFI] = 0.755, normed of fit indices [NFI]=0.70 and root mean square error of approximation [RMSEA] = 0.161), AGFI= 0.601 (Hu and Bentler, 1999). Therefore, there is room for some re-specifications and purification (Byrne, 2010).

Table 3. Model-second order Factor: Quality of Financial Reporting

Fit indices	Cut-off point	Initial measurement model	Modified measurement model
CMIN/DF	$\leq$3.000	13.565	1.808
GFI	$\geq$ 0.90	0.8687	0. 918
AGFI	$\geq$ 0.80	0.601	0. 887
NFI	$\geq$ 0.90	0.700	0. 959
CFI	$\geq$ 0.90	0.756	0. 973
RMSEA	$\leq$ 0.08	0.161	0. 071

Fundamentally, a refinement process followed a number of criteria to enhance the model's fitness including inspection of standardized regression weights (factor loading), modification indices, and standardized covariance matrix (Byrne, 2010; Hair *et al.*, 2010; Holmes-Smith *et al.*, 2006). By looking at standardized regression weights for each item, it was found that R4 (relevance), R6 (relevance), F2 (faithful representation), U3 (understandability), CC4 (Comparability) all have a value less than the cut-off value (>0.5), and accordingly, a decision was made to delete them. According to the modification indices' table, error terms of R7, U5, U7, and CC6 were found to have a higher error term value, and accordingly these items were deleted (Hooper *et al.*, 2008). By doing so, the CFA for the second order factor regarding the quality of financial reporting was tested again as suggested by Byrne (2010). The yielded fit indices indicted that the goodness of fit of the modified measurement model was adequately improved; all the fit indices this time were found within their recommended level as such: CMIN/DF was 2.720, GFI= 0.918, AGFI= 0.887, NFI= 0.959, CFI= 0.973 and RMSEA= 0.071 (see Table 3).

5.2.2 Model fitness for all constructs

A number of fit indices (CMIN/DF; GFI; AGFI; NFI; CFI; RMSEA) have been tested to ensure an adequate level of model goodness of fit to the data (Byrne, 2010; Hooper *et al.*, 2008). As seen in Figure (3), seven latent constructs [Availability, security, processing integrity, confidentiality, and privacy, quality of financial reporting] formed the measurement model and therefore are subjected to the confirmatory factor analysis (CFA). Furthermore, 88 indictors (items) were adopted to measure these latent constructs as illustrated in the research methodology. As shown in Table 4, the preliminary measurement fit indices were found as follows: chi-square (CMIN/DF= 2.323; GFI= 0.730; AGFI = 0.710, RMSEA= 0.062; NFI = 0.837; CFI = 0.900. Having a closer look at some of the fit indices (e.g. GFI, AGFI, NFI), the model does not seem to have adequate fit to data, and therefore, there is room for some re-specifications and purification (Byrne, 2010). Fundamentally, a refinement process followed a number of criteria to enhance the model's fitness beginning with inspection of standardized regression weights (factor loading), modification indices, and standardized covariance matrix (Byrne, 2010; Hair *et al.*, 2010).

Table 4. Results of Measurement Model all constructs

Fit indices	Cut-off point	Initial measurement model	Modified measurement model
CMIN/DF	≤ 3.000	2.232	1.892
GFI	≥ 0.90	0.730	0.901
AGFI	≥ 0.80	0.710	0.818
NFI	≥ 0.90	0.837	0.903
CFI	≥ 0.90	0.900	0.953
RMSEA	≤ 0.08	0.062	0.046

By doing so, the CFA was tested again as suggested by Byrne (2010) and Kline (2005) without problematic items. The yielded fit indices indicted that the goodness of fit of the modified measurement model was adequately improved; all the fit indices this time were found within their recommended level as such: (Chi-square minimum discrepancy/degree of freedom) CMIN/DF was 1.892,(Goodness- of- Fit Index) GFI= 0.901, (Adjusted goodness- of -Fit) AGFI= 0.818, (non-normed fit index) NFI= 0.903, (comparative fit index) CFI= 0.953 and (the root mean square error of approximation) RMSEA= 0.046 (see Table 4). Furthermore, the rest of the estimates were found within their recommended values; for instance, all remaining items were observed to have factors loading above the threshold value (>0.5). Standardized residual values were also found within the acceptable range of ±2.58 (Hair *et al.*, 2017). These fit indices collectively indicate that the overall fit of the measurement model is acceptable. Thus, there was no need to conduct any extra modifications or amendments in the measurement study's model (Byrne, 2010).

5.2.3 Reliability & validity

As shown in Table 5, all constructs were tested to ensure an adequate level of scales reliability using Cronbach's alpha, composite reliability (CR) and average variance extracted (AVE). Statistical findings in this regard indicated that all latent constructs have Cronbach's alpha **(α)** value above the cut-off point of 0.70 ranging between 0.965 for integrity processing and 0.965 for Security (Nunnally, 1978). By the same token, CR for all latent constructs existed within their respective level of 0.70 as reported by Hair *et al.* (2010). Table 5 indicates that while the highest CR (0.906) was noticed for the quality of financial reporting, the minimum value was exhibited by the availability of AIS (0.832). Moreover, as seen in Table 5, the AVE value of the latent constructs ranged from 0.555 availability to 0.709 quality of financial reporting, which all above the cut-off value of 0.50 as are recommended by Hair *et al.* (2017). Both convergent and discriminate validity were inspected to measure the constructs validity. Relating to the convergent validity, we note (Table 6) that all un-removable items had s significant standardized regression weight with their latent constructs above the cut-off value of 0.50 and were statistically significant with the *p* value less than 0.0001 (Hair *et al.*, 2017). By investigating the correlation among latent constructs, the highest value of inter-correlation estimates was less than 0.85 (Brown, 2006; Kline, 2005). Furthermore, as shown in Table 6 all latent constructs had squared root of AVE higher than the inter-correlation estimated as well as with other corresponding constructs. In light of these results, the model measures had attained an adequate level of convergent and discriminate validity.

Table 5. Composite Reliability and Average Variance Extracted

Constructs	Construct Reliability(CR)	Average Variance Extracted (AVE)	Cronbach's alpha (α)
Quality of Financial reporting	0.906	0.709	0.947
Confidentiality	0.879	0.646	0.948
Availability	0.832	0.555	0.943
Privacy	0.897.	0.686	0.962
Integrity Processing	0.873	0.633	0.931
Security	0.901	0.694	0.965

Table 6. Standardized Regression Weights

Items		Construct	Factor Loading	Items		Construct	Factor Loading
RE	<---	Quality	0.795	A1	<---	Availability	0.682
Fait	<---	Quality	0.912	A2	<---	Availability	0.850
Under	<---	Quality	0.753	A5	<---	Availability	0.764
Com	<---	Quality	0.897	A9	<---	Availability	0.670
R1	<---	Relevance	0.710	P3	<---	Privacy	0.815
R2	<---	Relevance	0.987	P4	<---	Privacy	0.871
R5	<---	Relevance	0.987	P6	<---	Privacy	0.818
R3	<---	Relevance	0.702	P7	<---	Privacy	0.807
F1	<---	Faith Rep.	0.786	IG2	<---	Integrity Processing	0.778
F3	<---	Faith Rep.	0.819	IG4	<---	Integrity Processing	0.858
F4	<---	Faith Rep.	0.811	IG6	<---	Integrity Processing	0.772
F5	<---	Faith Rep.	0.822	IG7	<---	Integrity Processing	0.771
U6	<---	Understand.	0.990	C3	<---	Confidentiality	0.768
U4	<---	Understand.	.0965	C4	<---	Confidentiality	0.863
U2	<---	Understand.	0.998	C6	<---	Confidentiality	0.789
CC3	<---	Comparability	0.857	C7	<---	Confidentiality	0.792
CC2	<---	Comparability	0.830	S3	<---	Security	0.828
CC1	<---	Comparability	0.832	S5	<---	Security	0.874
CC5	<---	Comparability	.0796	S6	<---	Security	0.843
				S7	<---	Security	0.785

Table 7. Discriminant Validity

Constructs	QFR	Confidentiality	Availability	Privacy	Integrity Processing	Security
QFR	**0.842**					
Confidentiality	0.790	**0.804**				
Availability	0.567	0.620	**0.745**			

Constructs	QFR	Confidentiality	Availability	Privacy	Integrity Processing	Security
Privacy	0.805	0.789	0.566	**0.828**		
Integrity Processing	0.671	0.629	0.633	0.660	**0.796**	
Security	0.601	0.664	0.696	0.568	0.672	**0.833**

5.2.4 Structural model and hypotheses testing

The structural model is used to validate the conceptual model and test the research hypotheses (Byrne, 2010; Hair *et al.*, 2010). An inspection of structural model was conducted with 9 causal paths between independent factors (exogenous factors) and dependent factors (endogenous factors). As summarized in Table 6, the main statistical results indicated all the fit indices of the structural model were found to be within their threshold values as such CMIN/DF was 1.970, GFI= 0.903, AGFI= 0.807, NFI= 0.901, CFI= 0.954 and RMSEA= 0.053. Thus, suggesting that structural model adequately fit the data. Moreover, statistical results largely supported the conceptual model via explaining 74 per cent of variance in quality of financial reporting.

Table 8. Fit Indices of Structural Model

Fit indices	Cut of point	Model fit
CMIN/DF	**≤3.000**	1.970
GFI	**≥ 0.90**	0.903
AGFI	**≥ 0.80**	0.807
NFI	**≥ 0.90**	0.90
CFI	**≥ 0.90**	0.954
RMSEA	**≤ 0.08**	0.053

With regard to the path coefficients analyses, the coefficient values of the paths ending to quality of financial reporting including: Processing Integrity of AIS (γ=0.29, p<0.0159); Confidentiality (γ=0.400, p<0.000); and Privacy (γ=-0.397, p<0.000) security (γ=0.2705, p=0.046) and Availability of AIS (γ=-0.2911, p<0.030) and quality of financial reporting were found to be statistically significant. This result is supported by Konrath, 2002), Ricchiute, 2006,). Daneilia, (2013), and Toposh (2014). In summary, the magnitude and significance of the loading estimates indicate that all of these five principles of SysTrust are relevant in predicating the quality of financial reporting. Moreover, the reliability of AIS by implementation of these five principles of SysTrust have significant impact on the quality of financial reporting, as the structural coefficient for these paths are significant. Thus, in order to enhance the quality of financial reporting, companies should fully implement all these main requirements of SysTrust; s framework (principles and criteria).

6. Contributions and implications

This study has extended the understanding of the practice and implementation of the main constructs of the SysTrust's framework (Availability, Security, Integrity processing, Confidentiality and Privacy) as an internal control method for assuring the reliability of AIS by testing the phenomenon in a new environment. In the literature review, it was pointed out that most of the researches in this area were conducted in developed countries. To the best knowledge of the researchers, the implementation of the SysTrust and its relationship with the quality of financial reporting as proposed in this study has never been investigated in Jordan or any other developing countries, particularly within MENA. This study contributes to the existing body of knowledge by enhancing current understanding of importance of the implementation of the SysTrust's framework requirements (functions, policies, procedures and criteria) as internal control system for assessing AIS reliability, which is an under-researched area in Jordan as a developing country. However, explanations of several findings mentioned above, indicate the importance of contextual factors within organizations and its environment. By highlighting the significance of several contextual factors, this study also hopes to expand the focus of SysTrust's principles.

This study provides some insights into the implementation of SysTrus's framework by Jordanian shareholding companies, which should help accounting managers, auditors and practitioners, acquire a better understanding of the current SysTrust's principles implementation status and the importance of its relationship with the quality of financial reporting. The present study has many important implications for accounting managers, auditors and financial practitioners and top managers in the surveyed companies and in similar organizations. The authors believe that the decision-makers of business organizations could benefit from this study's findings by achieving better understanding of implementation of the SysTrust's framework requirements for assuring the reliability of AIS (functions, policies, procedures and criteria) as well as its influence upon the level of quality of financial reporting. This might help them in implementing the required actions and important changes within their organizations. Decision-makers should also be aware of the important of each principle of the SysTrust's framework and its major requirements that highly related to the quality of financial reporting, so that they can make the right decision and directions for any change within their organizations. All the principles of the SysTrust are relevant and should be emphasized. The reliability of AIS in shareholdings companies should be enhanced by the implementation of all the principles of SysTrust's framework (availability, security, confidentiality, integrity processing and privacy). The indicators for each SysTrust's principle suggest how that principle should be impacted by management action.

However, this study has several limitations that should be considered when evaluating and generalizing its conclusions. However, the limitations discussed below can provide a starting point for future research. The study was conducted in one country, Jordan. Although Jordan is a valid indicator of prevalent factors in the wider MENA region and developing countries, the lack of external validity of this research means that any generalizations of the research findings should be taken with caution. Future research can be orientated in other national and cultural settings and compared with the results of this study. The data analysis was cross-sectional. As with all cross sectional studies, the parameters tended to be static rather than dynamic. This drawback limits the generalization of the study's findings to further situations and beyond the specific population from which the data was gathered. Future longitudinal studies could provide a better understanding of the implementation of AIS over time. The study used the multiple informant approach for data collections. This approach might not provide the consistent view about the organization. However, by using single informant approach in future research, the problem of consistent responses should be solved.

References

AICPA (1999) CPA SysTrust: assuring reliability of systems. AICPA, New York

AICPA (2000) "Assurance Services– Definition and Interpretive Commentary", available online at http://www.aicpa.org/assurance/scas/comstud/defincom /index.tm

AICPA/CICA (2006) "Trust Services Principles, Criteria and Illustrations for Security, Availability, Processing Integrity, Confidentiality, and Privacy (Including WebTrust and SysTrust)", American Institute of Certified Public Accountants and Canadian Institute of Chartered Accountants, available at: www.webtrust.org/principles-and-criteria/item27818

AICPA (2013) National Conference on Current SEC and PCAOB Developments http://www.aicpa.org/assurance/scas/comstud/defincom/index.htm

AICPA (2017) Trust Services Criteria, AICPA Publishing

Al-Dmour, A, Abbod, M. & Al-Dmour, H. (2018) "The implementation of SysTrust principles and criteria for assuring reliability of AIS: empirical study", *International Journal of Accounting and Information Management*, Vol. 26 iss. 3, *in press*

Arnold, V., Lampe, J., Masselli, J. & Sutton, S. (2000) "An analysis of the market for systems reliability assurance services", *Journal of Information Systems*, vol. 14: 65-82 [Supplement]

Azhar, S. (2004) *Management Information Systems*, 3rd Edition, Linga Jakarta, Bandung

Bedard, J.C., Jackson, C.M. & Graham, L. (2005) "Issues and risks in performing SysTrust engagements: implications for research and practice", *International Journal of Accounting Information Systems*, Vol. 6: 55-79

Bharath, S.T., Sunder, J. & Sunder, S.V. (2006) "Accounting quality and debt contracting", *The Accounting Review*, vol. 83(1): 1-28

Boritz, E. & Hunton, J. (2002) "Investigating the impact of auditor-provided systems reliability assurance on potential service recipients", *Journal of Information Systems, Supplement*, Vol. 16: 69-88

Boritz, E., Mackler, E. & McPhie, D. (1999) "Reporting on systems reliability", *Journal of Accountancy*, Vol. 188, Issue 5: 75-83

Boritz, J.E. & Kearns, J. H (2000) "1999 Symposium in IS assurance panel discussion on SysTrust", *Journal of Information Systems*, Vol. 14 No 1: 163-176

Boritz, J.E. (2005) "IS practitioners' view on core concepts of information integrity", *International Journal of Accounting Information Systems*, Vol. 6: 260-279

Botosan, C. (2004) "Discussion of a framework for the analysis of risk communication", *The International Journal of Accounting*, vol. 39: 289-295

Brown, T. A. (2006) *Confirmatory factor analysis for applied research*, New York, NY: Guilford Press

Burton, F., Emett, S., Simon, C. & Wood, D. (2012) "Corporate managers' reliance on internal auditor recommendations", *Auditing: A Journal of Practice & Theory*, Vol. 31, No. 2, May: 151-166

Byrne, B. (2010) *Structural equation modeling with AMOS: Basic concepts, applications and programming*, 6th Ed., New York, USA: Taylor & Francis Group

Canada, J, Sutton, S.G. & Kuhn J. Jr. (2009) "The pervasive nature of IT controls: An examination of material weaknesses in IT controls and audit fees", *International Journal of Accounting & Information Management*, Vol. 17 Issue: 1: 106-119

Casolaro, L. & Gobbi, G. (2004) "Information Technology & Productivity Changes in the Italian Banking Industry", Report Published by Bank of Italy Economic Research Department, pp. 1-26

Coe, M.J. (2005) "Trust Services: A better way to evaluate IT controls", *Journal of Accountancy*, Vol. 199, Issue 3: 23-34

Committee of Sponsoring Organizations of the Treadway Commission (COSO) (1992) *Internal Control-Integrated Framework*, Coopers & Lybrand, September, Vol. 1-4

Daneila, M., Vassen, E.H.J. & Dameri, R, P. (2013) *Accounting Information System for Decision Making*, Springer - Verlag: Berlin

Daske, H. & Gebhardt, G. (2006) "International Financial Reporting Standards and Experts' Perceptions of Disclosure Quality", *Abacus*, vol. 42(3-4): 461-498

Dechow, P. & Dichev, I. (2002) "The Quality of Accruals and Earnings: The Role of Accrual Estimation Errors", *The Accounting Review*, vol. 77: 35-59

Dechow, P.M., Sloan, R.G. & Sweeney, A.P. (1996) "Causes and consequences of earnings manipulation: An analysis of firms subject to enforcement actions by the SEC", *Contemporary Accounting Research*, vol. 13(1): 1-36

Dehning, B. & Richardson, V.J. (2002) "Returns on Investments in Information Technology: A Research Synthesis", *Journal of Information Systems,* vol. 16(1): 7-30

DeLone, W.H. & McLean, E.R. (2003) "The DeLone and McLean model of information systems success: A ten-year update", *Journal of Management Information Systems*, vol. 19, iss. 4: 9-30

Fornell, C. & Larcker, D.F. (1981) "Evaluating structural equation models with unobservable variables and measurement error", *Journal of Marketing Research*, vol. 18(1): 39-50

Francis, J., LaFond, R., Olsson, P. & Schipper, K. (2005) "The market pricing of accrual quality", *Journal of Accounting and Economics*, vol. 39(2): 295-327

Gelinas *et al*. (2005) *Accounting Information Systems*, 6th edition, Thomson

Gerry, H.G., Miller, K.C., Alali, F. (2008) "The effect of IT controls on financial reporting", *Managerial Auditing Journal*, Vol. 23 Issue: 8: 803-823

Gray, G.L. (2002) "Discussion of investigating the impact of auditor-provided systems reliability assurance on potential service recipients", Journal of Information Systems, Vol. 16, No. s-1: 91-95

Greenberg, R., W., Li, & Wing, B. (2012) "The Effect of Trust in System Reliability on the Intention to Adopt Online Accounting Systems", *International Journal of Accounting and Information Management*, Vol. 20 No. 4: 363-376

Hair Jr., J. F., Anderson, R. E., Tatham, R. L. & Black, W. C. (1995) *Multivariate data analysis with readings*. Englewood Cliffs, NJ: Prentice-Hall

Hair Jr., J. F., Black, W. C., Babin, B. J. & Anderson, R. E. (2010) *Multivariate data analysis: A global perspective*, 7th Ed., Pearson Education International

Hall, J.A. (2011) *Accounting Information Systems*, 7th Edition, South-Western Cengage Learning, USA

Havelka, W. A., Henderson, R. & Oesterhelt, D. (1995) "Three-dimensional structure of halorhodopsin at 7 Å resolution", *Journal of Molecular Biology*, 247: 726-738

Holmes-Smith, P., Coote, L. & Cunningham, E. (2006) *Structural equation modelling: From the fundamentals to advanced topics*. Melbourne: School Research, Evaluation and Measurement Services

Hooper, D., Coughlan, J., & Mullen, M. (2008) "Structural Equation Modelling: Guidelines for Determining Model Fit", *Electronic Journal of Business Research Methods*, 6: 53-60

Hunton, JE, Benford, T, Arnold, V. & Sutton, S.G. (2000) "The impact of electronic commerce assurance on financial analysts' earnings forecasts and stock price estimates", *Auditing: A Journal of Practice and Theory*, vol. 18: 5-22

Hunton, J. E. (2002) "Blending Information and Communication Technology with Accounting Research", *Accounting Horizons*, vol. 16(1): 55-67

IASB (2008) Exposure Draft on an improved Conceptual Framework for Financial Reporting: The Objective of Financial Reporting and Qualitative Characteristics of Decision-useful Financial Reporting Information. London

IASB (2008) Exposure Draft on an improved Conceptual Framework for Financial Reporting: The Objective of Financial Reporting and Qualitative Characteristics of Decision-useful Financial Reporting Information. London

IASB, (2010) The conceptual framework for financial reporting. London: International Accounting Standards Board

Jamal, K. & Maier, M. (2002) "Can WebTrust survive?", *Working paper*, University of Alberta, Canada

Kaliski, B. (2001) *Encyclopedia of Business and Finance,* Macmillan Reference USA

Khazanchi, D. & Sutton, S.G. (2001) "Assurance services for business-to-business electronic commerce: a framework and implications", *Journal of the Association for Information Systems*, vol. 1(1): 1-53

Kline, R. (2005) *Principles and practices of structural equation modeling,* 2nd ed., New York: Guilford Press

Konrath, L, F. (2002) *Auditing - A Risk Analysis Approach*, 5th Edition, Thomson Learning: Canada

Lala, V., Arnold, V., Sutton, S. G., & Guan, L. (2002) "The impact of relative information quality of ecommerce assurance seals on Internet purchasing behavior", *International Journal of Accounting Information Systems*, vol. 3(4): 237-253

McMullen, D. (1996) "Audit committee performance: An investigation of the consequences associated with audit committees", *Auditing: A Journal of Practice & Theory*, vol. 15(1): 87-103

McPhie, D. (2000) "AICPA/CICA SYSTRUST™ Principles and Criteria", *Journal of Information Systems*, Supp., Vol. 14, No. s-1: 1-7

Meharia, P. (2012) "Assurance on the reliability of mobile payment system and its effects on its use: an empirical examination', *Accounting and Management Information Systems*, Vol. 11, No. 1: 97-111

Nelson, R. R., Todd, P. A. & Wixom, B. H. (2005) "Antecedents of information and system quality: An empirical examination within the context of data warehousing", *Journal of Management Information Systems*, vol. 21 (4): 199–235 *The Updated DeLone and McLean Model of Information Systems Success*. Available from: https://www.researchgate.net/publication/226710735_The_Updated_DeLone_and_McLean_Model_of_Information_Systems_Success [accessed Mar 10, 2017].

Perego, P., (2009) "Causes and Consequences of Choosing Different Assurance Providers: An International Study of Sustainability Reporting", *International Journal of Management*, December, Vol. 26, No. 3: 412-425

Pugliese, A. & Halse, R (2000) "SysTrust and WebTrust: technology assurance opportunities", *CPA Journal*, vol. 70(11): 28-34

Raupeliene, A. & Stabingis, L. (2003) "Development of A model for Evaluating Effectiveness of Accounting Information Systems", *Efita Conference*, EFITA Conference, 339-345

Ricchiute, D, N. (2006) *Auditing*, 8th t Edition, Thomson Learning: Singapore

Schipper, K. & Vincent, L. (2003) "Earnings Quality", *Accounting Horizons*, 17: 97-110

Shoorvarzy, M.R. (2008) "Using NAA qualitative characteristics for evolution of earnings quality", PhD thesis, Islamic Azad University

Siponen, M. T. & Oinas-Kukkonen, H. (2007) "A Review of Information Security Issues and Respective Research Contributions", ACM SIGMIS Database, (38:1): 60-80

Strong, D. M., Lee, Y. W. & Wang, R. Y. (1997) "Data Quality in Context," *Communications of the ACM* (40:5): 103-110

Talebian, M (2008) "Quality of financial reporting, informational risk, capital cost", *MA thesis*, Islamic Azad University

Topash, N.K (2014) "Evaluation of Efficiency of Accounting Information Systems: A Study on Mobile Telecommunication Companies in Bangladesh", *Global Disclosure of Economics and Business*, vol. 3(1): 40-55

9

How do the foreign direct investments flow? The case of the cross-border M&As in the European Union

George Marian Aevoae[a1], Roxana Dicu[a] and Daniela Mardiros[a]

[a] *"Alexandru Ioan Cuza" University of Iasi, Romania*

Abstract: Mergers and acquisitions (M&As) have been a popular strategy for firms and represent an important alternative for strategic expansion. At European Union (EU) level there are companies which choose this strategic option in order to expand their activity overboard, by merging or acquiring a company from EU or from a country outside the Union. The purpose of this paper is to present a quantitative analysis, for the 2005-2016 period of time, of the cross-border mergers and acquisitions (CBM&As) in the EU, by considering the mergers and the acquisitions of a controlling interest (100%), taking into account only the companies that developed their activity in the EU. The paper will follow two directions. On a side, we will analyze the number and the volume of the CBM&As for the EU member states, which will be categorized as developed, advanced emerging, secondary emerging and frontier economies, according to FTSE Russell criteria. On the other side, we will discuss the volume of the inward and outward foreign direct investments (FDI) related to CBM&As for these countries, to confirm that the most of these funds are flowing between developed economies. The flows are correlated to the merger waves in the Europe, according to the data provided by the Institute of Mergers, Acquisitions and Alliances (IMAA) in 2018.

Keywords: cross-border mergers and acquisitions; developed, emerging and frontier economies; foreign direct investments; Lucas' paradox

---

[1] *Corresponding author*: Department of Accounting, Business Information Systems and Statistics, "Alexandru Ioan Cuza" University of Iasi, Romania; Carol I Blvd no. 22; e-mail address: aevoae@gmail.com

1. Introduction

Mergers and acquisitions (M&As) are seen worldwide as business transformation mechanisms which allow the involved entities the diversification or the expansion of their activities. However, these processes of ownership change and corporate value transformation are based on expectations regarding an increase of the future economic benefits for the entities, known as synergistic effects. The development of this processes led to their expansion outside the frontiers of the countries, with the title of cross-border merger and acquisitions (CBM&As). The raise of the CBM&As appeared after the development of national merger markets, because it allowed worldwide access to human capital competences, a better circulation of information for the stakeholders, more complex regulatory frameworks, and a better public perception on M&As as managerial strategic tools. The cross-border deals are more complex than the domestic ones and we noticed there are studies on the differences between countries in terms of how these transactions are regulated and used (Feito-Ruiz & Menéndez-Requejo, 2011; Martynova & Renneboog, 2008; Martynova & Renneboog, 2011; Višić & Škrabić Perić, 2011).

Companies access foreign markets as a result of their growth strategies, through greenfield investments, brownfield investments and CBM&As, known, as a total, under the well-known name of foreign direct investments (FDI). In this paper, we aim to demonstrate that the FDI flow mainly between developed economies, despite the fact that the economic theory states that the emerging markets could be better choices in terms of costs and levels of return on factors of production.

According to Nocke and Yeaple (2007), a cross-border merger or acquisition allows a bidder to get costly access to the country-specific capabilities of the acquired firm, and the price of such a transaction is governed by demand and supply of firms in the market for corporate control. In contrast, by engaging in greenfield FDI, a firm brings only its own capabilities to work abroad. Thus, choosing between the two main forms is a decision of the company itself, but there are studies that conclude, based on empirical evidence, that more companies choose greenfield FDI over M&A when investing on foreign markets (Stepanok, 2015; UNCTAD, 2018). Blonigen and Piger (2014) stated that, when deciding to develop FDI activity, the companies rely mainly on factors like trade agreements, relative labour endowments and cultural distance factors. On the same idea, Hennart and Reddy (1997) consider that these activities are based on the relevance of resource-accessing alliance formations.

Nevertheless, the flows of capital, technology, knowledge and skills across national boundaries through FDI can have both substantial positive effects of the economic development of the involved economies, especially host countries (Dike, 2018; Girma *et al.*, 2015; Wang, 2009) and negative consequences, especially in the case of acquirers from developed economies who crowd out domestic entrepreneurs from least developed economies (Danakol *et al.*, 2017). On the same page, FDI can have direct and indirect consequences, the latter being known as the "spillovers", which can appear in productivity (Javorcik, 2004), on workers (Agrawal & Tambe, 2016; Fosfuri *et al.*, 2001) or on the shared knowledge (Fu, 2012; Wang, 2009).

The reminder of this paper is structured as follows: Section 2 presents a theoretical delimitation between CBM&As and greenfield investment, with an emphasis on the factors of influence. Section 3 of the paper details the aforementioned concepts in terms of figures and numbers. Section 4 discusses the main concepts and theories related to the circulation of capital between different types of economies. Section 5 presents the data used to describe the FDI situation in the European Union and to demonstrate Lucas' paradox, while Section 6 is dedicated to the results of the research. The last part of the paper is dedicated to the main conclusions of our study.

2. CBM&As vs. greenfield investments: alternatives for FDI in world economies

In nowadays, globalization is an adjective we add to everything: markets, institutions, risks, finances, communications, etc. Actually, mostly from an economic point of view, this process fades the borders of the nations, allowing the interconnection of the economies. Usually, it is defined as the process by which geographical distance becomes an ever less important factor in the establishment and development of cross-border economic, political and socio-cultural relations (Bari, 2005: 30).

As a global finance tool, a FDI represents a long-term investment relationship between a resident and a non-resident entity; it usually involves a significant degree of influence exerted by the investor on the management of the direct investment enterprise in which he has invested. According to the United Nations Conference on Trade and Development (UNCTAD), a company can undertake FDI in two ways: greenfield investment in new assets (this is known as the situation where a company builds its operations in a foreign country from the ground up) or acquiring / merging with an existing local company (UNCTAD, 2000: 99, Calderón *et al.*, 2004), the latter being either private or state owned. Thus, the link between FDI and CBM&As is the fact that privatizations involving foreign investors count as CBM&As. In the conference's yearly World Investment Report, information related to specific topics is presented, including CBM&As, which were the theme of the report in 2000 (UNCTAD, 2000). In contrast to domestic M&As, CBM&As imply that the bidder company applies a growth strategy oriented towards foreign markets, sensing business opportunities that domestic enterprises have not yet perceived or have lacked the ability to exploit (Ahammad *et al.*, 2017; Boateng *et al.*, 2008).

The choice for CBM&As is one related to a number of factors that are influencing it. Obviously, when considering such factors, one should keep in mind that their range goes from firm-level to national-level, because the experience of the company is as important as country risks (Neto *et al.*, 2009). Our own projection related to factors influencing the choice for CBM&As is reflected in Figure 1.

Figure 1 Factors which influence CBM&As

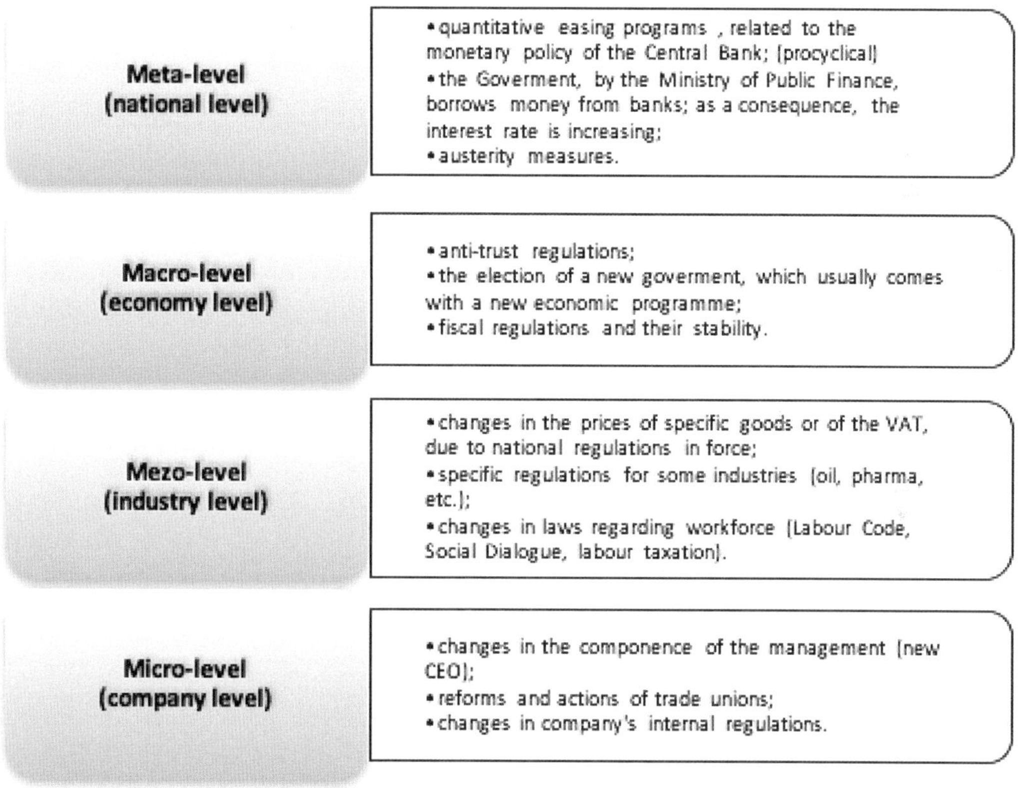

Source: Own processing after Whitaker (2016: 24)

The quantitative easing programs are procyclical, their purpose being to decrease the interest rate by creating money in the banking system. Actually, the Central banks are buying bonds from the banks and, through the infusion of money, the interest rates fall, loans are cheaper, and population is able to spend more. As a consequence, both the investments and the consumption increase. From an acquirer's point of view, a situation like this could be considered as beneficial for the CBM&As, because, in such economies, the population is willing to spend. The opposite situation, the anticyclical one, is related to the internal public debt and its impact on the interest rate. The latter is increasing, thus limiting the access of companies and population to loans. Regarding the elections and their impact on these transactions, it is recommended that the CBM&As take place a year before these events. This way, the companies are prepared to cope easier with potential domestic laws or regulatory changes. The regulatory changes which can appear as a result of a new Government appointment can increase or decrease the trust of the investors in the economy, according to the political programme they propose. At a green-level (industry level), there can be changes that affect a specific industry (a lower VAT for food or books, like the case of Romania (Fiscal Code, 2015: art. 291), the clawback tax for pharma industry, etc.) or changes in the laws regarding workforce (the minimum wage, social insurance, unemployment, etc.). For the involved companies, the changes in management or in employees' organization can have an important influence in the decision of participating in a CBM&A. All these factors influence, on a higher or a lower level, the management's decision to involve in M&As.

The same level perspective we found at Shimizu *et al.* (2004). They consider that the choice of CBM&As as a tool for strategic expansion is often influenced by (1) firm-level factors such as multinational experience, local experience, product diversity, internal isomorphism, and international strategy; (2) industry-level factors such as technological intensity, advertising intensity, and sales force intensity; and (3) country-level factors such as market growth in the host country, cultural idiosyncrasies between the home and host countries, and the specific culture of the acquiring firm's home country (particularly in terms of uncertainty avoidance and risk propensity).

By surveying a large number of journal articles, Xie *et al.* (2017) classify, summarize and integrate various cross-country determinants for M&As into seven major taxonomies: macroeconomic and financial markets environment, institutional and regulatory framework, political environment and corruption, tax and taxation laws, accounting standards, geographical factors, and cultural issues.

3. FDI and CBM&As at a global level

United Nations Conference on Trade and Development (UNCTAD) is the main UN body dealing with trade, investment and development issues. Since 1991, it has been presenting, yearly, a World Investment Report, which can be described as a timely contribution to both an important debate and an image of the international investment and development community. A consistent part of their yearly report consists of the situation of the FDI in and out of developed, developing and transition economies (according to UNCTAD country classification), which allows us a historical perspective on these flows.

According to UNCTAD, in 2013, the outstanding funds of private equity firms increased to a record level of more than 1 trillion $. Their cross-border investment was 171 billion $, recording a decline of 11%, and they accounted for 21% of the value of CMB&As. With funds available for investment, and relatively subdued activity in recent years, the potential for increased private equity FDI was significant (UNCTAD, 2014). When mentioning this, we have to keep in mind that the low level of flows to developed countries persisted in 2014, compared to 2013. Despite a revival in CBM&As, overall FDI flows to this group of economies declined by 28% to 499 billion $. They were significantly affected by a single large-scale disinvestment from the United States (UNCTAD, 2015). But the recovery in FDI was strong in 2015. Global foreign direct investment flows jumped by 38% to 1,76 trillion $, their highest level since the global economic and financial crisis of 2008-2009. A surge in CBM&As to 721 billion $, from 432 billion $ in 2014, was the principal factor behind the global rebound. The value of announced greenfield investment remained at a high level, at 766 billion $ (UNCTAD, 2016). For the 2016-2017 period of time, the values of FDI inflows and outflows are presented in Table 1.

Table 1. The value of FDI inflows and outflows, in 2016-2017 period of time

Region	FDI inflows (billions $)		FDI outflows (billions $)	
	2016	2017	2016	2017
Total	1.868	1.430	1.461	1.421
Developed economies, out of which:	1.133	712	1.031	1.000
Europe	565	334	529	418
Developing economies	670	671	405	381
Transition economies	64	47	25	40

(*Source:* Own processing after UNCTAD (2018), World Investment Report. Investment and New Investment Policies, United Nations, New York and Geneva, 2018, available online at http://unctad.org/en/PublicationsLibrary/wir2018_en.pdf)

Given the fact that CBM&As and the greenfield project are the main components of the FDI, they will be presented in the following tables. For the 2016-2017 period of time, the values of CBM&As are presented in Table 2.

Table 2. The value and number of CBM&As in 2016-2017 period of time

Industry	CBM&As (value – billions of $)		CBM&As (number)	
	2016	2017	2016	2017
Total	887	694	6.607	6.967
Primary	83	24	206	550
Manufacturing	406	327	1.745	1.690
Services	398	343	4.656	4.727

(*Source:* UNCTAD (2018), World Investment Report. Investment and New Investment Policies, United Nations, New York and Geneva, 2018, page 8, available online at http://unctad.org/en/PublicationsLibrary/wir2018_en.pdf)

For the 2016-2017 period of time, the values of the greenfield investments are presented in Table 3.

Table 3. The value and number of greenfield investments in 2016-2017 period of time

Industry	Greenfield projects (value – billions of $)		Greenfield projects (number)	
	2016	2017	2016	2017
Total	833	720	15.766	15.927
Primary	54	21	52	63
Manufacturing	295	338	7.703	7.678
Services	484	362	8.011	8.186

(*Source:* UNCTAD (2018), World Investment Report. Investment and New Investment Policies, United Nations, New York and Geneva, 2018, page 8, available online at http://unctad.org/en/PublicationsLibrary/wir2018_en.pdf)

Global FDI flows fell 13% in 2016, reaching an estimated 1.52 trillion $, in a context of weak global economic growth and a lackluster increase in the volume of world trade (UNCTAD, 2017). The decrease continued in 2017, by 23%, to 1,43 trillion $, in stark contrast to the accelerated growth in GDP and trade. The fall was determined, partly, in the value of the M&As. In 2017, although the number of CBM&As increased from 6.607 in 2016 to 6.967, their value dropped to 694 billion $, representing a decrease of 21,76% (Table 2). Equity investments at the global level were boosted by a 13% increase in the value of CBM&As, which rose to their highest level since 2007, reaching 887 billion $. The value of greenfield projects announcements reached an estimated 833 billion $ – a 5% rise from the previous year, although this was largely due to several very large projects announced in a handful of countries (UNCTAD, 2018; World Bank, 2017).

CBM&As constitute a large share of FDI flows, reaching, in the years of merger waves, their higher peak of 80% of the total, given the fact that target firms can benefit from the acquisition or merger of a foreign company (Stiebale & Reize, 2011). In other words, foreign investments help companies overcome constraints like: (1) difficult and adverse funding sources, (2) outdated technology and business organization, (3) saturated and/or insufficient domestic market, (4) a slow adjustment to market conditions etc. (Višić & Škrabić Perić, 2011:174).

4. The circulation of capital between developed and emerging economies

When discussing CBM&As, another focal point, which complements the FDI approach, is related to the circulation of capital. Brouthers and Dikova (2010) analyzed a sample of Western Europe companies which entered the Eastern Europe market, arguing that greenfield investments are a better option than acquisitions. The benefits of the CBAs between companies located in developed economies (as acquirers) and the ones from emerging markets (as targets) were also noticed by Bednarczyk *et al.* (2010) and Chari *et al.* (2010). Rabbiosi *et al.* (2012) argue that the companies from emerging economies build an organizational learning perspective if they enter developed economies markets, by closing transactions as CBM&As. Lebedev *et al.* (2015) studied the M&As in and out of the emerging economies and consider that the main focus when comparing the CBM&As between markets is on antecedents (motivation) and outcomes (performance). Erel *et al.* (2012) analyzed a sample of 56.978 CBM&As closed by USA companies, arguing that companies from countries with appreciated currencies, increased stock market value, and quality of disclosures requested by law tend to be acquirers of target from weaker-performing economies.

As the empirical evidence underlines, a major difference appears between developed and emerging economies. The standard neoclassical theory predicts that when two countries produce the same good with the same constant returns to scale production function, then the law of diminishing returns dictates that the marginal product of capital is higher in the less productive economy (Lucas, 1990; Višić & Škrabić Perić, 2011). The law of diminishing returns states that, by increasing one factor of production, while the others remain constant (*caeteris paribus*), inevitably the return per product decreases. Thus, the capital should flow from developed economies to the emerging ones. But funds go to the most advanced economies. This is known as Lucas paradox (Lucas, 1990). The explanations are multiple, but the firsts that come to mind are those related to antagonistic relation between higher returns on capital, on a side, and the laws, the economic performance and the quality of the institutions, specific to emerging and frontier economies, on the other side. In other words, the criteria which don't allow an economy to be classified as developed are the ones that stand in the way of progress, in our case in the way of developing commercial deals as CBM&As.

Regarding the transactions between developed economies, although they seem comparable in terms of laws and quality of institutions, they do vary in terms of regulations, and those referring to CBM&As are not an exception. The differences are subtle and related to banking and their relation to companies, the circulation of information between stakeholders, the treatment of human resources, the way corporate growth strategies are supported by the government, etc. Likewise, a focus point regarding CBM&As regulations is related to the perception of the owners of the entities involved in the process on the fact that they should pay attention to the ones from the other countries and not continuing the deal on the assumption that the home regulations are replicated worldwide (*"principle of caution"*) (Whitaker, 2016).

5. Research design and methodology

Through an empirical, descriptive research, we will study the CBM&As in which the countries of the European Union were involved, for the 2005-2016 period of time, aiming at identifying and presenting the characteristics of the studied phenomenon. The data regarding M&As were collected from the Zephyr database. One important characteristic of the dataset is that it covers a large fraction of companies, across all industries. Further, it provides information on both listed and unlisted companies. This feature of the data allows for a wide degree of observations in our sample. The search strategy took into consideration the deal status (completed-assumed, completed-confirmed, rumored, announced), the deal type (merger, acquisition), the geography criterion (European Union enlarged – 28 countries, as acquirer or target or vendor), for 2005-2016 period of time. As a result of the search, a number of 8.105 transactions were generated.

The transactions with other deal status than "completed-assumed" and "completed" were eliminated (3.160 transactions). The transactions that were eliminated and their status are presented in Table 4.

Table 4. The eliminated transactions from the zephyr database

Name	Total
Total deals	**8.105**
(-) Announced	106
(-) Pending	20
(-) Pending awaiting regulatory for approval	42
(-) Pending shareholder	2
(-) Postponed	8
(-) Rumor	453
(-) Rumor analyst speculation	78
(-) Rumor expired	1.674
(-) Rumor informal offer/non-binding	27
(-) Rumor withdrawn	245
(-) Withdrawn	505
Completed, out of which:	**4.945**
- completed	*4.290*
- completed assumed	*655*

(*Source*: Zephyr database 2005-2016 (Bureau Van Dijk))

To obtain our sample, which consists of the transactions representing mergers and acquisitions of a controlling interest (100%), we eliminate as follows:

1. the domestic M&As and CBM&As that involved a target and an acquiring company from outside of the European Union (641 transactions). These transactions were included in the database because the vendor of the securities was from the European Union, but they are of no interest for our study;
2. the transactions from 2017 (123 transactions), because the year is not completed, and our research takes into account the 2005-2016 period of time;
3. the domestic M&As, because the focal point of our study is to analyze the CBM&As (1.326 transactions);

4. the acquisitions which represent investments in associated entities (3 transactions) and investments in jointly controlled entities (1 transaction);
5. the transactions between more than two entities and we keep only transactions 1:1, mergers and acquisitions of a controlling interest of 100% (1.362 transactions).

The cross-border mergers and acquisitions of a controlling interest of 100% which are to be analyzed are in number of 1.489. The mergers and the acquisitions in percentage of 100% were applying the provisions of the Regulation no. 139/2004 on the control of concentrations between undertakings and are presented on the European Commission website (European Commission, 2017).

For the data collection, we use the observation method, considered useful to highlight the characteristics of the participating companies and understand the motivations behind the M&As.

As a result, in the quantitative part of the paper, we will present: the FDI situation at country level, as inflows (the target company has the residence in an EU country) and outflows (the acquiring company with the appurtenance in an EU country), on a side, and geographical area (Western and Eastern Europe), on the other side. This information will be correlated with the merger waves in Western and Eastern Europe. Given the fact that the quantitative study is referring to the 2005-2016 period of time, we will group the years according to the merger waves in Western Europe (using the value criterion): 2004-2009 (the third wave), 2010-2014 (the fourth wave), 2015-2016 (the fifth wave) and Eastern Europe: 2004-2013 (third wave), 2014-2016 (the fourth wave) (IMAA, 2018). Also, we want to demonstrate Lucas' paradox, taking into account the transactions between EU countries, grouped according to the FTSE Russell criteria into Not indexed, Frontier, Secondary Emerging, Advanced Emerging, Developed.

6. The results of the research

The approach of CBM&As is better made in terms of inflows and outflows, because these strategic transactions are a part of the foreign direct investments. In Figure 2 we can notice the evolution of the outflows from EU countries. Considering the years 2006, 2011, 2015, the peaks of the merger weaves we find appropriate presenting the countries and the value of the transactions with community dimension in the mentioned years.

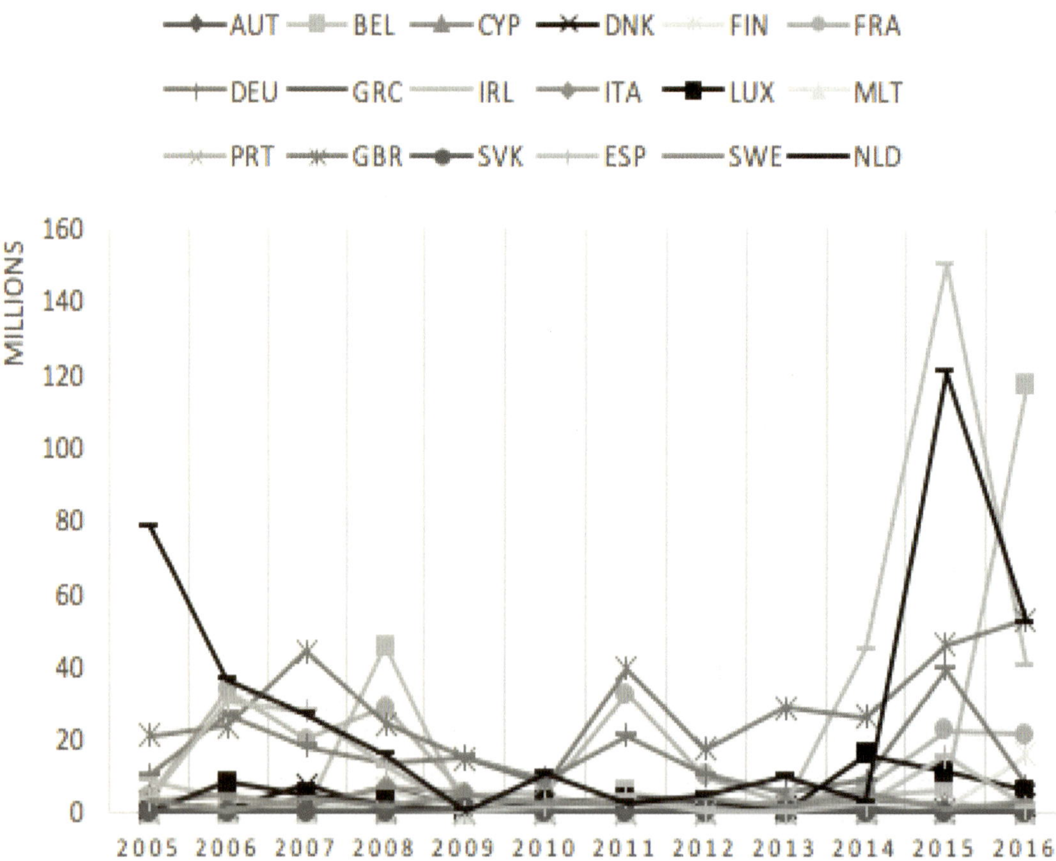

Figure 2. The outflows of FDI from EU countries (Western Europe)

Thus in 2006 the most significant registered value belongs to Netherlands (NDL) with the amount of 36.017 million dollars. In 2011 we find GBR and the amount was 39.077 million dollars and in the year of 2015 the country which registered the biggest outflow value of FDI representing CBM&As was Ireland (IRL), with a value of 149.970 million dollars. The results are consistent with total values for Western EU CMB&As transactions, which registered the top values in the same years mentioned above (2006 - 169.952 mil dollars, 2011 – 112.564 mil dollars, 2015 – 414.701 mil dollars).

The inflows of the FDI from CBM&As in the Western Europe, represented in Figure 3, follow the same trend as the outflows. In this case, we also notice that Netherlands registers the best trend for the inflows of FDI, and the total values for the 2005-2016 period of time also registered their picks in the years 2006 (149.363 mil dollars), 2011 (103.685 mil dollars) and 2015 (311.373 mil dollars).

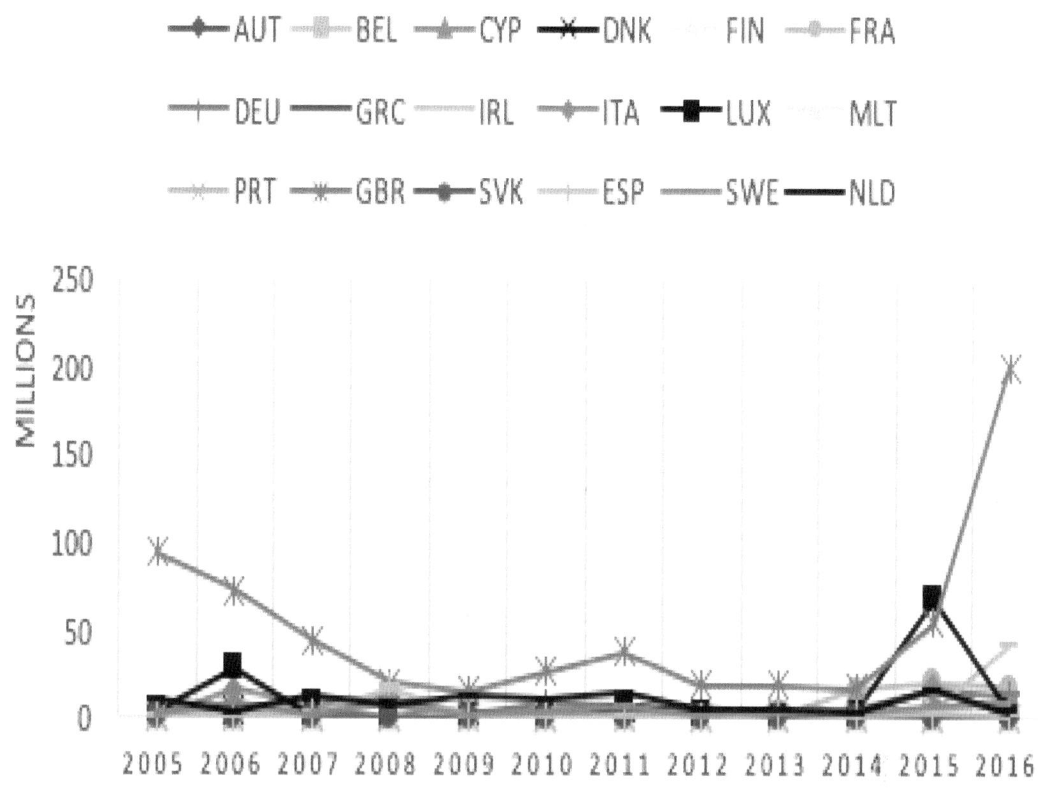

Figure 3. The inflows of FDI in EU countries (Western Europe)

In the case of Eastern Europe, the things are different, because the merger waves followed a different trend as the Western Europe (2004-2013 and 2014-2016, for the considered period). Given the fact that there were few transactions with community dimension for the Eastern Europe, it is difficult to consider a trend. The values for each country are represented in Figure 4. For Eastern Europe, the values are represented in thousands of dollars compared to Western Europe where they are presented in millions of dollars. We decide this due to the fact that the values of the FDIs in Eastern Europe are showing a lower level compared to the opposite side of Europe. More, it seems that the countries from the Western Europe reacted to the financial crisis. The years 2009 and 2010 are a fall in the value of the CBM&As (outflows 2009 – 47.121 mil dollars; outflows 2010 – 45.711 mil dollars; inflows 2009 – 48.775 mil dollars; inflows 2010 – 62.619 mil dollars). We cannot draw such a conclusion referring to the Eastern Europe.

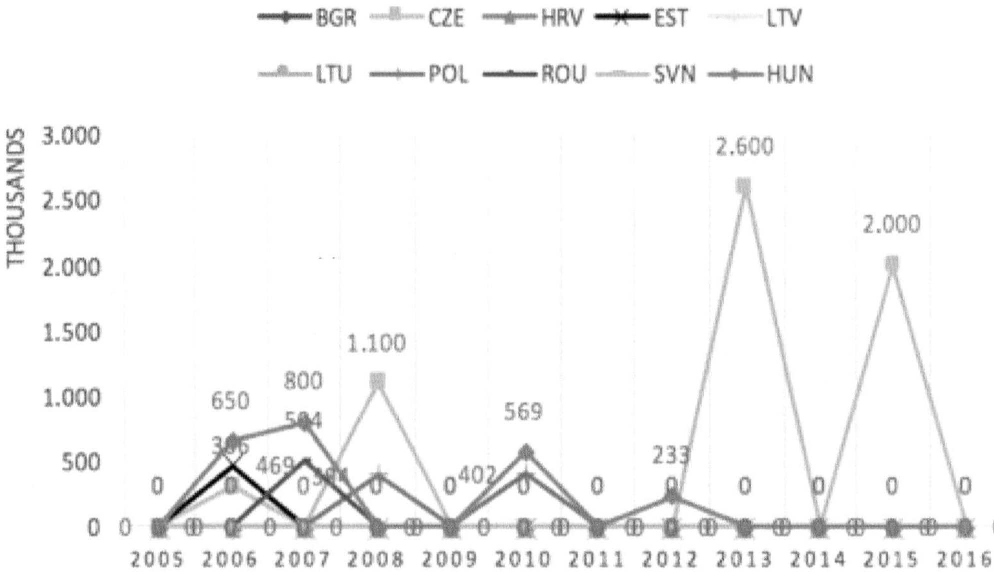

Figure 4. The outflows of FDI from EU countries (Eastern Europe)

For the inflows of FDI in the countries from Eastern Europe (the target companies are located in these countries), the values are displayed in Figure 5.

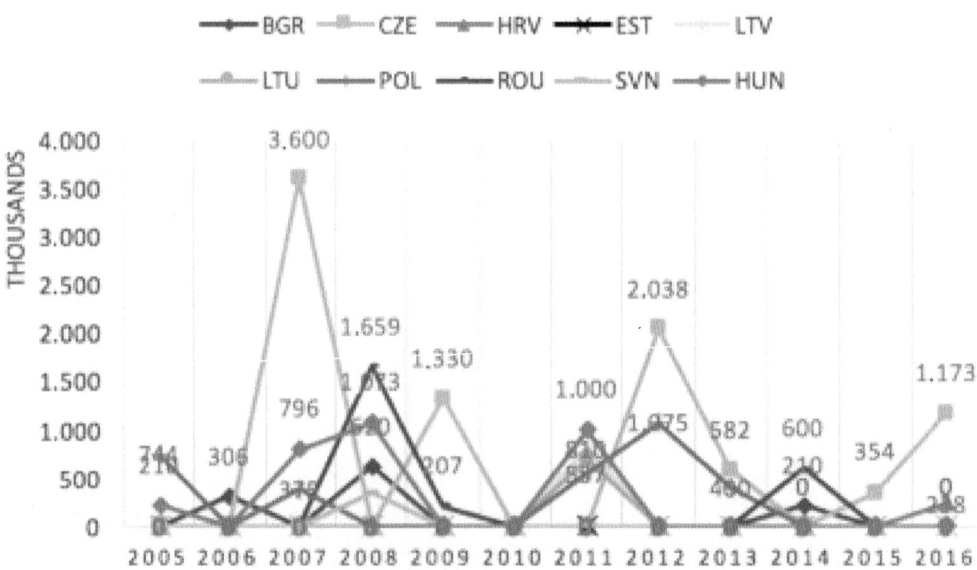

Figure 5. The inflows of FDI in EU countries (Eastern Europe)

In Table 5 we present the total values of inflows and outflows of the countries from the European Union enlarged, for the 2005-2016 period of time, taking into account all the mergers and acquisitions of a controlling interest (100%). As noticed in Table 5 and Figure 6, Netherlands presents the best situation of outflows of FDI (considering all the transactions in which a Dutch acquiring company was involved, the host country of the target being from anywhere in the world – 19,84%) and the United Kingdom for the inflows of FDI (the situation when British companies where in the position of target – 34,36%). Since the second position for the outflow FDI also belongs to United Kingdom, this speaks volumes about the financial power of this country in the European Union, before activating the article 50 from the Lisbon Treaty on March 29, 2017, in order to leave the EU at 11 pm (2300 GMT), on the same day in 2019 (Reuters, 2018). At the other end of the spectrum, we find Bulgaria (BGR), Croatia (HRV), Lithuania (LTU), Latvia (LTV) and Slovenia (SVN), all of them belonging to Eastern Europe, with 0 investments with community dimension from their companies, as acquirers. If we consider the inflows of FDI, we didn't find investments in Estonia, also an Eastern European country.

Table 5. The inflows and outflows of FDI – European Union enlarged

-thousand dollars-

			Country Code		
Indicator	**AUT**	**BEL**	**BGR**	**CYP**	**CZE**
FDI outflows	13.121.177	182.849.692	0	8.440.750	6.006.000
% total	0.73%	10.12%	0%	0.47%	0.33%
FDI inflows	14.169.188	32.082.019	1.136.458	5.310.825	9.076.782
% total	0.78%	1.78%	0.06%	0.29%	0.50%
Indicator	**DEU**	**DNK**	**ESP**	**EST**	**FIN**
FDI outflows	183.405.641	15.813.019	98.074.489	468.850	29.076.052
% total	10.15%	0.87%	5.43%	0.03%	1.61%
FDI inflows	91.078.359	19.239.879	35.605.075	0	14.074.458
% total	5.04%	1.06%	1.97%	0%	0.78%
Indicator	**FRA**	**GBR**	**GRC**	**HRV**	**HUN**
FDI outflows	190.889.180	343.049.485	706.439	0	2.252.040
% total	10.56%	18.98%	0.04%	0%	0.12%
FDI inflows	93.489.669	620.985.717	5.749.608	237.500	3.078.765
% total	5.17%	34.36%	0.32%	0.01%	0.17%
Indicator	**IRL**	**ITA**	**LTU**	**LTV**	**LUX**
FDI outflows	257.190.021	26.430.040	0	0	56.696.452
% total	14.23%	1.46%	0%	0%	3.14%
FDI inflows	72.743.546	77.580.948	701.000	810.000	123.767.848
% total	4.02%	4.29%	0.04%	0.04%	6.85%

	Country Code				
Indicator	**MLT**	**NLD**	**POL**	**PRT**	**ROU**
FDI outflows	0	358.556.482	796.877	883.200	504.380
% total	0%	19.84%	0.04%	0.05%	0.03%
FDI inflows	1.366.285	106.017.717	3.151.138	3.265.197	2.465.700
% total	0.08%	5.87%	0.17%	0.18%	0.14%
Indicator	**SVK**	**SVN**	**SWE**		
FDI outflows	881.567	0	31.283.082		
% total	0.05%	0%	1.73%		
FDI inflows	266.670	350.000	59.066.181		
% total	0.01%	0.02%	3.27%		
Indicator	**Total**				
FDI outflows	1.807.374.914 – 100%				
FDI inflows	1.396.866.534 – 100%				

(*Source*: own processing after Zephyr database 2005-2016 (Bureau Van Dijk))

Analyzing the Figure 6, it is obvious which are the countries who had the highest inflows (United Kingdom – GBR, followed by far by Luxembourg – LUX and Netherlands – NDL) and outflows of FDI (Netherlands – NDL, followed by the United Kingdom – GBR and Ireland – IRL), considering the CBM&As with a community dimension, in which at least one EU country was involved, as target or acquirer.

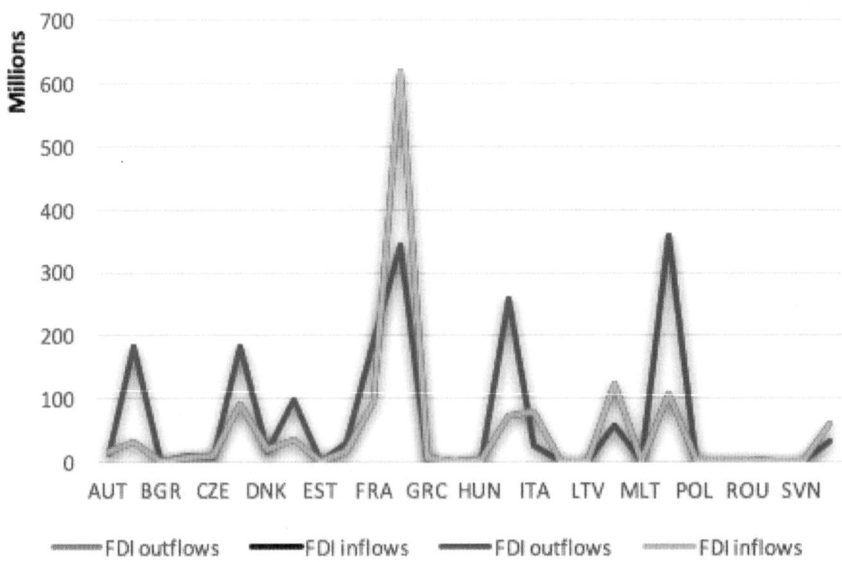

Figure 6. The total of inflows and outflows for the EU enlarged

In Figure 6, we present an analysis of the target countries from the EU, considering the statistical classification of economic activities in the European Community (NACE Rev.2) (Eurostat, 2008).

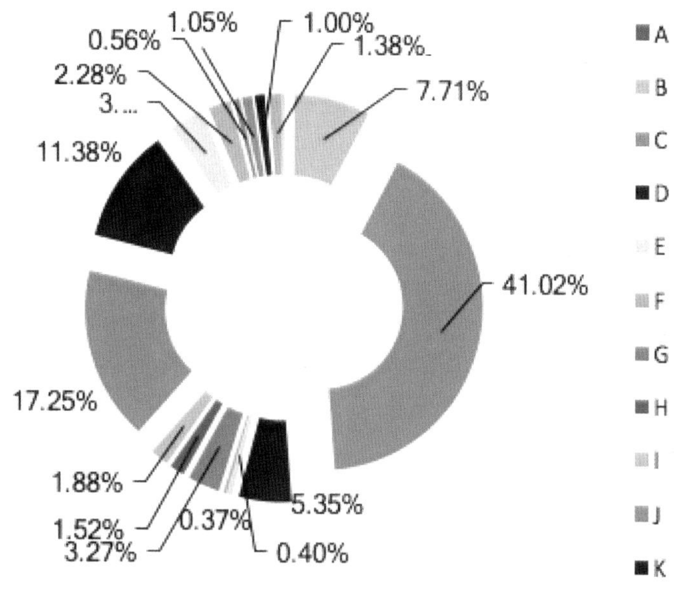

Figure 7. Distribution of target companies according to NACE Rev.2

As seen in Figure 7, the most transactions involved a target company which declared, as the main activity, one from section C *Manufacturing* (41,02%), followed by J *Information and communication* (17,25%) and K *Financial and insurance activities* (11,38%).

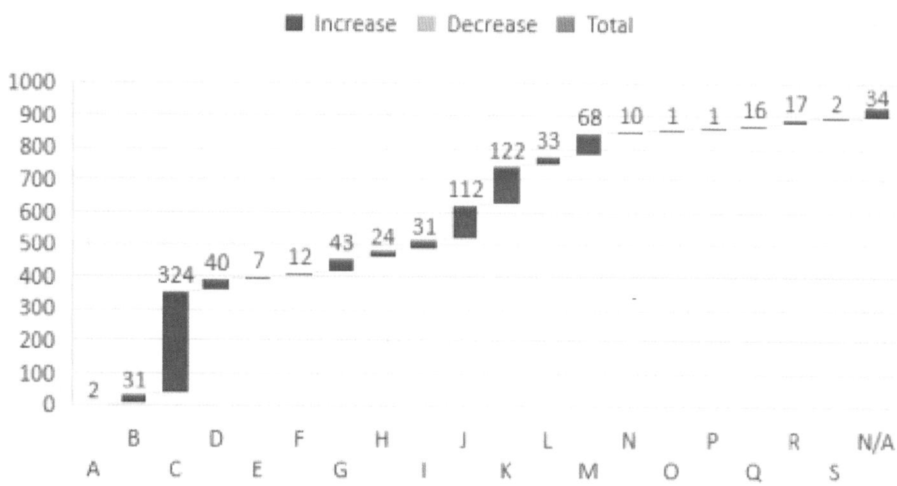

Figure 8. Number of transactions by target from the European Union

Although the funds should flow from the developed economies to the emerging and frontier ones, as the economic theory states (as presented above), funds go to the most advanced economies. This assertion is known as Lucas' paradox, presented in the qualitative part of our paper, which we manage to demonstrate using information from the 930 transactions with community dimension, which involved exclusively countries from EU, as target or acquirer (their number is structured by NACE Rev. 2 in Figure 8). Beyond the fact that these are the most representative M&A transactions in the EU, given the criteria which must be accomplished by a transaction to be considered having that dimension, their values help us affirm that, in the European Union, the FDI circulate, in a very large proportion, between the developed economies in the Union (96,10%, using data from Table 7). To sustain this affirmation, we also present the data from Table 6, which synthesizes the values of transactions between different types of economies, for the 2005-2016 period of time.

Table 6. The flows of FDI between types of economies for 2006-2016

\- thousand dollars -

	Type of economy	NI	F	SE	AE	D
2006	**NI**					468.850
2006	**SE**	306.000				
2006	**D**					98.078.245
2007	**NI**					945.553
2007	**SE**					800.000
2007	**D**	4.050.000		4.301.033		54.992.624
2008	**SE**		1.100.000			
2008	**AE**					394.451
2008	**D**		1.783.700		1.072.732	66.406.194
2009	**F**					881.567
2009	**D**		207.000			33.972.650
2010	**AE**					236.500
2010	**D**					12.936.556
2011	**D**	810.000	701.000		1.000.000	42.320.301
2012	**D**				3.113.617	16.581.520
2013	**AE**					2.600.000
2013	**D**				400.000	17.420.352
2014	**D**		600.000			29.681.627
2015	**F**					10.263.380
2015	**AE**					2.000.000
2015	**D**		66.485.000			58.334.042
2016	**F**					5.799.925
2016	**D**		3.199.450		1.173.185	171.032.069
Total		**5.166.000**	**74.076.150**	**4.301.033**	**6.759.534**	**626.146.406**

(*Source*: own processing after Zephyr database 2005-2016 (Bureau Van Dijk))

The most significant value of transactions between developed economies appears in 2016, representing 27,32% from the total of the transactions between this type of economies. The investments of acquirers from developed economies in companies located in advanced emerging economies present the highest value in 2012 (3.113.617 th dollars), in secondary emerging economies in 2007 (4.301.033 th dollars), and in frontier economies in 2015 (66.485.000 th dollars).

Cumulating the data from Table 6, we get the data from Table 7, which presents the total volume of transactions, considering the types of economies (not indexed - NI, frontier – F, secondary emerging – SE, advanced emerging – AE, developed - D), for the 2006-2016 period of time. Also, the Table 7 includes the percentage of presented flows in the total of 817.515.883 th dollars, representing the total of CBM&As, which involved exclusively countries from the EU enlarged.

Table 7. The total values of transactions, by types of economies, for the period 2005-2016 (thousand dollars)

TARGET / ACQUIRER	NI	F	SE	AE	D
NI					1.414.403 0.17%
F					16.944.872 2.07%
SE	306.000 0.04%	1.100.000 0.13%			800.000 0.10%
AE					5.230.951 0.64%
D	4.860.000 0.59%	72.976.150 8.93%	4.301.033 0.53%	6.759.534 0.83%	601.756.180 73.61%
Total	**5.166.000**	**74.076.150**	**4.301.033**	**6.759.534**	**626.146.406**

(*Source*: own processing after Zephyr database 2005-2016 (Bureau Van Dijk))

We can see that in Table 7, at the intersection of rows and columns, we find the values, as total for the 2006-2016 period of time. We have excluded the year 2005 because, according to FTSE Russell classification, all the economies to which we refer in this paper have no classification for the mentioned year. Although there is no information available for 2005, referring to country classification, the volume of transactions for the year was up to 101.066.760 th dollars, representing 12,36% out the total of 817.515.883 th dollars (the amount of transactions which involved only countries from EU, as target or acquiring company). The difference is 716.449.123 th dollars, split between different types of flows between economies, presented in Table 7.

7. Conclusions

Globalization offers enormous opportunities for economic growth and sustainable development with potential benefits on a scale difficult to imagine. As a result, FDI flows have recorded high values in the last years, with oscillations due to financial crisis, Brexit and other local or global events that affected the worldwide economy. In this context, developed economies attracted/invested funds from/to the countries with the same ranking. In the same time, developing countries, and least developed countries in particular, face considerable challenges. They range from structural constraints, such as the lack of adequate infrastructure and scarce access to finance, to strategic issues. In 2018, the projections for global FDI show fragile growth. Global flows are forecast to increase marginally, by up to 10%, but remain well below the average over the past 10 years.

At EU level, the M&As are considered having a strategic importance. For this purpose, the Regulation no. 139/2004 sets the rules for controlling the transactions with community dimension, in order to avoid a negative impact towards society. Our study is based on 1.489 CBM&As, and we conclude that the developed economies from the Western Europe are involved in the most transactions, that usually the manufacturing companies are involved in M&As (in order to control a market or to optimize their supply chain) and, at EU level exclusively, the Lucas' paradox is proved (73,61% of the M&As are closed between companies located in developed economies). Thus, in an environment marked by strong economic growth and elevated political risks, investors' pursuit of profitable businesses, mostly beyond the borders of their residence countries, raises the importance of FDI.

A second conclusion refers to the fact that, in our sample, only two transactions were declared as mergers 100%, the rest of 1.487 are reported as acquisitions of a controlling interest (100%). Even when mergers are supposedly between relatively equal partners, most transactions are in fact acquisitions, with one company controlling the other. The real number of mergers is so low that, for practical purposes, the acronym M&As basically means acquisitions.

Acknowledgements

The authors acknowledge the guidance of the editor in chief of JAMIS. An earlier version of this paper was presented at the International Conference Accounting and Management Information Systems at the Bucharest University of Economic Studies, in 2018.

References

Agrawal, A. & Tambe, P. (2016) "M&A and Spillover Effects on Workers", Working paper, available online at http://www.research.mbs.ac.uk/accounting-finance/Portals/0/Users/002/02/2/M%20and%20A%20and%20Spillover%20Effects%20on%20Workers.pdf [on-line access: March 17th 2018]

Ahammad, M., Tarba, S., Frynas, J.G. & Scola, A. (2017) "Integration of Non-market and Market Activities in Cross-border Mergers and Acquisitions", *British Journal of Management*, vol. 28, no. 4: 629-648

Blonigen, B. & Piger, J. (2014) "Determinants of foreign direct investment", *Canadian Journal of Economics*, vol. 47, no. 3: 775-812

Boateng, A., Qian, W. & Tianle, Y. (2008) "Cross-border M&As by Chinese firms: An analysis of strategic motives and performance", *Thunderbird International Business Review*, vol. 50, no. 4: 259-270

Brouthers, K.D. & Dikova, D. (2010) "Acquisitions and Real Options: the Greenfield Alternative", *Journal of Management Studies*, vol. 47, no. 6: 1048-1071

Calderón, C., Loayza, N. & Servén, L. (2004) "Greenfield Foreign Direct Investment and mergers and acquisitions: Feedback and macroeconomic effects", World Bank Group, available online at https://openknowledge.worldbank.org/handle/10986/13941, (on-line access: February 20th, 2018)

Chari, A., Ouimet, P. & Tesar L. (2010) "The value of control in emerging markets", *The Review of Financial Studies,* vol. 23, no. 4: 1741–1770

Danakol, S., Estrin S., Reynolds, P. & Weitzel, U. (2017) "Foreign direct investment via M&A and domestic entrepreneurship: blessing or curse?", *Small Business Economics*, vol. 48, no. 3: 599-612

Dike, C. (2018) "Effects of Foreign Direct Investment in Sub-Saharan Africa economic growth: evidence from panel data analysis", *International Journal of Economics and Financial Issues, Econjournals*, vol. 8, no. 2: 255-261

Erel, I., Liao, R. & Weisbach, M. (2012) "Determinants of cross-border mergers and acquisitions", *The Journal of Finance*, vol. 67, no. 3: 1045-1082

European Commission (2017) Mergers cases http://ec.europa.eu/competition/elojade/isef/index.cfm?clear=1&policy_area_id=2 [on-line access: March 1st 2018]

European Commission (2004) Council Regulation (EC) No 139/2004 of 20 January 2004 on the control of concentrations between undertakings, published in the Official Journal of the European Union no. 24/29.01.2004, pages 1-21

Eurostat (2008) *NACE Rev.2. Statistical Classification of economic activities in the European Community* http://ec.europa.eu/eurostat/documents/3859598/5902521/KS-RA-07-015-EN.PDF [On-line access: February 2nd 2018]

Feito-Ruiz, I. & Menéndez-Requejo, S. (2011) "Cross-border Mergers and Acquisitions in different legal environments", *International Review of Law and Economics*, vol. 31: 169-187

Fosfuri, A., Motta, M. & Rønde, T. (2001) "Foreign Direct Investment and spillovers through workers' mobility", *Journal of International Economics*, vol. 53, no. 1: 205-222

Fu, X. (2012) "Foreign Direct Investment and managerial knowledge spillovers through the diffusion of management practices", *Journal of Management Studies*, vol. 49, no. 5: 970-999

Girma, S., Gong, Y., Görg, H. & Lancheros, S. (2015) "Estimating direct and indirect effects of foreign direct investment on firm productivity in the presence of interactions between firms", *Journal of International Economics*, vol. 95, no. 1: 157-169

Hennart, J.-F. & Reddy, S. (1997) "The choice between mergers/acquisitions and joint ventures: The case of Japanese investors in the United States", *Strategic Management Journal*, vol. 18: 1-12

Institute of Mergers, Acquisitions and Alliances (2017) *Number and value of M&A in Europe*, https://imaa-institute.org/mergers-and-acquisitions-statistics/, [On-line access February 15th, 2018]

Javorcik, B.S. (2004) "Does foreign direct investment increase the productivity of domestic firms? In search of spillovers through backward linkages", *American Economic Review*, vol. 94, no. 3: 605-627

Lebedev, S., Peng, M., Xie, E. & Stevens, C. (2015) "Mergers and Acquisitions in and out of the emerging economies", *Journal of World Business*, vol. 50, no. 4: 651-662

Lucas, R. (1990) "Why doesn't capital flow from rich to poor countries?", *The American Economic Review*, vol. 80, no. 2: 92-96

Martynova, M. & Renneboog, L. (2008) "Spillover of corporate governance standard in cross-border mergers and acquisitions", *Journal of Corporate Finance*, vol. 14: 200-223

Martynova, M. & Renneboog, L. (2011) "The performance of the European market for corporate control: Evidence from the firth takeover wave", *European Financial Management*, vol. 17, no. 2: 208-259

Neto, P., Brandão, A. & Cerqueira, A. (2009) "The Macroeconomic Determinants of Cross Border Mergers and Acquisitions and Greenfield Investments", available online at https://www.researchgate.net/publication/46466162 [On-line access: January 10th 2018]

Nocke, V. & Yeaple, S. (2007) "Cross-border mergers and acquisitions vs. greenfield foreign direct investment: The role of firm heterogeneity", *Journal of International Economics*, vol. 72, no. 2: 336-365

Rabbiosi, Larissa, Elis, S. & Bertoni, F. (2012) "Acquisitions by EMNCs in Developed Markets", *Management International Review*, vol. 52, no. 2: 193-212

Reuters (2018) Brexit at breaking point? Diary dates for Britain's EU departure, https://www.reuters.com/article/us-britain-eu-timeline/brexit-at-breaking-point-diary-dates-for-britains-eu-departure-idUSKCN1M60PE [On-line access September 26th 2018]

Shimizu, K., Hitt, M., Vaidyanath, D. & Pisano, V. (2004) "Theoretical foundations of cross-border mergers and acquisitions: A review of current research and recommendations for the future", *Journal of International Management*, vol. 10: 307-353

Stepanok, I. (2015) "Cross-border mergers and greenfield foreign direct investment", *Review of International Economics*, vol. 23, no. 1: 111-136

Stiebale, J. & Reize, F. (2011) "The impact of the FDI through mergers and acquisitions on innovation in target firms", *International Journal of Industrial Organization*, vol. 29, no. 2: 155-167

UNCTAD (2018) *World Investment Report. Investment and New Investment Policies*, http://unctad.org/en/PublicationsLibrary/wir2018_en.pdf [on-line access May 28th 2018]

UNCTAD (2017) Global Investment Trend Monitor no. 25, February 2017, http://unctad.org/en/PublicationsLibrary/webdiaeia2017d1_en.pdf [on-line access January 15th 2018]

UNCTAD (2016) *World Investment Report: Investor Nationality: Policy Challenges,* http://unctad.org/en/PublicationsLibrary/wir2016_en.pdf [on-line access January 15th 2018]

UNCTAD (2015) *World Investment Report: Reforming International Investment Governance*, http://unctad.org/en/PublicationsLibrary/wir2015_en.pdf [on-line access February 1st 2018]

UNCTAD (2014) *World Investment Report: Investing in SDGs: An Action Plan*, http://unctad.org/en/PublicationsLibrary/wir2014_en.pdf [on-line access January 21st 2018

UNCTAD (2000) *World Investment Report: Cross-border Mergers and Acquisitions and Development*, http://unctad.org/en/Docs/wir2000_en.pdf [on-line access: January 20th 2018]

Višić, J. & Škrabić Perić, B. (2011) "The determinants of value of incoming cross-border mergers & acquisitions in European transition countries", *Communist and Post-Communist Studies*, vol. 44: 173-182

Wang, M. (2009) "Manufacturing FDI and economic growth: evidence from Asian economics", *Journal Applied Economics*, vol. 41, no. 8: 991-1002

Whitaker, S. (2016) *Cross-border Mergers and Acquisitions,* USA: John Wiley &Sons, Inc.

World Bank (2017) Foreign Direct Investment, Net inflows (1970-2016) https://data.worldbank.org/indicator/BX.KLT.DINV.CD.WD [on-line access January 10th 2018]

Xie, E., Reddy, K.S. & Liang, J. (2017) "Country-specific determinants of cross-border mergers and acquisitions: A comprehensive review and future research directions", *Journal of World Business,* vol. 52, no. 2: 127-183

Permissions

All chapters in this book were first published in JAMIS, by Bucharest University of Economic Studies; hereby published with permission under the Creative Commons Attribution License or equivalent. Every chapter published in this book has been scrutinized by our experts. Their significance has been extensively debated. The topics covered herein carry significant findings which will fuel the growth of the discipline. They may even be implemented as practical applications or may be referred to as a beginning point for another development.

The contributors of this book come from diverse backgrounds, making this book a truly international effort. This book will bring forth new frontiers with its revolutionizing research information and detailed analysis of the nascent developments around the world.

We would like to thank all the contributing authors for lending their expertise to make the book truly unique. They have played a crucial role in the development of this book. Without their invaluable contributions this book wouldn't have been possible. They have made vital efforts to compile up to date information on the varied aspects of this subject to make this book a valuable addition to the collection of many professionals and students.

This book was conceptualized with the vision of imparting up-to-date information and advanced data in this field. To ensure the same, a matchless editorial board was set up. Every individual on the board went through rigorous rounds of assessment to prove their worth. After which they invested a large part of their time researching and compiling the most relevant data for our readers.

The editorial board has been involved in producing this book since its inception. They have spent rigorous hours researching and exploring the diverse topics which have resulted in the successful publishing of this book. They have passed on their knowledge of decades through this book. To expedite this challenging task, the publisher supported the team at every step. A small team of assistant editors was also appointed to further simplify the editing procedure and attain best results for the readers.

Apart from the editorial board, the designing team has also invested a significant amount of their time in understanding the subject and creating the most relevant covers. They scrutinized every image to scout for the most suitable representation of the subject and create an appropriate cover for the book.

The publishing team has been an ardent support to the editorial, designing and production team. Their endless efforts to recruit the best for this project, has resulted in the accomplishment of this book. They are a veteran in the field of academics and their pool of knowledge is as vast as their experience in printing. Their expertise and guidance has proved useful at every step. Their uncompromising quality standards have made this book an exceptional effort. Their encouragement from time to time has been an inspiration for everyone.

The publisher and the editorial board hope that this book will prove to be a valuable piece of knowledge for researchers, students, practitioners and scholars across the globe.

List of Contributors

Zayyad Abdul-Baki and Mubaraq Sannia
University of Ilorin, Nigeria

Ahmad Bukola Uthman
Al-Hikmah University, Ilorin, Nigeria

Chaima Koolia and Raoudha Trabelsi
Sfax Business School, Sfax University, Tunisia

Fethi Tlili
Tunis Higher School of Communication, Tunisia

İlhan Dalcı and Hasan Özyapıcı
Eastern Mediterranean University, North Cyprus, Turkey

Łukasz Matuszak and Ewa Różańska
Poznan University of Economics and Business, Poland

Selena Aureli
University of Bologna, Italy

Andrea Cardoni
University of Perugia, Italy

Mara Del Baldo
University of Urbino Carlo Bo, Italy

Rosa Lombardi
University of Rome La Sapienza, Italy

Oyerogba Ezekiel Oluwagbemiga
Bowen University, Iwo, Osun State, Nigeria

Ogungbade Oluyinka Isaiah
Afe Babalola University, Ekiti State, Nigeria

Idode Patrick Esiemogie
Bells University of Technology, Ogun State, Nigeria

Aurelia Ştefănescu, Ileana Cosmina Pitulice and Viorica Georgiana Mînzu
Bucharest University of Economic Studies, Romania

Ahmed Al-Dmour and Maysem Abbod
Brunel University, England

Rand Al-Dmour
University of Jordan, Jordan

George Marian Aevoae, Roxana Dicu and Daniela Mardiros
"Alexandru Ioan Cuza" University of Iasi, Romania

Index